Although Congress responded to the financial market crash and the growing federal deficit by including modest revenue-raising items as part of the Revenue Act of 1987, it has continued to stall passage of the technical-corrections bill needed to clarify many of the provisions of the Tax Reform Act of 1986. In addition, the Treasury Department has been slow to provide guidance on many complicated tax areas, including passive income activity and fringe benefits issues.

As tax advisers, we are continually consulting with the Treasury Department and the Internal Revenue Service on tax issues that are relevant to you. And we make every effort to ensure that you are informed of the most current tax strategies, through personal consultations and our booklets and periodicals, including this publication.

If the technical-corrections legislation currently being debated is enacted, we will prepare a special edition of *U.S. Taxes—Views and Reviews* summarizing the most important changes and highlighting any revisions that will affect 1988 individual income tax returns.

THE PRICE WATERHOUSE
PERSONAL
TAX ADVISER

BANTAM BOOKS
TORONTO • NEW YORK • LONDON • SYDNEY • AUCKLAND

This publication contains information on the tax law as of September 12, 1988, and does not reflect developments since that date. Such developments include amendments to the Internal Revenue Code, promulgation of new tax regulations, other actions and interpretations by the Internal Revenue Service, and court decisions relating to the law. This publication is intended to offer guidance on personal tax matters. It is sold with the understanding that the author and publisher are not herein engaged in rendering legal, tax, or other professional services. This book should not be used as a substitute for personal consultations with professional tax advisers.

THE PRICE WATERHOUSE PERSONAL TAX ADVISER

A Bantam Book / November 1988

ISBN 0-553-28018-X

Published simultaneously in the United States and Canada

Bantam Books are published by Bantam Books, a division of Bantam Doubleday Dell Publishing Group, Inc. Its trademark, consisting of the words "Bantam Books" and the portrayal of a rooster, is Registered in U.S. Patent and Trademark Office and in other countries. Marca Registrada. Bantam Books, 666 Fifth Avenue, New York, New York 10103.

PRINTED IN THE UNITED STATES OF AMERICA

O   0 9 8 7 6 5 4 3 2 1

A NOTE FROM THE AUTHOR

The best way—in fact the only way—to be absolutely certain that your annual tax bill is what it ought to be and not one dollar more is to devise and use effective tax strategies.

And for 1988 and 1989, this couldn't be more true. Even experienced tax advisers are continually updating their strategies to reflect the tax law changes enacted by Congress in 1986 and 1987.

The 1986 Tax Reform Act rewrote the tax law from the bottom up. Then in 1987 lawmakers changed the changes—for example, by revising the law on home mortgage deductions. And the IRS itself has issued lengthy new regulations defining passive income, which will affect your ability to use losses in one area to offset income in another.

This book will help you plan tax strategies to use at the end of 1988 and throughout 1989. It is not a line-by-line guide to preparing your tax return. Instead, it will help you ensure that when preparation time does roll around, the number that winds up on the tax-due line is as small as it legally can be.

CONTENTS

CHAPTER 1

How the Tax Rates
Affect Your Bottom Line

When Congress adopted the 1986 Tax Reform Act, it attempted to simplify our tax structure by replacing many graduated rates with an easier two-rate system.

Did it succeed? Well, not exactly. We do have two rates now, but the system isn't that simple.

In this chapter we help you understand how the new two-rate system works.

Having this understanding can affect the way you think about the money you earn. That last dollar you bring in each year is now worth a lot more to you than it has been in decades.

MARGINAL AND EFFECTIVE TAX RATES Before we start, a couple of definitions will be useful, because we use these terms frequently in this and other chapters.

Taxable Income

Your taxable income is, logically enough, the amount of income on which you actually pay taxes. You calculate your taxable income by adding up your income from all sources and subtracting all your allowable deductions.

As we'll see in the following chapters, allowable deductions include adjustments to income (a Keogh contribution, for example); itemized deductions or the standard deduction; and the deductions you claim for personal exemptions.

Marginal Tax Rate

Uncle Sam defines marginal tax rate as the rate on your last dollar of earnings. Take, for the sake of illustration, a purely

1

imaginary tax system with two rates. Income up to $10,000 is taxed at 5 percent. Income that tops $10,000 is taxed at 10 percent.

If you earned $12,000 in salary and pocketed a $1,000 bonus, your marginal tax rate on the bonus is 10 percent—that is, the rate on the last dollar you received.

You also use your marginal tax rate to determine the tax benefit of a deduction. If your marginal tax rate is 10 percent, a $1,000 deduction saves you $100 in income taxes.

Effective Tax Rate

Effective tax rate, on the other hand, is the *overall* rate at which your income is taxed. Assume the same simple two-rate system and an income of $15,000.

The tax on your first $10,000 in income is $500 ($10,000 times 5 percent), and on income of more than $10,000, the tax is $500 ($5,000 times 10 percent).

So your total tax comes to $1,000 ($500 plus $500). Your top marginal tax rate is 10 percent, but your effective tax rate is only 6.7 percent ($1,000 divided by $15,000).

The new law narrows the difference between marginal and effective tax rates. It contains only two regular tax brackets—15 percent and 28 percent.

The 15 percent rate applies to taxable income up to: $29,750 for married individuals filing joint returns, and surviving spouses; $23,900 for heads of households; $17,850 for single people; and $14,875 for married individuals who file separate returns.

Income that tops these amounts is taxed at 28 percent. However, the income levels at which the higher rate takes effect will be adjusted for inflation after 1988. Consequently, the examples we're about to give may not be precisely accurate after this year. The principles involved, however, remain the same.

HOW IT WORKS   So, let's see how the two-rate tax system works.

Say you're married, file a joint return, and your 1988 taxable income comes to $50,000. Your federal income taxes for the year add up to $10,133.

Here's how we arrived at that figure. Your first $29,750 in income is taxed at 15 percent. That comes to $4,463. The remaining $20,250 of your income falls in the 28 percent bracket, generating a tax of $5,670. The total ($4,463 plus $5,670) comes to $10,133.

What could be simpler? For taxpayers with modest incomes, the two-rate system *is* simple. It's not so simple, though, when your taxable income rises beyond certain levels—$43,150 for single filers and $71,900 for married joint filers.

Beyond these points, the tax law begins to phase out the lower 15 percent bracket until, eventually, all income—beginning with the very first dollar—is subject to a flat 28 percent tax rate. In effect, beyond certain income levels your effective tax rate and your marginal tax rate become the same: 28 percent.

The sneaky device that makes this flattening out happen is called a "phase-out surtax." How does it work?

The law imposes an additional 5 percent tax on taxable income that falls within certain ranges. On this income you pay a 33 percent marginal tax rate—the normal 28 percent rate plus the 5 percent phase-out surtax.

These ranges of taxable income vary with inflation adjustments made in 1989 and later, but in 1988 they run between: $71,900 and $149,250 for married individuals filing joint returns, and surviving spouses; $61,650 and $123,790 for heads of household; $43,150 and $89,560 for single individuals; and $35,950 and $113,300 for married individuals filing separate returns.

Congress didn't want married couples who file separate returns to enjoy a tax break not available to married couples who file joint returns.

So if you're married and file separate returns, the benefit of the 15 percent tax rate is subject to the phase-out surtax not once, but twice.

That means the maximum effective tax rate paid by married couples filing separately reaches 29.7 percent when your separate taxable income equals $113,300.

Now, let's run through a simple example that shows you how a two-rate system turns into a flat tax. Suppose that in 1988 you and your spouse report taxable income of $149,250. The first $29,750 is subject to tax at 15 percent. The tax comes to $4,463.

Between $29,750 and $71,900 your income is taxed at the 28 percent rate. The tax comes to $11,802 ($71,900 minus $29,750 times 28 percent).

Between $71,900 and $149,250 your tax rate is 33 percent—28 percent plus the 5 percent phase-out surtax. The tax comes to $25,526 ($149,250 minus $71,900 times 33 percent).

So your total tax is $41,791, and look what has happened to your effective tax rate. Divide $41,791 by $149,250 (taxable income), and you get 28 percent. The surtax, effectively, wipes out the lower 15 percent bracket for you and other higher-income taxpayers.

Caution: The surtax comes into play again when you claim personal exemptions for yourself and your dependents. We show you how in Chapter 2. (You'll find complete 1988 tax tables in the appendix.)

QUESTIONS AND ANSWERS

QUESTION: In the past I've heard my accountant say that the best tax strategy is to defer income and accelerate deductions. Does this advice apply to 1988?

In any year, making the decision to defer income and accelerate deductions (we'll get to deductions in Chapter 3) involves some fortune telling.

You have to project your income and deductions and decide whether you'll save tax dollars by deferring income or accelerating deductions.

In short, you have to run the numbers as best you can.

But you should be aware that 1988 is a special year—from a tax point of view, anyway. Rates are as low as they've been in many years.

So it's more important than ever to estimate your income and deductions for both 1988 and 1989. And you probably will want to enlist your tax adviser's assistance early on in the process.

Keep these considerations in mind too: With the low tax rates now in effect, many taxpayers will find themselves in the same marginal tax brackets in 1988 and in 1989. Moreover, most tax experts think that 1988's low rates won't last forever.

In short, it may make better sense for you to reverse the traditional wisdom by accelerating income into 1988 and deferring deductions until 1989. That way you'll take maximum advantage of 1988's low rates. But the best strategy for you depends entirely on your personal financial circumstances.

Some items you and your accountant should pay close attention to: the impact of the alternative minimum tax, passive losses and passive income, the phase-out surtax, and deductions (medical expenses, casualty and theft losses, and miscellaneous deductions, for example) that are subject to a so-called threshold amount.

We'll discuss all these tax issues—and present some strategies for dealing with them—in the following chapters.

Q: I've run the numbers and think it makes sense for me to postpone receiving some of my income until 1989. Do you have any ideas for doing so?

First a caution: Whatever good reason you may have to defer income, you should keep in mind the following considerations.

One key to whether it makes sense for you to postpone income: Can you afford to go without a portion of your earnings? And how long can you do without this money?

Another key for employees: the interest rate your company pays on your deferred money. First find out if your company will pay you any interest rate. If it does, see if it will pay a competitive rate.

Also, weigh the risks. When you defer compensation, you become a creditor of your company. And if it goes belly up, you stand to lose the amount owed you.

Now, here are some ways you can defer income. If you're self-employed and keep your books on the cash basis, you can easily defer income by postponing the billing of clients or customers until near the end of the year. That way, you receive payment after December 31.

You may also try to defer dividend income, although doing so isn't easy. You can petition the board of directors of a corporation in which you own stock to put off, say, a 1988 dividend until 1989. Of course, directors aren't likely to be moved by your request unless you own a huge chunk of the company's stock.

One good way to defer interest income: Purchase short-term financial instruments—such as Treasury bills or certificates of deposit—that mature a year or less from their date of issue and pay interest only at maturity. The law doesn't require you to pay taxes on the interest these investments earn until they mature.

Here's an example. Say on January 2, 1988, you bought a one-year certificate of deposit (CD) that pays interest at maturity. You don't have to pay tax on your interest until 1989, when your investment matures. And in 1989 you could start this tax-saving cycle over again by buying a one-year CD that matures on January 2, 1990.

Caution: This strategy won't work if you purchase CD's or other financial instruments that mature in more than one year. Special rules apply to these investments. These rules require you to recognize receipt-of-interest income each year—regardless of when you actually get the money.

Q: What types of transactions give me some leeway when it comes to deferring or accelerating income?

You should try to time financial transactions to best suit your tax-planning needs. For example:

  • Selling stock that may generate gains or losses (see Chapter 13 for more information)
  • Exercising taxable stock options (see Chapter 24)
  • Collecting pension and profit-sharing payouts (see Chapters 21 through 23)
  • Paying off bills for itemized deductions—a big medical bill, for example (see Chapter 6)
  • Renewing certificates of deposit

If you own a business, you should decide whether or not to elect the special $10,000 write-off for equipment purchases in 1988. And you should choose the most favorable depreciation method for your equipment purchase. (See Chapter 18 for the lowdown on depreciation.)

Q: I heard that Congress recently adopted legislation that would increase Medicare coverage but that the premium is somehow tied to my tax liability. Details, please.

Beginning in 1989, people who are sixty-five years of age or older and others who are eligible for Medicare must pay a supplemental Medicare premium based on their income tax liability. For each $150 in taxes you pay Uncle Sam, you must fork over $22.50 in Medicare premiums.

And this rate rises to $37.50 in 1990, $39.00 in 1991, $40.50 in 1992, and $42.00 in 1993.

Uncle Sam says the surtax applies only to people whose tax liability adds up to $150 or more. Also, he caps the surtax at $800 per person in 1989, $850 in 1990, $900 in 1991, $950 in 1992, and $1,050 in 1993. (If you're married and file jointly, the ceiling is double these amounts.)

Caution: The new law won't allow you to deduct your supplemental Medicare premiums as a medical expense on your tax return. Nor is the premium treated as a tax when it comes time to determine your alternative minimum tax liability.

Another important point: Starting in 1989, you must take the supplemental premium into account when you make your estimated tax payments. But the IRS may waive the penalty on underpayment of estimated taxes the first year you become liable for supplemental premiums.

CHAPTER 2

Making the Most of Your Personal Exemptions

You've heard of the personal exemption. It's the amount you subtract from your taxable income for yourself and each of your dependents.

The personal exemption equals $1,950 in 1988 and $2,000 in 1989. In 1990 and thereafter it's adjusted for inflation.

Who qualifies for this exemption? Read on to find out.

QUALIFYING AS A DEPENDENT Uncle Sam says that you may claim a personal exemption for yourself as long as you're not listed as a dependent on someone else's return. If you're married and file jointly, you're entitled to take two exemptions— one for yourself and one for your spouse.

You may also claim a personal exemption for each of your dependents. But to qualify as a dependent, a person must meet five tests. Let's run through each of these.

Support Test

If you provide more than half a person's total support during the tax year, you meet this test. Here's how you calculate how much support you provide.

First, you add up the amount you contribute toward the support of your prospective dependent. Then you compare this sum to the entire amount of support this person receives from other sources. And this figure includes the individual's own funds if he or she uses them for support.

You may add into the total the amounts you spend for necessities—that is, food, lodging, clothing, education, medical and dental care, recreation, and transportation.

But you may not include in your contribution any part of the support that your dependent pays with his or her own wages—even if you're the one forking over the wages.

Say, for example, that you pay your mother $100 a week to stuff envelopes. Under the law, you may not claim the amount you pay her in wages as support payments.

Another point: Money that a person receives isn't considered support unless the funds are actually spent on items Uncle Sam classifies as support. What does this rule mean?

Say your father receives $2,400 in Social Security benefits and $300 in interest on his savings. He pays $2,000 for lodging, $400 for recreation, and $300 for life insurance premiums.

Even though your father received a total of $2,700, he spent—in Uncle Sam's eyes—only $2,400 for his own support. The reason: Life insurance premiums aren't considered a support item. So if you spent more than $2,400 to support your father, you provided more than half his support.

Member of Household or Relationship Test

The law defines a dependent as either a relative *or* someone who lives with you in your principal residence on a full-time basis. So a person who is related to you passes this test even if he or she *isn't* a member of your household.

But who qualifies as a relative?

Your natural or legally adopted children or stepchildren qualify. And so do your brothers, sisters, half brothers, half sisters, stepbrothers, stepsisters, parents, grandparents, stepfathers, stepmothers, uncles, aunts, nieces, and nephews.

In the eyes of the IRS your father-in-law, mother-in-law, brother-in-law, and sister-in-law are relatives too. And their status as relatives doesn't change with death or divorce.

But your cousins do not count as relatives.

As we've seen, a person who isn't related to you for tax purposes qualifies as a dependent only if he or she lives with you at your principal residence. So if you allow a cousin to live in, say, a beach house on which you pay the rent, he or she doesn't qualify as a dependent.

Another important rule: A nonrelative who is temporarily absent from your home—on vacation, at school, or in the hospital, for example—may still meet the member-of-household test. And the absence is considered temporary, even if your dependent is in a nursing home for an indefinite period.

Gross Income Test

First, a word about how Uncle Sam defines gross income for this test. It's income—in the form of money, property, and services—that isn't exempt from tax.

So tax-exempt income, such as income from tax-exempt municipal bonds and some Social Security payments, isn't included in the definition.

The law says that the person you're claiming as a dependent must not report gross income that equals or exceeds the amount of the personal exemption. But there are exceptions to this rule. If the person is your child and is under age nineteen or a full-time student, the test does not apply.

To meet the student exemption, your dependent must be enrolled for at least five months of the year in an institution in which education is the primary purpose.

For example, a hospital providing programs for interns and residents does not qualify. Those programs fall into the category of on-the-job training.

However, if your dependent is studying in a division of the hospital where the primary purpose is teaching—a student nursing program, for example—he or she will qualify.

Why the gross income exception for full-time students? It's Uncle Sam's way of encouraging young scholars to work their way through school without jeopardizing the parents' dependency deduction. But keep in mind: You still must continue to provide over half the student's support to collect your deduction.

Another point you should keep in mind: The exception for children does not extend to a son-in-law or daughter-in-law.

Here's an example of how the gross income test works. Say your father retired five years ago and he now receives more than half his support from you. Your father is a partner in a real estate partnership and his share of gross rental income from it is $2,100 a year before expenses. After expenses his net rental income comes to $200.

So may you claim your father as a dependent? The answer is no. His share of the partnership's gross rental incomes exceeds the amount of the personal exemption.

Citizenship Test

This test requires that a dependent be a U.S. citizen, resident, or national, or a resident of Canada or Mexico for some part of the tax year.

Let's say you're a U.S. citizen married to a French citizen.

The two of you and your son make your home in the United States, and you file a joint return.

You may claim your child as a dependent regardless of your citizenship or your spouse's citizenship, because he is a U.S. resident.

Tip: A special rule applies to adopted children of U.S. taxpayers who live abroad. In such cases you may claim the child as a dependent—even if he or she isn't a U.S. citizen or resident—as long as the child lives with you.

Joint Return Test

Even if the other tests are met, you're not allowed to claim an exemption for a dependent if he or she files a joint return. Here's an example.

Say you supported your daughter for the entire year while her husband served in the armed forces. The couple files a joint return. You may not claim a dependency exemption for her, because she files a joint return with her husband.

However, Uncle Sam does carve out an exception to this rule. You may claim an exemption for a dependent if neither the dependent nor the dependent's spouse is *required* to file a return but they file a joint return to claim a refund.

MULTIPLE SUPPORT   Often, especially in the case of children supporting aging parents or other relatives, no one provides more than half the support of a person. Instead, two or more people—each of whom would be entitled to take the exemption if it weren't for the support test—together provide more than half the dependent's support.

In these cases of multiple support, the law says, you may agree that any one of you who individually provides more than 10 percent of the person's support—but only one—may claim an exemption for that person. You may not split the personal exemption among you.

Each of the others must sign a written statement (Form 2120, "Multiple Support Declaration") agreeing not to claim the exemption for that year. The statements must be filed with the income tax return of the person who claims the exemption.

Here's an example. Say you, your sister, and two brothers support your mother. You provide 45 percent of her support; your sister, 35 percent; and your two brothers, 10 percent each.

Either you or your sister may claim an exemption for your

mother. The other must sign a Form 2120 or a written statement agreeing not to claim an exemption for her.

Because neither of your brothers provides more than 10 percent of your mother's support, neither of them may claim the exemption. And they do not have to sign a Form 2120 or the statement.

You should consider taking advantage of this planning opportunity and allowing the person who would benefit most from the personal exemption to claim it—even if that person does not contribute the most support.

FAMILY MATTERS   Uncle Sam imposes special rules for a child of separated or divorced parents or parents who have lived apart from each other for the last six months of the year.

In the case of separated parents, the parent who has custody of the child for the greater part of the year may claim the child as a dependent. And it doesn't matter whether that parent actually provided any support—as long as both parents together provide at least half the child's support and the child is in the custody of one or both parents for more than half the year.

In the case of divorced parents, custody is usually determined either by the terms of your most recent divorce decree or separate maintenance agreement, or a later custody decree.

What happens if neither a decree nor agreement establishes custody? Then the law considers the parent who has physical custody of the child for the greater part of the year to have custody.

This rule also applies if the validity of a decree or agreement that awards custody is uncertain because of legal proceedings that may still be pending on the last day of the calendar year.

PERSONAL CONSIDERATIONS   If your taxable income is high, you begin to lose the benefits of any personal exemptions. In 1988, as your income rises beyond designated levels, you get hit with an extra 5 percent tax. And this tax continues to apply until all the tax savings of the personal exemption are wiped out.

Here are the triggering levels of adjusted gross income (AGI) for this surtax.

- $149,250 for married individuals filing joint returns, and surviving spouses
- $123,790 for heads of households
- $89,560 for single individuals
- $113,300 for married individuals filing separate returns

Uncle Sam will adjust these AGI levels for inflation beginning in 1989.

The surtax starts at the trigger point and stays with you until it recaptures all the tax saving you gained by claiming one or more personal deductions.

Up to what amount must you pay it?

The range of income over which the personal exemption surtax applies depends on how many personal exemptions you claim. It's easy to calculate.

One personal exemption in 1988 reduces your taxable income by $1,950. That's a tax saving of $546, or 28 percent (the maximum tax rate) times $1,950.

To recover the full $546 with a 5 percent surtax, the IRS must apply that tax to $10,920 of income ($10,920 times 5 percent equals $546).

So, if you claim one personal exemption, you pay the surtax on the first $10,920 you earn over your trigger point. If you claim two personal exemptions, you pay the tax on the first $21,840 (two increments of $10,920) in income over the trigger point—and so on.

Caution: Legislation now before Congress would change the rules governing married couples who file separate returns. The proposed law would prevent separate filers from enjoying a tax benefit that's not available to joint filers.

Under the pending legislation, separate filers would pay the 5 percent surtax not only on their own personal exemption but also on an "assumed" exemption of their spouse. That means each spouse would pay the surtax on two exemptions—one for themselves and one for their spouse.

Still confused? Let's look at an example.

Say you are married with two children. You file jointly and claim four personal exemptions. You pay the 5 percent surtax on taxable income between $149,250 (the trigger point for joint returns) and $192,930 ($149,250 plus four times $10,920). The surtax equals $2,184 (5 percent times $43,680).

Tip: This new personal-exemption surtax changes one long-held tenet of tax planning. The dependency exemption for children of divorced parents, which used to be far more valuable to the higher-paid parent, now may help only the lower-income parent.

Let's go back to our previous example. You and your spouse divorce. Your taxable income remains greater than $122,320 (your single $89,560 trigger point plus three increments of $10,920).

So the personal exemptions for your two children are worthless to you. Your spouse should claim the children as dependents—if he or she can benefit.

Another important point: Under the 1986 tax law, blind and elderly taxpayers no longer get the extra personal exemptions that they used to claim. (But they do get other benefits, such as a larger standard deduction. For more information on the standard deduction, see Chapter 3.)

QUESTIONS AND ANSWERS

Question: My child was born in November of this year. May we claim him as a dependent for part of the year?

You're in luck. You may claim a full dependency exemption for your child in the year he or she is born. And this rule holds true even if your child's birthday is December 31.

Q: I claim my mother as a dependent. She passed away in early 1988. Am I still entitled to a personal exemption?

You are. The IRS says that a person who died during the year but was a dependent until death meets the test, even if that person passed away on January 1.

CHAPTER 3

Adding Up Your Deductions

Who, what, where, when, why, and how much? When you claim deductions on your Form 1040, the IRS, like a good reporter, is going to want the facts.

Taking legitimate deductions is, of course, one of the best ways of reducing your taxable income. But the rules governing deductions are tight. And, in the event that it decides to ask questions later, the IRS will want to see records and receipts for the expenses you have written off.

So, in the chapters that follow, we show you how to deal with deductions. We'll tell you what's deductible and what's not and what records, if any, you have to maintain to back up your claim.

We'll also give you some deduction strategies to consider. *When* you claim certain deductible expenses, can affect the *amount* of the deduction.

In this chapter we'll begin with the deduction that everyone may claim—the standard deduction.

YOUR STANDARD DEDUCTION When it comes time to file your tax return, Uncle Sam gives you two options. You may claim the standard deduction, or you may itemize your deductions.

Here, arranged by filing status, are the latest standard deductions. They're larger than they used to be. And beginning in 1989, Uncle Sam will adjust the amount of the standard deduction to reflect the ravages—if any—of inflation.

Standard Deduction

Filing Status	1988
Married, filing jointly	$5,000
Married, filing separately	2,500
Head of household	4,400
Single	3,000

Tip: Here's a break for people who are sixty-five or older. If you're single, the law allows you to add $750 to your standard deduction. If you're married, the law says you may add $600 for each spouse who is aged sixty-five or older.

Say you're single and aged sixty-five or older. Your standard deduction for 1988 adds up to $3,750—that is, you claim the 1988 standard deduction of $3,000 and you add to that amount $750.

Now let's assume you're married and file a joint return. You add $600 to your 1988 standard deduction, $5,000, if you—or your spouse—are sixty-five or older. If you're both in the sixty-five-or-older category, you add $1,200.

Tip: A single taxpayer who is both blind and sixty-five or older may add $1,500 to the standard deduction. A married taxpayer may add $1,200 ($2,400 if you and your spouse are both blind, sixty-five or older, and file a joint return).

Caution: Say you claim your father as a dependent and he is both blind and aged sixty-five or older. May you claim a deduction for his blindness and advanced age?

Unfortunately, the rules say that you may not claim a deduction for the blindness or old age of a dependent. This tax break is available only to people who file their own tax returns.

Caution: Children and other dependents who file their own returns aren't always entitled to claim a full standard deduction. (For the details, see Chapter 25.)

FINE LINE Before we go further, two key definitions—"above the line" and "below the line." The "line" refers to your adjusted gross income (AGI).

Uncle Sam used to allow you to deduct above the line—that is, a part of your AGI calculation—such items as moving expenses and employee business expenses.

Now you must subtract these items below the line. That is,

they're itemized deductions that no longer figure in your AGI calculation.

What difference does this change make? Consider this example. Say that the year is 1985 and your only income is your salary—a hefty $100,000.

From this amount you subtracted moving expenses of $2,000. The result—$98,000—was your AGI. Once you calculated your AGI, you then deducted your itemized expenses or claimed the standard deduction, whichever was greater.

Now, say the year is 1988. Once again your only income is your salary of $100,000, and you report moving expenses of $2,000. This time, though, you may not subtract your moving expenses above the line—that is, to arrive at your AGI.

You must add your moving expenses to all your other itemized deductions—mortgage interest, property taxes, and so on—below the line. If these itemized write-offs top the standard deduction, you're entitled to itemize. If not, you take the standard deduction.

The bottom line: If you claim deductions above the line, you're guaranteed to receive a benefit. If you claim deductions below the line, you benefit only if you itemize.

STANDARD PROCEDURE   To itemize or not?

The answer: If you may itemize, do so. You always come out ahead. How do you know if you may itemize? You add up your deductible expenses to see whether they are more or less than the standard deduction. If they're more, itemize; if not, take the standard deduction.

In the chapters that follow, we take a look at those items that are deductible from your adjusted gross income. We also examine itemized deductions that don't kick in until they exceed a percentage of your gross income.

QUESTIONS AND ANSWERS

QUESTION: I can't itemize this year. Does that mean I totally lose the benefit of these deductions?

You will, unless you take steps now.

Say you've run your numbers for 1988 and you know you can't itemize. What should you do? Put off paying some deductible expenses until 1989. That way, you increase the amount of your deductions for 1989—and, with luck, you can write off the costs in that year.

In short, you should always try to bunch your deductions in one year—by either accelerating or deferring payments. In doing so, you may exceed the standard deduction—and itemize—at least every other year.

For instance, say you normally receive your bill for real estate taxes on December 20. And you paid last year's bill when it was due—January 15, 1988.

By accelerating your payment of the current bill to December 31, you pay two years' worth of property taxes in one year—and increase your deductions for that year.

Q: I'm trying to boost my deductions for the year. I know I'm going to owe my dentist more than $5,000 for the reconstruction work he'll be doing. Can I pay him now—before he works on my mouth—and increase my medical expense deduction this year?

Sorry, but Uncle Sam won't allow you to deduct payments for services not yet rendered. But say the dentist has already begun the reconstruction work and you've agreed to pay him a flat fee when he's done. In this case, you may claim the deduction this year.

Q: What about my mortgage interest payments and state income taxes? May I prepay and deduct these amounts?

The IRS says you may not write off mortgage interest payments in advance. (See Chapter 4 for more information on interest deductions.)

But you may prepay—and deduct—your state income taxes, as long as your payments are based on a reasonable estimate of your final tax bill at the time you make your payment. (For more information on prepaying state and local income taxes, see Chapter 7.)

CHAPTER 4

Those Late, Great Interest Deductions

The main concerns borrowers used to have were whether they would qualify for the loan they wanted and what rate of interest they'd have to pay. Interest was interest, and it was all deductible when Congress passed the original Internal Revenue Code in 1913.

In fact, until passage of the 1986 Tax Reform Act, the only interest you couldn't deduct was interest paid on loans taken out to buy tax-exempt bonds and single-premium life insurance contracts. And the only restrictions on interest deductibility involved limits on investment and prepaid interest.

Now, however, the simple life is over.

To begin with, interest is no longer interest. The tax laws now recognize five different categories of interest and contain complicated rules intended to prevent taxpayers from shifting debt from one category to another. The categories:

- Mortgage interest
- Business interest
- Personal interest
- Investment interest
- Passive activity interest

Special rules apply to the deductibility of each type of interest. Business interest, for instance, is completely deductible, while deductions for personal interest will soon be history.

In this chapter we'll explain the rules that determine when and how much of your interest expense you may deduct. And we'll show you how you can work within these rules to maximize the amount of interest you can deduct in order to minimize the after-tax cost of your borrowing.

Because the new interest rules are complicated, we've divided this chapter into clearly labeled sections. Each section covers a different interest category. And we try early on to give you the information you need to determine whether the category applies to you.

MORTGAGE INTEREST   When it comes time to calculate your taxes for 1988 and 1989, set aside what you thought you knew about mortgage interest deductions. Congress changed the rules when it adopted the Revenue Act of 1987.

For the typical taxpayer, home mortgage interest is still fully deductible—provided that the mortgage is recorded and the house is used as security for the loan. In fact, the interest on any mortgage signed prior to October 14, 1987, is fully deductible in 1988—even if it wouldn't have been deductible under the old rules. And this rule holds true regardless of whether the debt is a first or second mortgage or a home-equity loan.

But limitations on the deductibility of home mortgage interest do apply to some taxpayers. The bad news for individuals who face limitations on their ability to deduct mortgage interest is that they have a whole new set of rules to learn in 1988.

We'll look at the rules one at a time so that you'll be able to tell easily which do and don't apply to you.

You own more than two homes

If you own more than two residences, Uncle Sam classifies the mortgage interest on these additional homes according to how you use the houses and the money.

Say, for example, that you use your third home—a ski chalet—for personal purposes only. Interest on the loan you take out to purchase the chalet is treated for tax purposes as personal interest. That is, it is 40 percent deductible in 1988. (We'll cover personal interest later in this chapter.)

What if you borrow money on your third home and use it to purchase stock in your company? The rules say that you write off the interest according to how you spent the money. In this case, you deduct the interest as investment interest.

You purchased a new home, refinanced an existing home, or incurred additional mortgage debt after October 13, 1987

If you fall into this category, Uncle Sam divides your deductible mortgage debt into two categories—acquisition debt and home-equity debt.

How does he define these two terms?

Acquisition debt is secured by your primary or second home and is incurred when you buy, build, or substantially improve your home. Acquisition debt also includes debt from refinancing your old mortgage, up to the amount of the refinanced debt.

Home-equity debt is also secured by your primary or second home, but in contrast to acquisition debt, home-equity loans are *not* used to buy, build, or substantially improve your residence. Furthermore, one loan can be both acquisition debt and home-equity debt.

Say, for instance, that you refinance your mortgage, using part of the proceeds to pay off your original mortgage and the rest to pay off some personal debt. You don't have to take out two loans—one to refinance the mortgage and a second one to tap into your home's appreciation. A single debt may qualify partially as acquisition indebtedness and partially home-equity indebtedness.

The interest on a home-equity loan, or on the home-equity portion of a combined acquisition/home-equity loan, is fully deductible so long as the debt does not exceed the lesser of: the fair market value of your home minus the total acquisition debt, or $100,000 ($50,000 if you're married and file separate returns).

What if you own two homes? It doesn't matter. The cap on your home-equity debt, whether on one or two houses, still may not exceed $100,000.

Tip: The best idea, taxwise, is to maximize your acquisition debt. If you think you will need more money later on, borrow the money when you buy the house. That way, you don't eat into your $100,000 home-equity ceiling.

Your mortgage debts total more than $1 million

Uncle Sam says you may deduct mortgage interest only on acquisition debt of up to $1 million—$500,000 if you are married and file separate returns.

But he provides a break to taxpayers who incurred their mortgage debt before October 14, 1987. This debt is not subject to the $1 million ceiling.

However, if your pre–October 14, 1987, acquisition debt topped $1 million and you took out additional debt after that date—to improve your kitchen, for example—you're subject to the ceiling.

Caution: And here's another consideration for homeowners. Even if you may write off all the interest on a refinanced mortgage loan for regular tax purposes, you may not be able do so when you compute your alternative minimum tax.

The AMT is a flat tax of 21 percent. Who pays it? Taxpayers whose legitimate deductions reduce the regular tax they owe substantially below the amount their incomes suggest they ought to be paying. (Chapter 20 explains the AMT in detail.)

Here's an example of how you'd compute the deductibility of a refinanced mortgage for AMT purposes. Say that your house costs $80,000. The outstanding balance on your old mortgage is $70,000. Now, you refinance, and the bank loans you $125,000. What is the maximum amount of interest on this new loan that you may write off when computing your AMT?

You figure the difference between your old mortgage balance and the amount of the new loan—$55,000 in this case ($125,000 less $70,000). The interest on this $55,000 is not deductible for AMT purposes.

An easy way to calculate how much interest you may deduct is to divide your old mortgage balance ($70,000) by the total amount of your new loan ($125,000). That's the amount (56 percent) of the interest on your refinanced mortgage that you may write off when you figure your AMT.

Under the AMT rules you may also deduct interest on amounts you borrow to "substantially rehabilitate" your home—provided, of course, the loan is a mortgage secured by the house. Although Uncle Sam doesn't define "substantially rehabilitate," you can assume he means only major renovations.

BUSINESS INTEREST   The rules governing business interest are simple. Whether your business is Consolidated Worldwide Corp. or Wilbur's Window Washing, the interest you pay on loans taken out to operate your business is completely deductible.

But you should be sure a business loan is a business loan, not an employee loan. What's the difference?

A business owner may deduct the interest on a loan he or she takes out to purchase a car for the company. If, however, you borrow money to buy a car and use it in your employer's business, the IRS classifies the loan as personal, and the interest, as you are about to see, is only partially deductible.

PERSONAL INTEREST   Before Congress adopted the 1986 Tax Reform Act, interest you paid on personal loans—money you borrowed to take a vacation, for instance—was fully deductible. After 1990, the new law says, personal interest won't be deductible at all.

For the interim, Congress enacted a gradual phase-out period. So personal interest becomes increasingly less deductible according to the following schedule.

Your Personal Interest Deductions

Year	Amount Deductible
1988	40 percent
1989	20 percent
1990	10 percent
After 1990	0 percent

You can see that with this schedule, the after-tax cost of borrowing rises from year to year through 1990.

Let's say that you pay $1,000 in interest on an auto loan in 1988 and again in 1989. The first year you may deduct $400 ($1,000 times 40 percent) from your taxable income, but a year later you may write off only $200 ($1,000 times 20 percent). The debt costs you more in the second year than in the first.

So what are your options? You have four.

First, you can go on borrowing as in the past, knowing that the money you borrow is costing you more each year.

Or you might reduce your borrowing by, say, delaying purchases until you've accumulated all or even more of the cash required.

A third alternative? Convert personal interest into another category—mortgage interest, for instance—that is still deductible.

What types of personal interest might you convert to deductible interest? Any interest you must pay on loans for a car, a boat—even a vacation.

Many people, in fact, are using their homes to finance some of their borrowing. You can, too, but as we noted earlier, you should exercise caution of you go this route.

The fourth way to minimize your nondeductible interest: leasing. For some people the savings can be substantial. Here's an example.

Your neighbor, let's say, just bought a $20,000 car. With $3,000 down, she agreed to pay the bank 10 percent interest on her loan, or $431.16 a month for 48 months. So her total pre-tax cost comes to $23,696—the down payment plus $20,696 in principal and interest charges.

Of course, she can deduct some of the interest charges. In 1988 she can write off 40 percent of the $1,536 she pays in interest. In 1989 it's 20 percent of $1,155; and in 1990, 10 percent of $735. In 1991 she gets no tax deduction for her $269 in interest.

If she, like you, is in the 28 percent bracket in 1988 and beyond, her tax saving comes to $172 in 1988, $65 in 1989, $21 in 1990—or a total of $258. So, over the four years the car costs her $23,696 minus $258 in tax savings—or $23,438.

You, on the other hand, decide to lease the same car. Your monthly lease payments come to $350, which means that over 48 months you'll spend just $16,800. Of course, you don't need a down payment, so you invest your $3,000 in a four-year, 8 percent CD. After taxes, it earns you $753.

The total cost of the car to you at the end of four years: $16,800 minus $753, or $16,047.

Compared to your neighbor, you've paid $7,391 less and had the use of the same type of car as she. Of course, she now owns a car that she can continue to drive for several more years, while you have to buy or lease a new one. Is her car worth the extra $7,391 she shelled out?

That's a question you must answer for yourself. Run the numbers before you jump on the leasing bandwagon. And as you perform your calculations, keep these points in mind.

There are many different types of leases—some even require you to put down money up front. Read the lease carefully before you sign on the dotted line.

Tip: A key variable in determining whether to buy or lease is whether you use the car for employee business purposes.

As we've seen, the interest on a car you *buy* to use for employee business purposes is considered personal interest and subject to the phase-out rules through 1990. But when you *lease* a car, you may deduct the portion of the lease payment attributable to employee business use. One word of caution though: You may not get the full benefit of your business deduction, depending upon the value of your car. See Chapter 12 for a discussion of these rules.

Our advice: Before you go the leasing route, compare the total after-tax costs of leasing and buying. It's the only way to know for certain if leasing is right for you.

INVESTMENT INTEREST   Investment interest is the interest you pay on your stock margin account or on any other loan you take out to fund an investment.

Different rules apply, however, to interest on so-called passive activities or on a passive investment in a business, a subject we'll get to shortly. As a general rule, you may deduct investment interest only against investment income.

If, let's say, you earn $5,000 from various investments and pay your broker $1,000 interest on a margin account, you may deduct the entire $1,000 against the $5,000. If your investment earnings had totaled a mere $50, though, that's also the maximum amount of investment interest you could deduct.

On the other hand, what you may not deduct in one year you may carry forward into other years. In our previous example you had $950 in nondeductible investment-interest expense. The law allows you to carry that amount forward indefinitely, until you generate enough investment income against which to write it off.

And keep in mind: Investment income includes not only periodic earnings from your investments—dividends from blue-chip stocks, for instance—but also your gain from the sale of those stocks.

The specific rules governing investment interest are just a bit more complicated—at least for the years 1987 through 1990.

First, you may recall that before 1986 you could write off from your regular income investment interest that was as much as $10,000 more than your investment income for the year.

This $10,000 allowance is phased out through 1990 at the same rates as personal interest.

In 1988, for instance, you may deduct 40 percent of excess interest up to $10,000. The maximum interest you may deduct under this rule is $4,000—that is, $10,000 times 40 percent. So, if in 1988 you have investment interest of $4,000 but investment income of just $1,000, you may write off $2,200—$1,000 plus 40 percent of the balance, or $1,200 ($3,000 times 40 percent).

In 1989 you may write off only 20 percent of the excess; and in 1990, 10 percent. After that the investment interest you may deduct is limited to the investment income you earn—with the carry-forward provision we mentioned.

Another wrinkle: Any passive losses you claim during the phase-out period—for example, 40 percent in 1988—reduce the investment income against which you may deduct investment interest. (We get to passive investment losses in Chapter 19.)

Of course, just as with personal interest, you may convert investment interest to mortgage interest by borrowing against your first or second home. Doing so will make the interest totally deductible—as long as your borrowings don't top $100,000.

However, as we've seen, a caveat applies. Whether you're borrowing to buy a boat or a bond, putting your home up as collateral is serious business. You should think through all the pros and cons before making that decision.

PASSIVE ACTIVITY INTEREST   In 1986 Congress created a new category of interest expense—interest from passive activities. We'll get to the definition of this term in a minute.

First, though, you should know that the tax code treats this interest much like the investment interest we've already discussed.

For instance, just as you may deduct investment interest only against investment income, you may write off passive activity interest only against passive activity income. No passive activity income, no deduction.

Also, like investment interest, you may carry passive activity interest expenses forward indefinitely. That is, you may use them to offset passive income in future years.

But there is one difference: In the year you dispose of a passive investment, the law lets you deduct the passive activity interest that you hadn't been able to deduct in previous years. This break doesn't apply to investment interest.

But what in the world is a passive activity?

The tax code says that it's any business in which you do not "materially participate." So you must be involved in the operation of a business on a "regular, continuous, and substantial basis." If you're not, the business qualifies as a passive activity for you.

And if it's a passive activity, you may deduct any interest expense you incur only against income that you also derive from a passive activity. In other words, you may not deduct this interest from wage income, investment income, or business income.

Limited partnerships are, in the eyes of the law, always passive activities. Most rental activities, also, fall into the category of passive activities. (See Chapter 15 for information on exceptions to this rule. And see Chapter 19 for more information on passive activities.)

QUESTIONS AND ANSWERS

QUESTION: Can I boost my mortgage interest deductions by making my mortgage payments in advance?

The law won't allow you to claim a deduction for prepaid interest—no matter what category that interest falls into.

But most people actually pay their mortgage in arrears. That is, the payment you must make on January 1, for instance, is really for principal and interest due in December. So if you make this January 1 payment on December 31, the amount is not prepaid—and you may deduct it.

Tip: Banks and other lending institutions send out statements of interest paid. But lenders often omit from these statements the interest on the payment you made in December. Check the statements to make sure the interest listed is the actual interest you paid during the year.

Also, when you refinance, make sure you pick up interest you paid from the date of closing to the end of the month when you refinance. This amount is seldom reported on statements issued by lending institutions.

Q: Are points still deductible?

Points—the additional amount you pay when a loan is closed—are deductible in the year you buy your home. (One point is one percent of the amount of your loan.) But a word of warning: You may not deduct points currently if you pay them with money borrowed from the same bank that holds your mortgage. Our advice: Write a separate check to your lender for points attributable to any borrowings secured by your home.

Caution: The IRS maintains that you may not take a deduction in the current tax year for points that you pay as part of a refinancing. It says you must write off these points over the life of the mortgage.

Say, for example, that you refinance your home mortgage and pay points of $2,000. The term of the loan is twenty years. So you claim a deduction for $100 a year for twenty years.

Q: I'm going through a divorce and want to buy out my spouse's interest in our home. If I do so, using the house as security for the mortgage, what are the tax consequences?

Money you borrow to buy out your spouse's interest in a house qualifies as acquisition indebtedness. And as such, the interest is fully deductible.

Q: How can a loan I make to my kids to purchase a home qualify as acquisition indebtedness?

Make sure that the home secures the debt by filing the appropriate papers. Otherwise, the interest payments are personal interest and only 40 percent deductible in 1988.

Q: We bought our house ten years ago for $75,000. The fair market value of our home went up to more than $120,000. So, in January 1987, we refinanced our original mortgage and obtained a new loan. We used the money for personal purposes. Is the interest on our refinanced mortgage deductible?

The interest is fully deductible since the mortgage is secured by your home and was incurred before October 14, 1987. In the eyes of the IRS your mortgage is acquisition debt, even though it exceeds the cost of your home.

Q: I want to turn the equity in our house into cash. What's the best way?

You have three ways to get at your accumulated equity. You can refinance your house. You can take out a second mortgage. Or you can apply for a home-equity loan.

When you refinance, you apply for an entirely new mortgage. Doing so is usually costly, and it takes time. So you'll want to refinance only if the interest rate on the new mortgage is low enough to offset the cost of securing the new mortgage. Otherwise you'd be wise to consider one of the other two methods.

Second mortgages and home-equity loans are, technically, one and the same. Both allow you to borrow against a portion of the difference between the balance due on your existing mortgage and the current value of your home.

With a second mortgage you get a single check for the full amount of the loan. Home-equity loans, on the other hand, usually allow you to take the money as you need it by writing a check or using a credit card. While second mortgage loans usually run for five to fifteen years, home-equity loans can run longer or can even be open-ended.

More and more people are using one of these three devices to tap the equity in their homes in order to finance other purchases.

It's legal and it can be smart—provided you understand the limitations and are aware of the pitfalls.

The pitfalls, however, can be subtle.

First, there's the expense. Banks frequently charge "loan origination fees," or points of 2 or 3 percent on second mortgages and home-equity credit lines. And there are closing costs, which can add up to several hundred dollars. You pay all these fees up front, before you get the cash.

Less obvious, and more significant, is the risk you assume when you use your house as collateral. Suddenly you have tens of thousands of dollars available to you.

Feeling flush, you succumb to buying the boat you've dreamed of for years. But the payments and maintenance costs turn out to be more than you can handle and you fall behind. With a standard loan, you lose the boat. With a home-equity loan, though, it's your house the bank comes after.

Here's another example. Let's say you buy a new car.

A standard auto loan requires you to pay off the principal over a specified period—three to five years. Buy the same car with a home-equity line of credit, and all you have to pay is interest. Without self-discipline, at the end of five years you could easily have an old, unpaid-for car.

Another risk to the home-equity loan: rising interest rates. Because the rate on most home-equity loans floats with the market, you may start out with an easy payment. But you could wind up with a monthly payment you can no longer afford.

We're not advising you to avoid tapping the equity in your home, but we are urging caution. Also, if you do opt to refinance or sign up for a home-equity loan, shop around. The rates and terms of these loans vary enormously from institution to institution.

Q: Not all my mortgage interest is deductible. What do I do with the rest?

Write it off as personal interest. Although personal interest is only 40 percent deductible in 1988 and 20 percent deductible in 1989, a partial deduction is better than no deduction at all.

Q: My son fell on hard times, and I made three mortgage payments for him. May I deduct the interest?

Uncle Sam allows you to write off interest only on debts for which you are legally liable. You're not entitled to a write-off unless you're a signatory to your son's mortgage.

Q: Is it still worthwhile to check my credit card statements for personal interest I paid during the year?

It certainly is. After all, a small deduction is better than no deduction at all.

Q: How do I know whether interest is personal interest, say, or investment interest?

You trace how you use the money you borrowed. And you trace it from the day the money is in your hands until the day you repay the loan.

Say you go to the bank and take out a loan. You use the money to buy a new car for the family. The car is a personal asset, so the interest on the loan is personal interest.

Simple, you say, But wait a minute.

Let's say you borrow $25,000 and deposit the money in your checking account. Later in the year you use the money to purchase some stock, a car for your son, and a typewriter for your business.

In the eyes of the IRS, this single loan generates three types of interest—investment interest on the stock purchases, personal interest on the car, and business interest on the typewriter. And different rules govern the deductibility of these different types of interest.

Usually when you borrow money, you either use it immediately for a particular purpose or deposit it in your checking or savings account until you're ready to buy.

What happens if you deposit the money in an account that contains other funds? Uncle Sam says the interest on the loan is investment interest. And it remains investment interest until you take the money out of your account and use it.

What's more, you must spend the money you borrow within 15 days if you want interest on the loan classified according to how you use the money.

And if you wait longer than 15 days? The IRS bases the interest deduction on the first purchase you make from your account.

Here's how the 15-day rule works.

Say you borrow $1,000 on September 1 to purchase some stock. You put the money in your checking account, which already has a balance of $1,000.

On September 20 your washer goes on the blink. So you buy a new one, for $600, and write a check for that amount.

On October 9—39 days after you took out the loan—you purchase the stock. You fork over $1,000 for 100 shares of ABC Co. What are the tax consequences?

The IRS treats the interest on the entire $1,000 as investment interest until September 20, when you purchased the washer.

Then it classifies the interest on $600—the amount you paid for the washer—as personal interest. The remaining $400 is investment interest.

How do you avoid this paperwork nightmare? For starters, maintain separate accounts for funds you borrow for personal, business, investment, and passive purposes. That way you won't be tripped up by the tracing rules. The tax benefits outweigh any additional bank fees for segregating accounts.

If you don't go this route—that is, if you put your borrowed funds and personal stash in one account—observe the 15-day rule. Otherwise, be prepared to wade through the IRS debt allocation and tracing rules. And there's more than paperwork hassles involved. You could wind up with more nondeductible interest expenses than you bargained for.

Also, make sure you can trace debts you rack up for investments. For example, ask your lender to make the loan amount payable not to you but to a third party—your stockbroker, for instance.

Q: A friend tells me that there's a 90-day rule governing mortgage interest deductions. True?

Yes. Uncle Sam gives you 90 days from the time you purchase your house to secure a mortgage. If you wait longer, you're entitled to write off your mortgage interest as acquisition debt only if you can prove, under the tracing rules, that you spent the borrowed money to acquire or improve your home.

Q: We're building a new home. Does our construction loan qualify as acquisition debt?

The answer is yes—to the extent that you spend the money you borrowed within 24 months of completing your new home.

Q: I borrowed money to invest in tax-exempt bonds. Is the interest on my loan investment interest?

This interest indeed falls into the category of investment interest, but you may not claim a write-off. The reason is simple.

The rules don't allow you to deduct interest on money you borrow to invest in instruments that don't produce taxable income. Tax-exempt municipal bonds are a good example.

Q: I loaned my daughter $15,000. I'm not charging her interest. What are the tax implications of the loan?

Even though your daughter is paying you no interest, the law requires you to "impute," or assume, interest income. The interest equals the lesser of:

• The amount of the outstanding loan times the applicable federal rate (based on a rate the federal government pays on its borrowing)
• Or the net investment income of the borrower if it exceeds $1,000
• Or zero if the net investment income of the borrower is less than $1,000

Say, for example, that your daughter reports $200 of investment income for the year. There's no imputed interest to you, because her net investment income—$200—is less than $1,000.

But say she reports $10,000 in net investment income. In this case you must impute interest income on the loan—that is, $15,000 times the applicable federal rate, say 8 percent, or $1,200. And this imputed interest would be treated as a gift from you to your daughter.

The law does make an exception to the imputed interest rules for so-called *de minimis* loans of less than $10,000. If you make personal loans that total less than this amount, you don't have to impute interest income at all. But this exception doesn't apply if the loan is used to buy income-producing assets—rental property, for example.

Another wrinkle: If the primary purpose of the loan was to avoid paying income tax—for instance, you loaned your daughter money to make an investment so the investment income would be reported on her return instead of yours—the net investment income limitation doesn't apply. You must impute interest based on the applicable federal rate.

Depending on how your daughter used the money, she may be entitled to a deduction for the imputed interest—even though she never actually paid that amount to you.

Tip: The rules governing imputed interest are lengthy and complex. If you've borrowed or loaned money at no interest—or at a rate below the applicable federal rate—see your tax adviser.

Q: I'm a shareholder in an S corporation that operates a retail clothing store, and I don't participate in the management of the company. The corporation purchased some stock on margin. Is this interest passive interest or is it investment interest?

Your S corporation owes interest on a transaction that had nothing to do with selling clothing—its trade or business. So Uncle Sam considers the interest to be investment interest, not passive interest.

Your share of this interest passes through the S corporation to you. And you may deduct the expense if you have investment income. Otherwise, as we saw, you must carry the amount forward to future years. This same rule applies if the income came from dividends, annuities, or royalties.

Q: Should I pay this year the interest that has accrued on my life insurance policy loan?

The interest that accrues on policy loans is payable at any time. And if you have many years of interest due, it would probably make sense to pay up this year. After all, in 1988 personal interest is still 40 percent deductible.

Be careful, though. If you used your loan for an investment or for a passive activity, the interest is only deductible under the rules that apply to these categories.

CHAPTER 5

The Right Way to Write Off Charitable Contributions

Americans donate generously to charity, and one reason for their generosity is the tax code. The government encourages people to make charitable contributions by allowing them to write off donations on their personal tax returns.

Even so, there's a host of requirements governing charitable contributions, and it's important that you familiarize yourself with these rules.

In this chapter we tell you what you need to know to make the most of your allowable charitable deductions—and minimize your tax bill.

Let's start with a few general rules.

First, you may write off your charitable contributions only if you itemize deductions on Schedule A of your tax return. (The rule that allowed deductions for nonitemizers expired in 1986, and Congress decided not to extend it.)

The IRS defines a charitable contribution as a contribution or gift "to, or for the use of, a qualified organization." But don't let the jargon confuse you.

A qualified organization is simply a nonprofit charitable, religious, or educational group that meets government guidelines. In fact, an organization can—and undoubtedly will—tell you whether your contribution to it is tax deductible.

Moreover, a 1987 change in the tax law requires organizations to state clearly that donations are not deductible when that is the case. One note of caution, however: You are responsible for any additional tax if you are misled by an organization.

As a rule of thumb, your contribution is probably deductible if an organization is operated solely for charitable, religious, scientific, literary, or educational purposes, and you have no power to earmark a specific individual as the recipient of your generosity. But if the organization you favor substantially tries to influence legislation or gets involved in political campaigns, you're out of luck.

Note, too, that the law even permits you to write off contributions to federal, state, and local governments. The only requirement: The governmental body must use your gift solely for public purposes—to build a park or a playground, for example.

Tip: Legislation now before Congress would relax the rules governing some contributions to colleges and universities.

The proposal says that in addition to previously allowable educational contributions, you may deduct 80 percent of your donation to a school if, in exchange for that deduction, you receive the right to buy seating in its athletic stadium. At the moment these contributions aren't deductible at all.

Under current and proposed law, the amount you pay for your athletic tickets isn't deductible.

GIVING ITEMS OF VALUE   Something else you should know: The law allows you to contribute either money or property to a charity. If you donate money, you write off the amount of your gift. If you donate property, you deduct an amount equal to the fair market value of the property at the time you make the donation.

The government defines fair market value as "the price at which the property would change hands between a willing buyer and a willing seller," which only means the amount the property would bring if you sold it on the open market.

Fair market value isn't always easy to determine, however. One acceptable indication: a sale or purchase of similar property close to the date of your contribution.

So if you donate a Winslow Homer painting, for instance, to your local museum—and a comparable Homer just sold at auction for $1 million—you may be fairly confident that you'll be able to write off a full million with few questions asked.

The opinion of an appraiser is valid too. In fact, appraisals are required if you donate property with a total value of more than $5,000. For example, if you donate two automobiles—valued at $3,000 each—to an area vocational school, you'd be required to get an appraisal, because the value of the two cars tops the $5,000 limit.

Additionally, the IRS now requires you to attach color photographs to your income tax returns to support charitable donations of works of art with a total value of $20,000 or more.

As far as appraisals go, the tax law does carve out an exception for publicly traded securities. No appraisals are required for them. Appraisals are required, however, if you donate nonpublicly traded securities with a value of more than $10,000. As we've seen, if you make more than one gift, the value of your donations is added together to see if you exceed the $5,000 and $10,000 limits.

Caution: Make sure you get an accurate appraisal of property you donate. You may find yourself liable for a special penalty if you overstate your gift's value.

When does the penalty apply? Here are the two conditions. First, the value you claim on your personal return is more than 150 percent of the correct fair market value. And second, you underpaid your tax by at least $1,000 because of the overstatement.

The penalty is not insignificant. It adds up to 30 percent of the underpaid tax that the IRS attributes to the overvaluation.

Caution: Here's another rule to keep in mind. The IRS wants to make sure that an appraisal is not made by someone with a stake in overstating your gift's value.

So appraisals may not be made by you, the organization receiving the gift, the party from whom you acquired it, or any "related entity"—that is, a member of your family, or a corporation that is controlled by any of the above individuals or organizations. For the same reason, the appraiser must not base his or her fees on the gift's appraised value.

And note: You may deduct the cost of an appraisal, but only as a miscellaneous deduction, not as a charitable contribution. And miscellaneous deductions are subject to a 2 percent floor. (See Chapter 8 for more information on the 2 percent rule.)

Another rule to keep in mind: Using a trust, you may donate a partial interest in property, such as stocks or bonds, to a charitable organization and still collect a tax deduction. Under this arrangement, you—or another beneficiary—continue to get the annual income from the trust. When you die, however, the property passes to the charity.

You get your deduction—which equals the present value of the gift—the year you create the trust. If your gift consists of securities that have risen in value since you purchased them, you also avoid paying the capital gains tax on that appreciation.

Also, be aware that if you make noncash gifts of more than $500, you must file Form 8283, "Noncash Charitable Contributions," with your personal tax return. Form 8283 requires that you state when and how you acquired the property and the amount you paid for it.

For more information on how to value donated property, ask your local IRS office for a free copy of IRS Publication 561, *Determining the Value of Donated Property*.

Tip: The law also allows you to write off as charitable contributions expenses you run up when you provide volunteer services.

Say you work as a volunteer at a local nonprofit hospital. The hospital requires you to wear a bright yellow smock while you're on duty, and you purchase one from the hospital—for $20. Feel free to deduct the cost and cleaning of your garment.

The reason: It isn't suitable for everyday use, and you're required to wear it while you perform services for a charitable organization.

Or say that every Tuesday you drive twenty-four miles from your home to a nonprofit child-care center, where you donate three hours of your time. The law permits you to write off your out-of-pocket actual automobile expenses—that is, gas and oil—or claim a standard rate of 12 cents a mile.

You'll probably come out ahead if you deduct your actual expenses—even though Uncle Sam won't allow you to figure in the cost of general repairs, maintenance, insurance, and depreciation. (You may write off the cost of tolls and parking even if you opt for the standard mileage rate.)

But, as a practical matter, you may find that it's more trouble than it's worth to keep track of your actual car costs. So our advice is to opt for the standard rate of 12 cents a mile—unless you log substantial mileage each year.

Finally, let's say you serve on the board of a nonprofit group. You're asked to attend a two-day training session in your state capital.

The law says you may deduct your travel expenses—in this case, the cost of your meals and lodging during these two days—under one condition. Your trip must not include any "significant element of personal pleasure, recreation, or vacation."

Remember, however, that the cost of the meals you eat during these trips might fall under the 80 percent rule. This is the same rule that limits the deduction you claim for business meals to 80 percent of the cost. Unless the IRS changes its mind, this same limit on deductions will apply to meals eaten during charitable travel. Check with the IRS or your tax adviser at tax time.

You should know, too, that the rule about significant personal pleasure doesn't mean that you must get no enjoyment out of your charitable activity. You're free to have a dandy time if, say, you volunteer to take your daughter's Sunday school or kindergarten class on a field trip to a local zoo.

You'll pocket the write-off as long as you're genuinely on duty throughout the trip. You may not, however, write off the value of your time.

And you may not claim deductions for entertainment or for personal expenses, such as the cost of bringing your spouse or child along on the trip.

What if your charity pays you a per diem amount to cover the cost of meals and lodging while you're away from home?

If the per diem amounts exceeds your actual costs, you must report the extra cash as income on your personal tax return. But if the amount adds up to less than your actual expenses, you may write off the deficit as a charitable contribution.

Charitable groups often hold or sponsor events in order to raise money. You may write off the cost of tickets to these charitable events. But the amount shown on the ticket is not necessarily the amount of your gift. You may deduct only the amount of your actual contribution.

Say, for example, that you pay $50 to attend a special showing of a movie for the benefit of a charitable organization.

Printed on the ticket is "Contribution—$50." If the regular price for the movie is $4, you made a contribution of $46. If the regular price isn't indicated on the ticket or anywhere else, just note the normal price for similar events or activities in your area and reduce your donation by that amount.

Caution: If you purchase a ticket for a charitable event and the amount of the deductible contribution is not specified, Uncle Sam will assume that the total amount paid is for your personal benefit. That means you could lose your entire write-off unless the charity shows the deductible portion of the ticket price or you can prove that the amount you claim is a bona fide charitable donation.

Tip: You may deduct the entire cost of a benefit ticket if you donate it back to the organization for resale or to another charitable group.

WHEN YOU MAY DEDUCT YOUR CONTRIBUTION The law says that you may deduct charitable contributions in the year you make them. But it really means the year that you mail them.

Let's say the date is December 31, 1988, and you mail a

check for $200 to your church. The church receives your donation on January 2, 1989. Under the rules, you're entitled to write off the contribution on your 1988 return, because you mailed your check in 1988.

What if you charge your contribution to your bank credit card? You deduct these donations in the year you charge them.

If your gift is in the form of a stock, you claim a deduction in the year in which a properly endorsed stock certificate is mailed or delivered to the charity.

But let's say you give a stock certificate to your agent or to the issuing corporation—IBM, for example—for transfer to your favorite charity. Your gift doesn't count for tax purposes until the date the stock is actually transferred on the books of the corporation.

CHARITABLE DEDUCTION LISTS   Under a complicated set of rules, Uncle Sam limits your total deductions for charitable contributions. If your contributions for the year total 20 percent or less of your adjusted gross income (AGI), you have little to worry about.

Say, for example, that your AGI adds up to $50,000 in 1989. You should feel free to deduct up to $10,000 in charitable donations.

But let's say you're an exceptionally generous soul and you contribute 30 percent or even 50 percent of your AGI to charity. In this case, the amount you may write off depends on what you contributed and to whom you contributed it.

Our advice: If your charitable contributions top 20 percent of your adjusted gross income, you should consult your tax adviser.

QUESTIONS AND ANSWERS

QUESTION: My country club operates as a nonprofit organization. Are my annual dues deductible as a charitable contribution?

Sorry, but the answer is a resounding no.

The law won't allow you to deduct as charitable contributions dues, fees, or bills you pay to country clubs, business or civic leagues, social clubs, or other similar groups—even if they are nonprofit organizations. Also, contributions to fraternal orders or lodges are not deductible unless the organization is using the contribution solely for charitable, religious, or educational purposes.

Also forbidden: the cost of raffle, bingo, or lottery tickets, tuition expenses, the value of your time or services, the value of blood given to a blood bank, donations to homeowners associations, and gifts to individuals.

Q: I want to make a donation to a day-care center. May I deduct this amount as a charitable contribution?

Donations to nonprofit day-care centers are deductible—but only if certain conditions are met. Specifically, the center must provide care primarily to children whose parents are gainfully employed. Also, the center must make its services available to the public.

Q: Am I entitled to a deduction for the clothes I give to charity?

Many people donate used clothing to charities, then forget to claim a deduction. So be sure to write off the fair market value of these items on your tax return.

Tip: The IRS says the fair market value of used clothes is the amount people would pay for these items in thrift shops and used clothing stores. So check with stores in your area to find out the value of articles you donate.

Q: We donated our old couch to a local shelter for the homeless. Do we get a tax deduction?

The same rules that apply to gifts of used clothes apply to donations of used furniture and other household goods. Claim a deduction on your return equal to the fair market value of these items. Keep a detailed list of every item, and write down the value of each item separately.

Q: My spouse and I care for a foster child. Are any of our costs deductible?

You're entitled to tax deductions if a foster child is placed in your home by a charitable organization—as long as you provide the child with food, clothing, and general care.

Also, you must not have a profit motive. For example, it doesn't count if you're paid for your time or services as a foster parent.

You may deduct the excess of your out-of-pocket expenses over the amount you're reimbursed by the charitable organization. Even the cost of the child's tickets to attend sporting events and movies qualifies for the deduction.

Q: An exchange student from Sweden is living with our family this school year. Are we entitled to any tax breaks?

Uncle Sam knows it costs you money when an exchange student comes to live in your home. So part of the cost of housing an exchange student—whether from the United States or another country—is deductible as long as the student is not related to you and is not your dependent. Uncle Sam allows you to write off as much as $50 a month of these costs.

Here are the details: The student—who is enrolled in grade 12 or lower—must be a member of your household under a written agreement between you and a qualified nonprofit charitable organization. And the purpose of the exchange must be to provide educational opportunities for the student.

You may take your $50 deduction for each full calendar month the student lives with you. But the youngster must attend a U.S. school at least 15 days a month.

If, however, the organization reimburses you for your exchange student's costs, you may not take a deduction. In fact, Uncle Sams says you may not take a write-off if you receive any reimbursement either in the form of money or gifts to help defray your expenses—even, for instance, a series of food packages from your student's parents.

Reimbursement for extraordinary or one-time expenses, however, such as a hospital bill or vacation trip, won't deprive you of your deduction, provided you paid the cost at the request of the student's parents or the sponsoring organization.

And keep this fact in mind: You may not deduct the costs of a foreign student living in your home if the arrangement is part of a mutual exchange program that also allows your child to live with a family in a foreign country.

CHAPTER 6

How to Write Off Your Medical and Dental Expenses

In theory, Uncle Sam allows you to write off almost any medical expense. But in practice it's now difficult, if not impossible, for a person with health insurance to claim an actual deduction on his or her tax return. The reason is simple enough.

The law says you may write off only those medical expenses that exceed 7½ percent of your adjusted gross income (AGI). Say your AGI totals $50,000 in 1988. Your medical expenses, after insurance reimbursements, must top $3,750 before you can write off a single cent. Timing, therefore, could be an important tax tactic.

If, for instance, you expect to incur $3,500 in additional medical expenses in each of the next two years, try to arrange to pay the entire amount during one year. In that way at least part of your medical expenses would be deductible.

In this chapter we provide a checklist of deductible medical and dental expenses. Let's start, though, with the general rules for these write-offs.

DEFINING MEDICAL EXPENSES Uncle Sam defines medical expenses as amounts you pay for the "diagnosis, treatment, or prevention of disease, or for treatment affecting any part or function of the body."

Included in these expenses are the costs of medical and dental insurance and transportation for needed medical and dental care.

You may write off medical and dental expenses if you itemize your deductions on Schedule A of your Form 1040. But, as we've seen, you may deduct only those expenses that top 7½ percent of your AGI. And you must write off these expenses only in the year you pay them.

What happens if you mail a check to your doctor on December 31? The law allows you to claim the expense in the year you mail the check.

The same rule holds true for medical and dental expenses you charge to a credit card. You may deduct the expense in the year you make the charge.

You may also claim a deduction for medical expenses you pay for your dependents. (See Chapter 2 for more on who qualifies as a dependent.)

In addition to dependents, you may also claim medical expenses you incur on your children's behalf even if you're divorced and your ex-spouse is entitled to claim the kids as his or her dependents. Also, you may ignore the gross income test for dependents when claiming medical expense deductions. If, in other words, your aging father would qualify as your dependent except for the fact that his income was too high, he would still qualify for purposes of any medical payments you made on his behalf.

Our advice: If you're chipping in to cover your parents' living costs, pay for their medical bills—not their cable television.

CHECKLIST OF DEDUCTIONS   Now here's our alphabetical checklist of deductible medical and dental expenses.

First, though, a note: Uncle Sam imposes an 80 percent cap on deductions for business meals. This same limitation may apply to all medically related meals, including those you ingest while you're in the hospital. Our advice: Check with your tax preparer or the IRS before you claim such expenses.

Alcohol and Drug Abuse Treatment

The law allows you to deduct the cost of treatment at a center for substance abusers. You may write off charges for therapy and medical care. You may also write off the amount you pay the center for lodging and meals provided during your treatment.

Care for the Handicapped

Uncle Sam says you may deduct as a medical expense the cost of sending a mentally or physically handicapped person to a special school. There's just one catch: The primary purpose of the special school must be to treat the student's medical problem.

Tip: You may deduct payments you make in advance for the lifetime care of a handicapped person—as long as the prepayments aren't refundable and aren't for medical insurance premiums.

Fees for Hospital Services

You may deduct the cost of hospital services, including ambulances and fees for laboratory, surgical, obstetrical, and diagnostic services. You may also write off the expense of private nurses, including the cost of meals you provide for them.

Fees for Medical Services

Uncle Sam says you may write off fees you pay to any doctor, surgeon, or other qualified practitioner. Who qualifies? The list includes dentists, osteopaths, ophthalmologists, optometrists, acupuncturists, chiropractors, podiatrists, psychiatrists, and psychologists. You may even deduct fees paid to Indian medicine men—or so the courts ruled in one case.

Home Alterations to Accommodate a Handicap

If you install ramps or railings, widen hallways or doors, lower kitchen cabinets or adjust electrical outlets and fixtures to accommodate a physical handicap, you may write off the full cost of these home alterations as medical expenses.

Home Alterations to Accommodate a Medical Condition

The amount you deduct depends on how much the equipment you install or the improvement you make increases the value of your home. Here's an example.

Say you suffer from heart disease and you're unable to climb the stairs in your home. Your doctor suggests you install an elevator. And you do—at a cost of $2,000.

Next, you ask an appraiser to tell you how much the installation of the elevator increases the value of your home. The answer: $1,400.

You may deduct $600 as a medical expense—that is, the difference between the cost of the improvement ($2,000) and the value it adds to your home—$1,400.

What if the improvement doesn't increase the value of your home? You may write off the entire amount you pay—in this case $2,000.

Tip: Under special circumstances the rules allow you to write off as a medical expense the cost of removing lead-based paints from your walls and woodwork.

What are the conditions? You must perform the work to prevent a child who has or has had lead poisoning from eating the paint. And the walls and woodwork from which you remove the lead-based paint must be in poor repair and within the child's reach.

Caution: If the IRS audits your return, it may ask you to provide a written statement from the doctor who recommended you make your improvement. Our advice is to secure a statement from your physician before you undertake the work.

The IRS may also ask you to prove how much the value of your property was—or was not—increased by your improvement. So you should obtain a reliable written appraisal of the improvement from a qualified real estate appraiser or a valuation expert.

Meals and Lodging

The law says you may deduct as a medical expense the cost of meals while you are away from home for medical treatment, under one condition: The meals must be provided as part of your stay at an inpatient hospital or similar facility—for example, an alcohol or drug treatment center.

As for lodging outside a hospital, the rules say you may deduct $50 per person per night for the cost of a room. So if you travel with your sick child for out-of-town medical care, you could write off $100 per night for lodging expenses.

Tip: You may also write off the cost of trips you take on doctor's orders—to a warmer or drier climate, for instance. But the purpose of your trip must be to alleviate a specific ailment. You get no deduction if you travel for general health reasons.

Here's an example. Say you suffer from a respiratory disease and each winter you travel from your home in northern Ohio to Arizona. And you take the trip on the advice of your physician.

You may write off as a medical expense your transportation costs—in this case, air fare—between your home and your residence in Arizona.

You may also write off lodging expenses and the meal costs that you incur when you travel from Ohio to Arizona. But you may not deduct meals and lodging once you arrive at your destination.

Medical and Hospital Insurance Premiums

The cost of health and hospitalization insurance premiums are allowable deductions. And this includes Part B and voluntary

Part A Medicare premiums and the premium cost for contracts to repair or replace lost or damaged glasses or contact lenses.

When Congress adopted the 1986 Tax Reform Act, it provided an extra tax break for self-employed taxpayers, partners and S corporation shareholders who pay for their own and their family's health insurance. Until 1990, but only until then, these taxpayers may deduct 25 percent of the cost of this insurance above the line—or directly from their gross incomes.

The other 75 percent of the insurance bill is lumped together with other medical expenses. So it is deductible to the extent that it—when added to these other medical costs—totals more than 7½ percent of your adjusted gross income.

To qualify for this favorable treatment, you must make available the same coverage to all your employees on a nondiscriminatory basis.

Caution: The rules say that you qualify for the 25 percent write-off only if you aren't eligible to participate in the health insurance plan of another employer—including your spouse's employer.

Also, you may not take the deduction for health insurance premiums if the cost tops your earned income from your business.

Here's an example. Say that you report a $6,000 loss from your sole proprietorship. Your health insurance bill for the year adds up to $1,600.

You're not entitled to claim an above-the-line deduction of $400 (25 percent of your premiums), because doing so would simply allow you to claim a larger loss.

Medicines

You may deduct the cost of prescribed drugs.

You may also write off the cost of birth-control devices if they're prescribed by your doctor and aren't available for purchase over the counter.

Drugs that you buy without a prescription—aspirin, for instance—aren't deductible even if a physician recommends their use.

Mental Health Services

You may deduct as a medical expense amounts you pay for mental health services, including counseling and therapy.

Nursing Home Services

Uncle Sam allows you to write off the cost of nursing home services provided to you or one of your dependents—as long as the service is needed for medical reasons.

So if you have no medical problems and are perfectly able to care for yourself but just happen to live in a retirement or nursing home, you pocket no deduction.

Nursing Services

Amounts you pay for nursing services are deductible. And you may write off these costs even if the services are not performed by a licensed registered nurse.

The only requirement: The services must be similar to those provided by licensed nurses—for example, dispensing medicine, changing dressings, and bathing the patient.

You may claim as medical expenses: the cost of their salaries, any Social Security taxes paid on their wages, and the cost of any meals you provide them.

Special Equipment

The tax law allows you to deduct the cost of purchasing special medical equipment, including motorized wheelchairs.

Also, you may write off the expense of installing special equipment, such as hand controls in your automobile. And you may deduct repairs or other operating costs of this equipment, as long as the equipment helps you compensate for a specific disability.

But you're not allowed to deduct operating costs that are ordinarily considered a personal expense. For instance, you may not write off the cost of oil or gasoline for a specially equipped automobile.

Special Items

Included in this catchall category: false teeth, artificial limbs, eyeglasses, contact lenses, hearing aids, guide dogs, and crutches. The category also includes the cost of oxygen equipment and oxygen to relieve breathing problems caused by a medical condition.

Transportation

You may write off the cost of transportation to and from needed medical care. Transportation expenses include automobile (including tolls and parking), taxi, train, and plane fares, as well as ambulance service fees.

Tip: Calculate your automobile expenses either by using nine cents a mile (the amount the IRS allows) or your actual out-of-pocket costs. Actual costs include expenses for gas and oil. But they do not include interest on a car loan, insurance, depreciation, and so forth.

QUESTIONS AND ANSWERS

QUESTION: I know what's deductible as a medical expense. What's not deductible?

For starters, you may not write off the cost of bottled water, disability insurance, funeral, burial, or cremation expenses, health club dues, household help, illegal operations or treatment, and insurance that pays your ordinary living expenses if you are ill.

Nor may you deduct the cost of life insurance, diaper services, maternity clothes, nursing care for a healthy baby, toothpaste, toiletries, and cosmetics.

Q: What about the cost of stop-smoking and weight-loss programs? May I deduct these expenses?

You may deduct the cost of programs designed to help you lose weight or stop smoking only if the program is prescribed by a doctor to alleviate a specific ailment. For instance, if you're told to stop smoking because of your emphysema, the cost is deductible. If you enroll in a program just to improve your general health, however, the cost is entirely yours to shoulder.

Q: I ran up $5,000 in medical bills in December of 1988. But my insurance carrier didn't reimburse me until January of 1989. How do I handle these amounts on my tax return?

Uncle Sam requires you write off medical expenses in the year you pay them. So you must deduct your $5,000 medical bill on your 1988 return. Then you report the amount you received from your insurance carrier as income on your 1989 return.

Say you rack up $5,000 in medical expenses but you deduct only $3,000—that is the amount of your medical expenses that exceed 7½ percent of your AGI. The rules require you to report as income only the amounts you receive from your insurance carrier that are equal to or less than your medical expense deduction.

You received $5,000 from your insurance company but wrote off only $3,000. That means you don't have to claim $2,000 of your reimbursement as income on your return.

CHAPTER 7

Tips on Writing Off State and Local Taxes

When the income tax was first enacted back in 1913, your grandfather was allowed to deduct from his income virtually every other tax he paid. This practice was grounded in the belief that taxes are involuntary expenditures and that people shouldn't be taxed on income used to pay taxes.

But that was then, and this is now. And in the past seventy-five years the practice, if not the belief, has changed. Today you may deduct only a few taxes from your federal taxable income. Which ones, to what extent, and how? That's what this chapter is all about.

WHICH ONES? If you don't itemize deductions on your Form 1040, the answer to this question is short: none. You may not deduct any personal state and local taxes on your return. But if you do itemize, you may write off some or all of the following:

- State and local income taxes
- State and local real property taxes
- State and local personal property taxes

We say that you *may* write these taxes off because there are qualifications and exceptions. We cover these later. But, by and large, the deductibility of state and local income and property taxes is determined by a few general rules.

The tax must be imposed on you, not on someone else. If, for instance, you pay the property taxes on your mother's house, you may not deduct those taxes on your return.

And you must actually pay the tax in the calendar year for which you are filing. If you pay your taxes by check, the

IRS considers the day you mail or deliver the check the date of payment. If you use a pay-by-phone account, the date of payment is the payment date reported on the statement of the financial institution with which you have the account.

INCOME TAXES Every state—except Alaska, Florida, Nevada, South Dakota, Texas, Washington, and Wyoming—imposes some kind of personal income tax. Some cities—New York, Cincinnati, and Philadelphia, for instance—impose their own income taxes as well.

The law allows itemizers to deduct these state and local income taxes on Schedule A of Form 1040. Specifically, you may write off the income taxes that are withheld from your paycheck. You also may deduct estimated payments that you're required to make.

REAL ESTATE TAXES If you itemize, you may also deduct nonbusiness state and local real estate taxes on Schedule A on your Form 1040 in the year you pay them. Remember, though, that you may deduct only those real estate taxes that you actually pay.

Say, for example, that you and your spouse own your home jointly but file separate returns. Each of you may write off only the taxes that you respectively pay.

The one exception to this rule: taxpayers in community property states—that is, Arizona, California, Idaho, Louisiana, Nevada, New Mexico, Texas, and Washington. The IRS considers the taxes paid from community funds are paid on a 50/50 basis.

In some cases you may want to transfer property to another family member who could make better use of the property tax deduction than you can. Just keep in mind that there's a drawback to this strategy. When you transfer property to another person, you lose control of it.

One other note: You may not deduct real estate taxes placed in escrow—that is, in the care of a third party—until they're actually paid. Most often this issue crops up with a home mortgage.

If your monthly mortgage payment includes an amount placed in escrow for real estate taxes, you may not write off the total of those escrow payments. You may deduct only the amount of the tax that the lender actually paid to the taxing authority, such as a city or county.

Most lenders pay taxes out of escrow accounts on the tax due date. But if the due date is shortly after the end of the calendar year, you may want to ask your lender to accelerate the payment so you can claim the deduction a year earlier.

You may also deduct taxes on properties that produce rent or royalty income—such as an apartment building that you own. But you claim these deductions on Schedule E, not Schedule A, of your Form 1040.

Caution: Trash and garbage service fees that are listed separately on your real estate tax bill aren't deductible. However, if the municipality where you live provides these services but doesn't break out their separate costs on your real estate tax bill, you may continue to write off the entire amount.

Tip: The tax law treats real estate taxes differently in the year you sell your home. For the details, see Chapter 14.

PERSONAL PROPERTY TAXES   Uncle Sam allows you to write off personal property taxes on your federal return. But to qualify for the deduction, a personal property tax must meet the following three tests.

The tax is based on the value of your property.

Say your state imposes an annual motor-vehicle registration tax of one percent of the value of your car plus 75 cents per hundred pounds of weight. You pay a tax of $84 based on your automobile's value ($6,000) and its weight (3,200 pounds).

You may deduct $60 (the part of the tax that is based on your car's value) as a personal property tax. The remaining $24 (based on the car's weight) is not deductible.

The tax is imposed annually.

Your county mails you a personal property tax bill once a year. But it gives you the option of paying the tax quarterly. The tax qualifies as personal property tax—no matter when you pay it—because it is actually imposed annually.

The tax is imposed on personal property.

Here's a break. Uncle Sam considers a tax imposed on personal property even if it is for the "exercise of a privilege." What does this cryptic rule mean?

Here's an example. Your city imposes a yearly tax on your car based on its value. But it defines this tax as a registration fee for the privilege of registering your car or driving it on the highways. As long as the fee is based on your car's value, however, the law looks upon it as a tax on personal property.

OTHER TAXES   The law permits you to deduct taxes, such as windfall profits taxes, if they are "ordinary and necessary expenses of producing income." You should note that the windfall profit tax was repealed as of August 24, 1988.

The 1986 Tax Reform Act carves out an exception to this rule, though, for state transfer taxes on sales of securities, such as stocks and bonds.

The law won't allow you to deduct transfer taxes on your return, but you may subtract them when it comes time to calculate your gain or loss from the sale of securities.

Usually, foreign income and real property taxes are deductible. However, you may not deduct the foreign tax if you paid it on income that was excluded from your federal tax return. Besides, you may choose to take a credit for foreign taxes instead of claiming an itemized deduction.

As you remember, a credit reduces your tax by the amount of the foreign tax paid. A deduction reduces only the amount of your income subject to tax. If you paid foreign taxes, we suggest that you consult with your tax adviser.

Another important point: Social Security taxes for self-employed individuals become 50 percent deductible in 1990. But this change will simply offset a scheduled increase in the self-employment tax rate.

WHAT'S NOT DEDUCTIBLE   Which federal, state, and local government taxes and other fees may you not write off? Here's a checklist of these nondeductible taxes.

- Car inspection fees
- Cigarette, tobacco, liquor, beer, and wine taxes
- Dog tags and hunting licenses
- Driver's license fees
- Estate taxes
- Federal excise taxes on telephone service
- Federal gasoline taxes
- Federal income taxes
- Fines—for parking or speeding, for example
- Gift taxes
- Inheritance, legacy, or succession taxes
- Marriage licenses
- Mortgage recording taxes
- Occupancy taxes, such as taxes on hotel rooms
- Parking meter fees
- Passport fees

- Penalties assessed as taxes
- Sales taxes
- Social Security taxes
- Stamp taxes
- Tolls for bridges and roads
- Transfer taxes
- Utility taxes
- Water bills, sewer, and other service charges

Caution: Don't make the mistake some taxpayers do and deduct Social Security and other employment taxes you pay on the wages of a household worker. The law won't allow you to write off these amounts.

QUESTIONS AND ANSWERS

QUESTION: I make estimated payments of my state income taxes. My last payment for 1988 is due in January 1989. Do I deduct this amount in 1988 or 1989?

You write off a January 1989 payment of 1988 state income taxes on your 1989 return. But here's a way to claim the deduction in 1988.

Make your last quarterly estimated payment on December 31, 1988. If you speed up your payment by a few weeks, you accelerate your deduction by a full year.

Caution: We've seen IRS auditors deny deductions to taxpayers who wrote off state tax payments that substantially exceeded their state tax liability.

The only way you can guarantee yourself a deduction is to prove that your payments were based on a reasonable estimate of your final tax bill at the time you made your payment. (If circumstances change later on, your deduction is still safe in Uncle Sam's eyes.)

Say that you paid $3,000 in estimated state income taxes last year. But the payment you made was far beyond what you estimated you would actually owe. In fact, at tax time you discover you're entitled to a refund of the full amount you paid in.

The result: The IRS—on audit—may disallow the $3,000 in estimated payments you deducted from your income, because, in reality, you weren't required to pay an extra $3,000. In any case, the amount the IRS may disallow is the difference between what a reasonable estimate would have been and the estimate you claimed.

Q: I made a mistake on my 1987 return and, as a result, I owe an extra $210 in state taxes and a $40 penalty. How much is deductible?

If you owe additional state taxes because you filed an amended return or were audited, you may also deduct these additional tax payments. Claim the write-off in the year you make the payments. Penalties and fines, however, are not deductible.

So, if you file an amended 1987 state return in 1989 and pay an additional $210 in state income taxes plus a $40 fine, you deduct the $210 in 1989. You may not write off the $40 penalty.

Q: I overpaid my state taxes by $400 in 1987. I received a refund for that amount in 1988. Must I report the $400 as income?

The answer depends on whether you reduced your federal taxes by taking itemized deductions in the year you overpaid. If you itemized deductions in 1987, you must report the $400 refund as taxable income on your 1988 return. But if you claimed the standard deduction in 1987, you may pocket the $400 refund tax free.

Q: We're selling our house. Who gets the deduction for the property taxes—do we or do the people who are buying the home?

If you buy or sell real estate during the tax year, whether it's a home or income-producing property, you must divide real estate taxes between yourself and the buyer or seller. You split the taxes that each of you may deduct based on the number of days each of you owned the property. If you are the seller, for instance, you pay and deduct the taxes up to the date of the sale. The buyer pays and deducts the taxes after the sale. (See Chapter 14 for more information on this topic.)

Q: I'm self-employed and I pay personal property taxes on the business equipment I own. Where do I write off these local taxes?

You deduct taxes that you pay on operating your business—or on property used in the business—on Schedule C (Form 1040). Farmers use Schedule F (Form 1040).

CHAPTER 8

Make the Most of Your Miscellaneous Deductions

Remember all those itemized deductions you used to take for accountants' services, financial advice, professional journals, and a host of other miscellaneous items?

As you know from sad experience with your 1987 return, these items are now only partially deductible from your adjusted gross income (AGI). To be specific, you may write off only that portion of these costs that adds up to more than 2 percent of your AGI.

Here's an example. Let's say that in 1988 your AGI totals $50,000. And you report miscellaneous itemized deductions of $1,200. That means you may deduct $200—the amount of these expenditures that tops $1,000 ($50,000 times 2 percent).

And what are these partially deductible expenses? You find out in this chapter.

BASIC RULES First, let's run through a few basics.

You may write off your miscellaneous deductions only if you itemize. You claim these deductions on Schedule A of your Form 1040.

And Uncle Sam says you may write off as a miscellaneous deduction any expense that's related to your job, to your investments, or to your taxes.

Expenses other than these probably aren't deductible.

Tip: It makes sense to bunch your deductions in one year. By doing so, you may top the 2 percent limitation and be able to claim a write-off. For example, you might want to accelerate miscellaneous deductions into 1988. Of course, this tactic makes sense only if you're going to top the 2 percent limit in 1988. If you fall below the limit, a better strategy is to defer miscellaneous deductions until 1989, when you may be able to take a write-off.

EXPENSES RELATED TO YOUR JOB   The IRS wants you to play fair. So you may deduct expenses that are related to your job only if you pay them out of your own pocket. If your employer reimburses you, you're not entitled to write-offs. Here's our alphabetical checklist of the costs you may deduct.

Career Counseling

The law allows you to deduct the cost of career counseling, as long as you incur the expense as part of your efforts to find a new job.

Moreover, you must look for the same kind of work you're now doing. Otherwise, Uncle Sam won't help shoulder the cost. Here's an example.

Say you're a history teacher by training but are tired of the academic rat race. With the help of a career counselor, you find a position as a speechwriter for a local politician.

Pat yourself on the back. But don't even think about writing off the cost of your counseling. It's not deductible, because you landed a job in an entirely different profession.

Tip: You may write off career counseling expenses even if you don't in the end change jobs. But you may not claim a deduction if you're looking for your very first job or a job in a new profession.

Computers

When Congress adopted the 1984 Tax Reform Act, it imposed strict new rules on write-offs for personal computers. As a result, it's not so easy nowadays to claim a deduction for a personal computer if you're not self-employed.

Under the law, you may deduct a personal computer only if having one is a condition of your employment. Also, you must keep the computer for the convenience of your employer. And it must enable you to perform your duties as an employee.

Say you sign on with a wire service as a reporter and you're stationed in an outlying area. You work out of a spare bedroom in your house. As a condition of your employment, the wire service requires that you purchase a personal computer and modem so that you can transmit the stories you write.

You meet all three of these tests, so you're entitled to a deduction on Schedule A of your Form 1040. (See Chapter 18 for more on how to write off computers.)

Dues

You may write off dues you pay to professional organizations. You may also deduct union dues and expenses, such as initiation fees.

Education

Uncle Sam allows you to deduct the cost of employment-related education—as long as it meets one of two requirements.

Your courses must help you maintain or improve your present works skills. Or your education must be required either by your employer or by law to keep your salary, status, or job. For example, a nurse may write off the cost of continuing education courses that the state requires to maintain a nursing license.

Among the costs that you may deduct: tuition, books, supplies, lab fees, and the cost of travel to and from your courses.

Caution: Uncle Sam won't permit you to deduct education expenses that enable you to meet the minimum education requirements of your profession. The key word here is minimum.

Say that you're hired as a lab technician by a large corporation. You never graduated from college, and the company requires you to complete your education.

You may not deduct the cost of attending school. Why? Your education simply allows you to meet the minimum requirements of your profession. You may, however, write off the cost of continuing-education classes—but only after you secure your degree.

Also, you may not deduct professional accreditation fees, such as bar exam fees or medical and dental licensing fees, that you pay at the outset of your career.

Finally, you may not deduct education expenses that qualify you for a new trade or business. For example, even if earning a law degree would meet the requirement of improving your present work skills, you may not deduct the cost of obtaining the degree. Why? Because it will permit you to practice law, a new trade or business.

Employment Agency Fees

You may deduct employment agency and headhunter fees. But, as with career counseling, you must satisfy this condition: The agency must help you find a new job in the same occupation.

You may write off these fees even if the agency fails in its mission. Again, you may not claim a deduction if you're seeking a job for the first time.

Entertainment

You may write off some or all of the cost of business entertainment. (See Chapter 10 for the rules of deducting entertainment expenses.)

Gifts

Good news. You may deduct the cost of business gifts. But don't be too generous: You may write off gifts of only $25 a year to any single person in any single year.

Here's an example. Helen makes her living as a literary agent. Every Christmas she purchases a copy of a favorite hardcover book for each of the fifty authors she represents.

She may write off the cost of these books—up to $25 each—as long as she made no other gifts to these clients during the year. If she made other prior gifts, which, say, added up to $15 each, she may deduct only $10 per book per client for her Christmas gift.

Job Search Expenses

Keep track of all the expenses you pile up that are associated with changing jobs—everything from telephone calls to the cost of postage.

These expenses are deductible, as long as you're looking for a position—you guessed it—in your same profession, or not seeking employment for the first time.

Here's an example. You're set to graduate from a Boston-area college with a degree in computer science. And you travel to San Francisco for an interview with a computer manufacturer. Alas, you may not write off your travel expenses, because you're looking for your first job.

A few years pass. You landed the job with the computer manufacturer and are still employed there. In fact, you're doing so well that a Boston computer company contacts you about an exciting new position. So you travel to your old stomping grounds for an interview.

This time you may deduct your travel expenses, because you're seeking a new position in your current profession.

Medical Examinations

The cost of a physical examination required—but not paid for—by your employer is deductible as a miscellaneous itemized deduction.

Caution: Health club expenses aren't deductible, even if your job—as in the case of a police officer—requires that you stay in top physical condition.

Military Uniforms

If you're on active duty in the armed services, the law won't allow you to write off the cost of your uniforms. But it does permit people in the reserves to claim deductions.

If you're in the reserves, you may write off the unreimbursed cost of your uniform as long as military regulations prohibits you from wearing it off duty.

Caution: The law won't allow you to deduct the cost of uniforms that replace regular clothing—uniforms worn by students at military academies, for example, fall into this category. But you may write off the cost of insignia, shoulder boards, and related items.

Office Expenses

Turn to Chapter 15 for information on how to write off an office in your home.

Resumé Preparation

Keep tabs on how much you spend typing, printing, and mailing copes of your resumé to prospective employers. These costs are deductible—as long as you're looking for a new job in your present occupation.

Rewards

Most people don't know it, but you may also deduct a reward you pay for the return of lost business property. Say, for example, that you leave your briefcase on the train. You advertise in your local paper that you'll pay $100 for its return.

Your luck is good, and a fellow commuter returns your briefcase to you. You may write off both the reward and the cost of your advertisement.

Subscriptions

The law allows you to deduct subscriptions to professional and trade journals as long as these publications relate to your work.

Caution: Don't make the mistake some taxpayers do and write off the cost of a three-year subscription all in one year. The IRS may disallow a portion of your deduction. The rule says that you may write off magazine subscriptions only one year at a time. Here's how it works.

Say you pay $300 in December 1988 for a three-year subscription to a technical business journal. The subscription begins in January 1989.

You may deduct only $100 of the subscription price in 1988—subject, of course, to the 2 percent AGI limitation. And you may deduct $100 in 1989 and $100 in 1990.

The news isn't all bad, though. Since you paid in December, you get to deduct the portion representing your 1989 subscription a whole year in advance.

Telephone

You may deduct the cost of the unreimbursed business portion of your telephone expenses and long distance telephone calls. These costs may even include answering services and beeper expenses, so long as they are required for your job.

However, legislation now before Congress could limit your deduction. Beginning in 1989 you will no longer be able to deduct any portion of your standard monthly base charge for the first telephone line into your home. But you will be able to write off the cost of additional lines and work-related long distance calls.

Tools and Supplies

Say you purchase a $10 mechanical pencil for use in your work. Uncle Sam allows you to deduct this expense in the year you pay it.

He also permits you to write off the cost of larger items—a desk and couch for your office, for example—but you must depreciate these items, meaning you write off their cost over several years. (See Chapter 18 for more on depreciation.)

Transportation and Travel

You may write off the cost of business transportation and travel if your employer doesn't reimburse you for the full cost. (See chapters 11 and 12 for more on deducting transportation and travel expenses.)

Caution: The cost of commuting is never deductible. (See Chapter 12 for information on writing off the cost of your automobile.)

Work Clothes and Uniforms

The rules allow you to deduct the cost and upkeep of work clothes and uniforms as long as you meet two conditions. Your employer must require you to wear special clothes on the job, and the clothing must not be suitable for ordinary or everyday wear.

Say you work as a manager of a store that sells fashionable designer clothing. Your employer requires you to wear only clothes sold in the shop. You may not, however, write off the cost of your fancy duds, since they're also suitable for ordinary wear.

So write off the cost of your uniforms if you're a:

- Civilian faculty member of a military school
- Fire fighter
- Jockey
- Letter carrier
- Nurse
- Police officer
- Professional ballplayer
- Transportation worker, such as an airline pilot or bus driver

Tip: You may also deduct the cost of protective clothing required in your work—for instance, safety shoes and glasses, hard hats, or work gloves.

EXPENSES RELATED TO YOUR INVESTMENTS The government allows you to deduct costs associated with those investments that produce taxable income. Before we get to our alphabetical checklist of what you may write off, a few general rules.

You may not write off sales commissions and other expenses you pay when you purchase investments. These expenses are "capital costs." That is, they're considered part of the cost of your investment and contribute to its basis—the cost of your property for tax purposes.

When it comes time to sell, you subtract capital costs from the amount you receive. And these costs either decrease your gain or increase your loss.

Here's an example. Say you purchase 100 shares of stocks at $20 a share, for a total of $2,000. You pay your broker a sales commission of $150.

A year later you sell the stock for $25 a share, or a total of

$2,500. To calculate your gain, you add the amount you paid for the stock—in this case, $2,000—and your costs of acquiring your investment—your broker's commission of $150.

Next, you subtract this total—$2,150—from the amount you received when you sold the stock—$2,500. The result, $350, is your taxable gain.

Now, on to the checklist.

Accounting Fees

If you pay an accountant to keep track of your taxable investments or help you with planning, you may write off these fees.

Computers

If you use a computer to keep track of your investments, you're entitled to a deduction for the machine. (See Chapter 18 for more information on writing off computers.)

Custodial Fees for Dividend Reinvestment Plans

No doubt you've heard of dividend reinvestment plans. These programs allow you to use your dividends to purchase additional shares. Some companies offering these plans charge participants a custodial, or service, fee. And you're entitled to deduct these charges on your return.

Entertainment

The law says you may claim a deduction equal to 80 percent of those meal and entertainment expenses that are associated with your taxable investments. So if you take your stockbroker to lunch to discuss her recommendations, feel free to write off 80 percent of the cost of the meal. (See Chapter 10 for more information on entertainment deductions.)

Investment Adviser Fees

If you pay someone to manage your investments, you may deduct any amounts you pay that person. The only requirement: Your investments must produce taxable income.

Here's an example. Say you decide to put all your money in tax-free municipal bonds. And you pay someone to manage these bond investments. Under the rules, you may not deduct the fee you pay your money manager. The reason: Your investments don't produce taxable income.

Caution: You may not know it, but mutual funds often charge you for investment fees. They do this by reducing the amount of dividend income you receive.

Beginning in 1988, this "charge" becomes subject to the 2 percent floor on miscellaneous itemized deductions, and funds must notify you of the amount you pay.

How do you handle this fee on your tax return?

Include in your taxable income the gross amount of the dividend shown on your statement. Then claim the investment fees as miscellaneous itemized deductions.

Be aware, however, that legislation now before Congress would exempt these fees from the 2 percent floor. So check with your tax adviser before you file your return.

IRA Administration Fees

The law allows you to write off trustees' administration fees that you pay to maintain your Individual Retirement Accounts (IRA's).

Our advice: Pay this fee separately if your miscellaneous deductions for the year top the 2 percent floor. But if you fall below the floor, save yourself the trouble of writing a separate check. Let your IRA fork over the administration fee. But be aware, if you go this route, you'll have that much less in your IRA.

Legal Fees

The same rule that applies to fees for investment advisers applies to fees for legal services. You may deduct the amounts you pay as long as the lawyer's advice was related to producing taxable income.

Caution: You may write off only those legal fees that aren't part of the cost of acquiring an investment or defending title to it. Here's an example.

Say you purchase an apartment building and you hire an attorney to handle the closing. The lawyer's fee is a capital cost, meaning it's related to acquiring the property. So it's not deductible.

But all is not lost. The fee is added to your cost in the building, which increases the amount of depreciation you claim.

Office Expenses

The law won't allow you to deduct office expenses—such as rent—that are related to managing your investments and collecting taxable income from them. (See Chapter 15 for the details on how to write off home offices.)

Caution: The IRS says you may not write off the cost of hiring someone to guard your personal residence against burglary attempts—even if your home is loaded with evidence of your favorite hobby, collecting valuable art, for example. Nor may you write off a security system to protect coin or other collections.

Postage and Supplies

Again, as long as your investments produce taxable income, you may write off the cost of postage and supplies associated with these investments.

Safe Deposit Box Rental

Uncle Sam says you may deduct the cost of renting a safe deposit box if you use the box to store investments—or papers related to investments—that generate taxable income. But you may not write off the cost if you use the box only for personal items or tax-exempt securities.

Service Fees

You may write off fees you pay to a broker, a bank, a trustee, or other agent to collect your taxable interest or dividends on shares of stock.

But, as we've seen, you may not deduct a fee you pay to a broker to buy investment property, such as stocks or bonds. You must add this fee to the cost of your property.

Caution: The IRS won't allow you to write off bank check-writing fees on an interest-bearing personal checking account.

Subscriptions

You're allowed to claim a deduction for subscriptions to investment-related publications. But remember, you may not write off in one year the cost of a multiple-year subscription. You may, however, deduct that portion of your payment that represents the current year of your subscription.

Telephone

You may deduct the cost of investment-related telephone expenses and long distance calls. As we noted earlier, legislation now before Congress would limit your deduction after 1988 by excluding any portion of your standard monthly basic charge for the first telephone line into your house. You may still write off the cost of any other investment-related telephone expenses.

Transportation and Travel

The rules let you write off the cost of transportation and travel associated with investments that produce taxable income. For example, you may claim a deduction for your mileage and parking fees when you visit your stockbroker—as long as you don't invest solely in tax-exempt instruments.

Caution: Sorry, but Uncle Sam won't allow you to write off the cost of travel to an investment seminar or convention. Nor may you deduct the cost of the seminar or convention itself.

You're also out of luck when it comes to writing off transportation and other expenses you pay to attend stockholders' meetings of companies in which you own stock but have no other interest. You may not deduct these expense—even if you're attending the meeting to get information that would be useful in making future investments. (See chapters 11 and 12 for more on transportation and travel expenses.)

EXPENSES RELATED TO YOUR TAXES   Here's our checklist of deductions related to tax planning and preparation.

Appraisal Fees

You may deduct these fees if you pay them to determine the fair market value of property you donate to charity. The reason: The fees go to determine the amount of your deduction.

Legal Fees

If you pay for tax advice, it's deductible. You may even deduct legal expenses for tax advice related to a divorce, as long as your attorney's bill specifies how much is for tax advice.

Tax Planning and Preparation Fees

Usually you may write off—in the year you pay them—tax counsel and assistance fees, such as fees you pay to have your tax return prepared. So you may deduct on your 1988 return those fees you pay in 1988 for preparing your 1987 return, as well as fees for an early start on your 1988 return.

You also may write off expenses you pay for determining, collecting, or refunding any tax—including income tax, estate tax, gift tax, sales tax, or property tax. And you may deduct fees you pay to a consultant to advise you on the tax consequences of a transaction.

More good news: If you contest a tax assessment, any fees you pay are deductible, even if your defense is unsuccessful.

And you may deduct professional fees you pay to obtain federal tax rulings. Finally, you may also write off the cost of defending yourself if you're audited.

Tip: Uncle Sam allows you to claim a deduction for tax preparation and planning books—including *The Price Waterhouse Personal Tax Adviser*.

QUESTIONS AND ANSWERS

QUESTION: In addition to my regular work, I operate a small kennel. This year my little business was awash in red ink. How much may I deduct?

It depends. Uncle Sam doesn't mind if you dabble in a small business just for the fun of it. But he doesn't want to help foot the bill—hence, the so-called hobby loss limitation rule.

Under the rule, you may deduct hobby expenses that are not otherwise deductible, only up to the amount of your hobby income. What does "not otherwise deductible" mean? Well, let's say that you breed and sell show dogs. Dog food is not ordinarily a deductible cost, but in your case it is—subject to the hobby loss rules.

You're not allowed to create a tax loss from your hobby to slash your overall tax bill.

One other point: You claim your hobby losses as miscellaneous itemized deductions—not on Schedule C.

How does the IRS determine if your enterprise is a hobby or a for-profit business?

First, the IRS provides an objective test. If you meet this test, the government presumes—at least for this year—that you are engaged in a legitimate business.

Under the objective test, you must realize a profit from an activity in three out of the most recent five consecutive years. If horse breeding and racing are your passions, you need to make a profit from these activities in two out of seven consecutive years.

And second, there is a subjective "facts-and-circumstances" test. Under it, the IRS considers whether you operate your business in a businesslike way. It also examines your expertise in your chosen activity, the time and effort you devote to it, and the amount of personal pleasure you derive from it.

Caution: The rules on itemized deductions may also restrict your hobby write-offs to an amount less than your hobby income. Here's how.

You know that hobby deductions—other than taxes you may deduct as a personal expense, such as property taxes—are classified as miscellaneous itemized deductions. And as we've seen, you may deduct them only to the extent that they exceed 2 percent of your AGI.

So while you must include the full amount of your hobby earnings in taxable income, your hobby write-offs will offset this income only to the extent your combined miscellaneous itemized deductions top the 2 percent floor. If your combined miscellaneous itemized deductions are less than 2 percent of AGI, you get no tax deduction for your hobby expenses.

Q: I now know what I may write off as a miscellaneous deduction. But what may I not deduct?

Here's an alphabetical checklist of items you may not deduct:

- Burial or funeral expenses
- Campaign expenses
- Fees and licenses, such as car licenses, marriage licenses, and dog tags
- Fines and penalties, such as parking tickets
- Home repairs, insurance, and rent
- Life insurance
- Losses from the sale of your home, furniture, personal car, and so forth
- Lost or misplaced cash or property
- Lunches and meals you eat while working late
- Personal legal expenses
- Personal living or family expenses
- Political contributions
- Self-improvement expenses, such as the cost of attending a self-enrichment workshop
- Voluntary unemployment-benefit fund contributions

One last word on final expenses: While you may not deduct funeral and burial expenses on your personal return, your estate gets to write them off on your federal estate tax return.

Q: I started a new job this year that required me to move to another city. May I write off my moving expenses?

The law allows you to deduct moving expenses that are due to a change in your employment. So if you accept a job in a new city, you may deduct the expenses of moving to that city—as long as you meet IRS guidelines. What, you ask, are the IRS guidelines?

The rules say that you must stay in your new job at least 39 weeks. Also, you must relocate within one year of the date you assume your new post, and your new job must be at least 35 miles farther away from your existing home than your old job.

You deduct moving expenses as miscellaneous itemized deductions. But moving expenses aren't subject to the 2 percent floor that applies to most miscellaneous deductions.

Q: What may I deduct as moving expenses?

Uncle Sam says that you may write off the cost of moving your household belongings, including your car and your pets, to a new location. And he imposes no ceiling on this write-off—as long as the amount you claim is reasonable in light of the circumstances of your move.

You may also deduct travel expenses, including the cost of meals and lodgings for you and your family, that you rack up on your way to your new home.

And if you aren't able to move into your new home right away, you may write off temporary living expenses—for up to 30 days.

What's more, you may deduct the cost of house-hunting trips. And, if you're a homeowner, you may deduct the cost of selling your old home and buying a new one. If you rent, you may write off the cost of cancelling your old lease and securing a new one.

Caution: The rules cap deductions for purchase and lease costs, housing-hunting expenses, and temporary living expenses to a total of $3,000. Of this amount, house hunting and temporary living expenses may not exceed $1,500.

CHAPTER 9

Safeguarding Your Travel and Entertainment Deductions

There's a whole host of rules that you must follow—and follow to the letter—when you write off business travel, meal, and entertainment expenses. And these standards are the same whether you work for yourself or for someone else.

One of the most important of these rules: You may not deduct these expenses unless you can prove that you actually spent the amount you claim.

In this chapter we'll tell you what records you must maintain to safeguard your travel, meal, and entertainment deductions. Then, in the next two chapters, we tell you what else you need to know to make the most of these write-offs.

WHAT YOU NEED FOR THE RECORD Suppose the IRS decides to audit you. And it asks you to prove your outlays for business travel, meal, and entertainment expenses.

What kinds of evidence should you provide? Actually, Uncle Sam considers two types. The first is documentary evidence, which the IRS defines as any kind of receipt that is corroborated by a third party. Cancelled checks meet this requirement, and so do credit card slips.

The second is a log or diary. The government, however, doesn't require you to keep a log as long as you note all the required information on your documentary evidence—on the back of credit card slips, for example. Here's the information you're required to record.

Business Purpose

For each expense, note the business reason or nature of the business benefit you've realized—or expect to realize—from the trip or entertainment.

Say you purchase drinks for a customer and yourself. The drinks follow a lengthy sales presentation during which you describe your company's new computer. The business purpose of the drinks: to try to clinch the sale.

You must document the topic of business conversation that took place before, during, or after the entertainment. Example: "Discussed possible purchase by XYZ Corporation of ten computers."

Business Relationship

Identify each person you entertain by name and your business relationship—for example, Joe Jones, President, XYZ Corporation. Also, write down the names and business relationships of any people you visit on a business trip.

Cost

You should jot down the amount you spend for each item—dinner, say, and theater tickets, followed by a round of drinks at your favorite nightspot. And don't overlook tips and incidental items, such as taxi fares and telephone calls.

Time

If you conduct a business discussion during a meal or while you entertain, there's no need to record the length of your business conversation, but you must note the date.

If you don't discuss business during the meal or entertainment, the rules require you to jot down both the date and the length of the business discussion that took place before or after the meal or entertainment.

In the case of travel expenses, write down the dates you leave and return from your trip and the number of days you spend away from home.

Place

The rules require you to record where you run up the expense—the name of a restaurant, for example. If you don't discuss business during the meal or entertainment, note where the business conversation took place before or after the meal or entertainment. When it comes to travel, jot down your destination—the name of a city will do.

Caution: Special record-keeping rules apply if you write off dues to social, luncheon, athletic, or sporting clubs. Each time you use the club, you must document whether your use was business or personal.

NOTE IT NOW   You should document your expenses as close as possible to the time you take a business trip or entertain business colleagues. The reason: The IRS places greater value on records that you keep currently.

Say you dine out on business three times a week. The morning after each business meal, you jot down on the back of your charge slip all the data Uncle Sam requires—the time, date, and place of your meal, the nature of your business discussion, and so on. The IRS is unlikely to challenge the validity of your deduction.

Now let's say your office mate also wines and dines customers several nights a week. But she doesn't write down anything until the end of the month.

Uncle Sam is far more likely to challenge her evidence. The reason: The information isn't timely, and it's based on memory.

Of course, a log where you record all your business engagements and a file of your receipts are the best evidence, as far as Uncle Sam is concerned.

Tip: Stationery stores offer a variety of easy-to-maintain log books that are no bigger than a checkbook. You may find one of these logs useful.

A word to the wise: Never underestimate the importance of writing down the required information. Without this documentation, the IRS may disallow your perfectly legitimate deductions.

RECORDS YOU DON'T HAVE TO KEEP   Here's one category of expenses you don't need to keep receipts for. That category includes anything, except lodging, costing less than $25.

The IRS requires you to keep documentary evidence only for outlays of that amount or more. If you spend less than $25, you don't need receipts. Simply write down the proper information in your log or on a slip of paper.

QUESTIONS AND ANSWERS

QUESTION: My employer reimburses me for my travel, meal, and entertainment expenses. I don't have to keep records for the IRS, too, do I?

If you make an adequate accounting of your expenses to your employer, chances are you don't have to substantiate them again for your personal tax return.

But if you claim any deductions on your personal return—say, for expenses beyond those reimbursed by your employer—you must keep records to back up these claims.

The IRS also requires you to document your expenses if you're related to your employer or if your employer doesn't require you to account for your expenses.

Q: When it comes to the $25 rule, do I add up what I spent the entire evening or only at each spot?

The IRS looks at each expenditure separately.

For example, if you take a client to dinner and a play, the cost of dinner is treated as one expenditure, the play as another. If you spend less than $25 for dinner and less than $25 for theater tickets, receipts aren't required for either expense.

Caution: Say you purchase several rounds of drinks at your favorite watering hole. The amount you spend is treated as one item for purposes of the $25 rule.

CHAPTER 10

How to Write Off Business Meals and Entertainment

Whether a meal is a partially deductible business expense or just a bite to eat depends, in part, on who's doing the eating and why. The deductibility of entertainment expenses also depends on who and why, but it can also depend on where.

You may, for instance, pay for a skybox view of the ball game for you and your clients. But so far as the IRS is concerned, you might as well head for the bleachers.

If you understand them, the tax rules covering business meals and entertainment aren't incompatible with either a refined palate or a keen feel for the game. You can, however, avoid indigestion and a losing season by reading the rules here first.

LAVISH OR EXTRAVAGANT Let's start with the basics. Uncle Sam allows you to write off business meals and entertainment expenses as long as they're not "lavish or extravagant."

What, you ask, is lavish or extravagant?

The government doesn't say. But we've never seen IRS auditors disallow a deduction simply because it exceeded a certain dollar amount.

Our advice: Dine and entertain in any style you think is reasonable. The IRS won't label a deduction as lavish or extravagant unless it's totally outrageous.

And "outrageous" is usually easy to spot.

Say you're a plumbing contractor and you do business in Texas. You take your favorite customer to lunch in Paris—not Paris, Texas, but Paris, France.

You may write off the cost of the meal, but, chances are, the IRS will consider the cost of your two round-trip airline tickets as lavish and extravagant. The reason is simple: The trip to France is neither ordinary nor necessary to your business.

WHICH MEALS AND ENTERTAINMENT QUALIFY? The law allows an 80 percent deduction for meals and entertainment expenses that are *directly* related to the active conduct of your business. An 80 percent deduction is also allowed for meals and entertainment costs that are *associated* with the conduct of your business.

What's the difference?

Uncle Sam defines "directly related entertainment" as any entertainment during which you "actively" discuss or conduct your business. Also, your primary purpose must be to transact business. That is, you must expect to gain some benefit from your entertainment—other than goodwill.

An example: Say you're an accountant and you're at a client's office going over her business plan. Your meeting starts at ten A.M. and continues through four P.M., but the two of you don't break for lunch. Instead, you order out and munch your sandwiches while sitting at her conference room table.

Under the rules, the meal qualifies as directly related entertainment, because you continue your business discussion through lunch.

But the IRS assumes the meal or entertainment isn't directly related if it takes place in a setting that makes doing business difficult—if not impossible. For example, the IRS presumes you can't conduct business in a noisy nightclub or a theater.

"Associated entertainment" is far more common among businesspeople—and far harder to pin down. The IRS rule for this type of entertainment: It must precede or follow a bona fide business discussion. Also, you must prove that your expense was for a specific business purpose—to obtain a new client, for instance, or keep an old one.

Simply taking your attorney to a baseball game to cultivate good feelings doesn't qualify as associated entertainment. But if you met before the game to discuss your plans to acquire another company, you could write off 80 percent of the cost.

It's not enough, in other words, that the person you take to the baseball game has a business relationship with you—as an important potential sales account, for instance. You must actually conduct business before or after the game.

BUSINESS MEALS   When is a meal a business meal?

It's a business meal—and therefore 80 percent deductible—if it's directly related or associated with the active conduct of your trade or business. If it's not, it's not deductible at all.

Here's an example: Say you sell paper products and one of your best customers is the XYZ Corporation. You take the president of XYZ out for a fancy dinner.

You don't discuss business before, during, or after the meal. You didn't expect to talk shop, because all sales to XYZ are negotiated by the company's purchasing agent.

The cost of the meal is not deductible, because it doesn't meet the requirements of directly related or associated entertainment— that is, you didn't actually discuss business before, during, or after the meal.

Something else you should know: When we refer to the cost of the meal, we mean the cost of the food you consume plus the cost of tips and taxes. Also included are cover charges, room-rental fees, and other entertainment expenses.

Here are some other rules governing business meal deductions.

A company representative must be present at the meal, or your write-off isn't going to fly. You may not, in other words, treat visiting clients to a deductible dinner and night on the town unless someone from the company is willing to share the repast. But you may deduct the cost if your attorney, accountant, or other professional adviser attends the business meal as your representative.

The 80 percent limit on deductibility applies to all business meals—whether you're entertaining someone in your own city or dining solo at some out-of-town motel during a business trip. But transportation costs to the restaurant—taxi or limo fares—are still fully deductible.

The 80 percent rule also applies to so-called "single sum expenditures." What's a single-sum expenditure? Here's an example to illustrate.

Say a hotel includes one or more meals in its room charge. In this case, Uncle Sam says, you must allocate a portion of the room charge for food and a portion for lodging. The part for lodging is fully deductible, but you may write off only 80 percent of the food costs.

The single-sum rule also applies to per diem arrangements.

But the 80 percent rule doesn't affect employer reimbursement policies at all. Your employer may still reimburse you 100 percent for the cost of your business meals, as long as you account to him or her for the money you spend.

Nor does the 80 percent rule apply to most food-related employee fringe benefits. The holiday ham, the employee cafeteria that qualifies as a *de minimis* fringe benefit (one too small to really matter), and the food and refreshments served at the company picnic, are still fully deductible expenses to your employer and nontaxable to you.

Caution: Also not subject to the 80 percent rule are taxable employee benefits, such as the vacation packages awarded to salespeople for meeting quotas. (The value of these benefits, however, must be reported on employees' W-2 forms and is subject to withholding.)

The cost of food and beverages served at conventions, seminars, and meetings is also fully deductible, provided the confab meets several conditions.

For starters, there must be a speaker. Also, there must be no separate charge for food and beverages. And there must be a minimum of forty attendees, more than half of whom must be traveling away from home.

But even this exception expires. After December 31, 1988, food and beverage costs at this kind of meeting will be subject to the 80 percent rule.

Tip: Under the rules, you may deduct 80 percent of the cost of business meals you prepare and serve in your own home—as long as you can prove the meals were for business, not pleasure.

BUSINESS ENTERTAINMENT   The rules for deducting business entertainment expenses parallel those for business meals. The basic rule: 80 percent of the cost of legitimate entertainment expenses are deductible. Of course, even after you meet this rule, you're faced with the particulars and the exceptions.

Parking costs at a sporting event, unlike the cab fare to a restaurant, are not considered transportation expenses. Rather, your parking tab is part of the entertainment expense—and only 80 percent deductible.

Furthermore, with one exception, only 80 percent of the price printed on the entertainment ticket is deductible. If you pay a premium to an agent or a scalper, that part of the cost is strictly on you.

The only exception to this rule is the charitable sporting event—one in which all the proceeds go to charity and practically all the labor is voluntary. You may deduct as a business entertainment expense the full cost of these tickets, plus the agent's fee, if any.

Moreover, any food and beverage costs that are part of the ticket package are also 100 percent deductible. Note, sadly: High-school and college games do not qualify as charity events.

Caution: Skyboxes are out as deductible business entertainment expenses—or at least they're on their way. In 1988 you may claim as a deduction only one third of the extra cost of a skybox. In future years the extra cost is totally nondeductible.

QUESTIONS AND ANSWERS

QUESTION: I belong to a luncheon club. May I write off the dues I pay?

The IRS allows you to deduct the *business* portion of the dues you pay to a luncheon club—or dues to any other social, athletic, or country club, for that matter—as long as you can prove that you use the club more than 50 percent of the time for business.

But you may write off only that portion of your dues you can attribute to directly related entertainment, meaning meals during which you actively discuss business.

One other catch: The amount of dues you may write off—that is, the amount attributable to business—is subject to the 80 percent rule.

Say, for example, that you use the club 60 percent of the time for directly related entertainment. Your dues times 60 percent times 80 percent is the amount that's deductible.

Tip: If you're near—but not over—the 50 percent mark, make a conscious effort to increase the business entertaining you do at your club.

Q: I belong to a professional society. Once a month we hold a breakfast meeting. The cost of these breakfasts is not broken out but is included with my dues. How do I write off the breakfasts?

You deduct these meals as meals. It's up to you to calculate how much of the amount you pay is for dues—and 100 percent deductible—and how much for breakfasts, which is 80 percent deductible.

Q: What's the "quiet business meals" rule?

In the old days you could deduct the cost of a "quiet business meal." As long as the environment was conducive to a business discussion, you weren't required to discuss business before, during, or after the meal to make the cost deductible.

In 1986, Congress—in a belt-tightening mood—zapped this rule. You may no longer claim a deduction for quiet business meals.

You may deduct only the cost of business meals that meet the definition of directly related or associated entertainment.

Q: Are meals I eat while I'm out of town on a business trip subject to the 80 percent rule?

The law says that you may write off only 80 percent of the cost of business meals. And it makes no difference if you ingest them during out-of-town business trips. (See Chapter 11 for more information on travel expenses.)

Q: I own my own company. And I pay a per diem amount to my employees when they travel. Do I write off the whole amount?

Companies that pay their employees a per diem when they travel will have to find out how much of that goes toward meals and how much toward other expenses.

They may ask employees to document how they spend the money given to them. Then they may deduct only 80 percent of the amount that goes for meals.

Another idea: Companies may determine how much employees spend on average for meals when they travel and deduct 80 percent of that amount.

Q: My employer reimbursed me for my moving expenses, including the cost of meals we ate traveling from our old home to our new home. What are the tax consequences?

Your employer reimburses you for full moving expenses, including the cost of the meals you ate while you were on the road.

You report the amount you received from your employer as income. Then you write off 100 percent of the cost of the meals on your return as an itemized deduction. You report this information to the IRS using Form 3903, "Moving Expenses."

If your employer didn't reimburse you for these expenses, you could claim 80 percent of the cost of your meals as an itemized expense in your moving-expense deduction. Moving expenses aren't subject to the 2 percent floor.

Caution: Legislation now before Congress would cap deductions for meals you consume when you relocate to 80 percent of their cost, even if your employer reimburses you.

Q: My employer pays me a flat $100 a month for entertainment, and I don't have to account for how I spend this money. How do I treat this amount on my tax return?

Since you didn't account for how you spent this money, the IRS does not consider these amounts to be reimbursement. Rather, it considers them taxable income.

So your employer reports your monthly entertainment allowance as income on your Form W-2, and the amount is subject to all payroll taxes.

If you want to claim deductions for business meals or entertainment expenses actually incurred, those are subject to the 80 percent rule and to the 2 percent floor on itemized deductions (see Chapter 8).

Q: I'm self-employed and run up about $2,000 a year in business meal and entertainment expenses. May I still write off at least 80 percent of this amount from my self-employment income?

Self-employed people may deduct the expense of business meals before they determine their self-employment income—so long as they abide by the 80 percent limit.

CHAPTER 11

How to Write Off Travel Expenses

You may not know it, but there's still ample opportunity to collect generous write-offs for business travel. And combining business with pleasure may still pay off as well. Just be sure that you know—and follow—the IRS regulations.

In this chapter we'll run through the rules governing write-offs for business travel. We'll tell you what's deductible and what's not.

HOME AWAY FROM HOME When you travel strictly on business, your write-offs are clear-cut. The amount you spend for lodging and transportation—hotel bills, taxi fares, and so on—is deductible. So is the cost of tips, baggage handling, business calls, telegrams, laundry, and dry cleaning.

And Uncle Sam allows a write-off for the cost of the meals you consume while you're away from home—although these expenses are deductible only up to 80 percent of the final tab. (See Chapter 10 for more on deducting business meals.)

But your travel deductions become less clear-cut when you combine business with pleasure—sightseeing, or visiting old friends, for example.

Let's say you take a vacation or other trip primarily for personal reasons. You may not deduct any of your transportation costs. You may, however, write off any business expenses you run up once you arrive at your destination.

Here's an example. Suppose you take your family to New York for a holiday. While you're there, you take time out from your vacation to see a customer. You may deduct the cost of the cab fare between your customer's office and your hotel. And you may also write off 80 percent of the meal you buy her.

But if your primary reason for the trip was business, you're entitled to a deduction for transportation, as well. And it makes no difference if you add a few days to a business trip to see the sights.

Say, for example, that your company requires you to attend its annual sales conference. So you fly from New York to Palm Springs, where the conference is being held. You spend a week at the conference, then five days vacationing.

You could deduct your hotel bill and other expenses for attending the one-week meeting. You could also write off your air fare to Palm Springs, because—in the eyes of the IRS—you took the trip for bona fide business reasons.

Caution: The IRS scrutinizes borderline "business" trips, meaning trips that are part personal and part business. But as long as you can document that the main reason for your trip was business, you may deduct the entire travel cost—even if your trip includes some personal R&R.

FOREIGN TRAVELS   When you travel overseas, the law requires you to allocate all costs between the business and personal portions of your trip.

And it makes absolutely no difference that the reason you took the trip was for business. It only matters how you spend your time on the trip.

Say, for example, that your trip consisted of 70 percent business and 30 percent vacation. You could deduce only 70 percent of your transportation and lodging costs.

But there are exceptions to this rule. The IRS will allow all your transportation costs if:

• You spend less than a quarter of your travel days on personal affairs
• You're overseas for less than seven days
• You're not in "substantial control over arranging the trip"—that is, as far as the IRS is concerned, you're not self-employed, a managing executive, or you're not related to your employer
• Your major reason for taking the trip was not a holiday or vacation

Another special rule: Uncle Sam may disallow a deduction for a trip to a convention outside North America if he concludes that holding the convention in, say, Peking or Hong Kong was less reasonable than holding it here.

Also, the rules require you to show that the convention you attend is related to the active conduct of your trade or business.

Obviously, if you belong to the International Association of Criminal Attorneys, you may write off the cost of your participation in a meeting held in London. But if you belong to the Green County Pipefitter's Association, forget about deducting the cost of attending your annual confab in Amsterdam.

Caution: Uncle Sam won't allow you to write off the cost of travel expenses that are "lavish or extravagant." What meets the definition? Let's say you own and operate a chain of dry cleaning stores. And you charter the Concorde to take you and a customer to a business meeting in London. You can be pretty certain that Uncle Sam will disallow your deduction for the trip.

LIMITS ON CRUISES The law limits the amount you may write off for luxury cruise expenses, even if the ship takes you from one place to another on business.

The limit? It comes to twice the highest federal government allowance for U.S. travel by executive branch employees. Currently, that amount is $136 per day. So you may deduct no more than $272 per day for luxury cruise travel expenses.

Unless the cruise company breaks out food and beverage expenses separately, these costs are fully deductible—up to the $272 per day limit, of course. If the company does itemize your meal and beverage expenses, they're only 80 percent deductible.

What happens if you attend a convention or seminar aboard a cruise ship? You're not subject to the rules we just described.

For starters, the IRS says that you get no deduction unless you can show the convention is directly related to the active conduct of your trade or business.

Also, the cruise ship must be registered in the United States—and few are—and you must sail to ports of call in the United States or its possessions.

Finally, to pocket your deduction, the IRS requires you to attach a statement to your tax return specifying, among other items, the length of your trip, the schedule of business activities, and the number of hours you attended these sessions. And the statement must be signed by an officer of the sponsoring organization.

One final point: The rules cap deductions for conventions or seminars aboard cruise ships to $2,000 per year per person.

QUESTIONS AND ANSWERS

QUESTION: May I deduct the cost of taking my spouse along with me on a business trip?

Uncle Sam won't allow you to write off the expenses of bringing along your spouse—or any other relative, for that matter—on a business trip.

But the government provides an exception to this rule in cases where a spouse's presence serves a bona fide business purpose.

Taking notes at meetings doesn't fit the definition of a bona fide business purpose. But entertaining clients may. The courts have upheld deductions for a spouse's traveling expenses in cases where entertaining constituted a reason for his or her presence.

Q: I took my spouse with me on a business trip. I don't intend to claim a deduction for his expenses. But how do I write off my own expenses?

If you traveled by automobile, the law allows you to deduct the full expense—even though your companion was riding in the car with you.

But if you traveled by any other mode of transportation—an airline or train, for example—you may write off only the price of your ticket.

In the case of lodging, claim a deduction for the single room rate—$100 a night, say—rather than the double room rate you paid—$120 a night, for example.

CHAPTER 12

The Right Way to Write Off Business Automobiles

The company car has been around longer than the Internal Revenue Code. So you'd think that by now the rules governing write-offs for business cars would be clear-cut and easy to understand. Well, think again.

In this chapter we'll try to make sense of the complicated rules for writing off business automobiles. First, though, a few words about record keeping.

KEEPING THE RECORDS Uncle Sam says that you must substantiate the business use of your car, and that means you must maintain adequate records. You're not off the hook if you use a car owned by your employer, either. These record-keeping rules apply whether you own the car or it is provided to you by your company.

The best way: Keep a log handy to record your business miles, your destination, and the business purpose of your trip. (See the Appendix for a copy of a sample log.)

These records aren't just for show. When you or your employer file annual tax returns, the IRS wants proof of your automobile expenses and usage.

It wants to see the number of miles you logged for business. It wants to know the total number of miles you drove. And if you're driving a company car, the IRS wants to know if your employer allows you to use the automobile to commute.

Finally—and most important—the IRS wants to know if you have support for your deduction. If the answer is yes, you're better off if your evidence is written.

BUSINESS DRIVING DEFINED When it comes time to write off automobile expenses, here's the first question you must ask yourself: What percentage of my car's use may I attribute to business?

The IRS defines business use as the miles you drive your car between two business locations—your office, say, and the office of a customer.

Commuting is never business use. It makes no difference what type of work you do, how far you travel to your office, or what crisis you're about to face.

A trip to work is personal and not deductible. And making a business phone call or holding a business meeting in your car while you drive won't change that fact.

Furthermore, commuting—in the eyes of the government— involves more than driving your car to and from your home to your place of business.

For an employee, the IRS defines commuting as the first trip in the morning and the last trip home. So if you drive from your home to a customer's office, you are—in the eyes of the IRS— commuting. And you're not entitled to classify the trip as business.

Tip: You skirt this rule if you are temporarily assigned to work at a client's place of business, which is located some distance from your office.

In this case, you can argue that you are temporarily away from your "tax home," or your principal place of business. The result: You may claim as business miles the distance from your home to your client's office.

Say you're a salesperson for ABC Furniture Co., which is located five miles from your home. You're due at a client's office at nine A.M. on a Monday morning. And you decide to drive directly from your house to your client's place of business.

Your client is based in a city 80 miles from your home and 75 miles from your office. The IRS lets you classify 80 miles as business use.

Tip: The law also carves out an exception to the commuting rule for people who are self-employed and do business from a bona fide home office. These taxpayers may claim—as business mileage—trips to and from home.

Let's say you're a physician in private practice in Chicago and you maintain an office on the first floor of your town house. You see patients in your office, but once a day you drive 12 miles to a local hospital to make your rounds.

Under the rules, you may claim as business mileage the 12

miles to the hospital—and the 12 miles back—even though you're driving to and from your home. The reason: Your home is also your office.

Here's another example. Say you're employed full-time by a computer manufacturer and spend your days working at its headquarters. But at night you freelance as a computer programmer. And you maintain an office in your home for this purpose.

Your largest freelance client is a small software manufacturing company. One evening a week you drive from your home to that company's office, where you advise it on the development of new software. Uncle Sam allows you to claim as business mileage the miles you drive from your home to your client's office—again, because your home is your office.

But here's where the scenario gets complicated.

Say you drive from the office of your employer to the office of the software manufacturer and then drive home. You may classify the miles you drive from the office of your employer to the software manufacturer as business miles. But—and here's the kicker—the IRS would consider the drive from the software manufacturer to your home to be commuting. The reason: The IRS says that your last trip of the day is commuting—even if the trip isn't between your regular office and home.

DRIVING THE COMPANY CAR   If your employer provides you with a company car, you need to concern yourself with the following issues.

The law requires your employer to report the value of your personal use of the car on your W-2 form. And your employer must also withhold income and Social Security taxes (FICA) on the value of this benefit. However, with the exception of FICA, your employer may choose not to withhold taxes, as long as he lets you know by January 31 of each year.

Tip: If your employer does not withhold income taxes, you may need to pay estimated taxes to cover what you'll owe on this fringe benefit.

When it comes time for your company to report the value of your personal use of the company car on your W-2, it has two options. It can report only the value of your personal use, or it can report the total value of your use of the car as personal use.

Let's take a look at each option.

If your company reports only personal use, you must submit evidence to your employer that documents how you used the car. Say you log 23,176 miles—based on odometer readings at the beginning and end of the year—in your company car in 1988. You drive 15,677 miles on business, 3,466 miles commuting to and from work, and 4,033 on personal trips.

At the end of the year your employer asks you to submit a form detailing how you used your car. So you report 15,677 business miles and 7,499 personal miles—that is, the mileage you post for commuting and personal trips.

Based on these numbers, your employer determines that your business use added up to 68 percent of your total miles and your personal use 32 percent.

Now, your employer—following IRS regulations—reports the value of your personal use on your W-2 form. That amount equals your personal use multiplied by the total value of the use of the car.

And your employer may determine the value of your use of the company car in a number of ways. The most popular way: the annual lease value tables—based on fair market value—issued by the IRS. (You'll find a copy of the IRS lease table in the Appendix.)

Another method is to use standard car-lease rates in your area. One important point: The IRS tables include the cost of maintenance and insurance. You can't subtract these amounts from the tables even if your employer makes you pay for insurance or maintenance.

Your company may also report the total value of your use of the car on your W-2 form. In this case, you may deduct the value of the business use of your car on your personal return.

Here's an example. Say the year is 1988 and the value of your use of the company car, based on the annual lease value method, is $5,100. Your employer adds that amount to your W-2 form.

When it comes time to file your 1988 tax return, you provide your tax preparer with a copy of your W-2 and a statement summarizing how you used your company car. Let's say you used it 12,433 miles for business and 5,321 miles for personal purposes.

You or your tax preparer multiplies the percentage of business use—in our example, 70 percent—times your car's value as recorded on your W-2—$5,100. The result, $3,570, is the amount you may deduct on your return as a business expense.

You take this deduction above the line—that is, against your total income, to get your adjusted gross income. (See Chapter 3 for an explanation of above the line and below the line.)

You may also deduct any other expenses you paid based upon your percentage of business use.

Caution: If your company reports the total value of your car use on your W-2, you and your employer are paying Social Security taxes on that amount. And that means money out of your pocket.

Here's an example. Assume your employer reports the total value of the use of your company car to you—$5,100, for example. You and your employer pay Social Security taxes on the entire amount—unless you've already paid all the Social Security tax you owe (in 1988, that means 7.51 percent on income up to $45,000).

Now, let's say your employer changes his method. Your company reports the value of only your personal usage of your company car—or $2,800. Clearly, you're better off paying Social Security taxes on $2,800 than on $5,100.

Caution: Are you an officer or owner of 5 percent or more of the stock in your company? If so, the rules won't allow you to depreciate your car using the accelerated method, unless you use the vehicle more than 50 percent of the time for business. (For more on depreciation, see Chapter 18.)

OTHER POINTS TO KEEP IN MIND If you aren't an officer or a 5 percent shareholder of your company, and the only personal use of your company car allowed by your employer is commuting, your employer may use a different method to calculate the value of your fringe benefit.

If you drive to and from work, your employer credits you with an extra $3 a day in taxable income. A one-way commute is valued at $1.50.

There's yet another option available to your company when it comes time to report the value of your company car. This option applies to cars that are valued at less than $12,060, that log at least 10,000 miles a year, and that are used primarily for business. The rules say that your employer may report your personal usage of the company car at the rate of 22.5 cents a mile for the first 15,000 miles and 11 cents a mile thereafter.

BUSINESS USE OF PERSONAL CAR If you use your personal automobile for work, there are three requirements you must meet before you may deduct business-related automobile expenses on your personal tax return.

First, you must use your automobile "for the convenience of your employer"—that is, your employer must require that you have a car to properly perform your duties as an employee.

Second, your employer must require the automobile as a condition of employment. In other words, no car would mean no job. Last but most important, you need to substantiate business use and maintain adequate records.

An example of an employee who would meet these two tests: A messenger service's representative who must deliver packages to customers.

When you deduct car expenses, you have two choices: You may claim a flat amount for each business mile you drive—known as the standard rate—or you may write off the actual costs of operating your automobile. Here's how the two methods work.

Using the Standard Rate

The standard mileage rate currently equals 22.5 cents a mile for the first 15,000 miles of business travel in a year and 11 cents a mile thereafter.

There's one catch, though: You may not use the standard 22.5-cents-a-mile deduction on cars that you have fully depreciated—that is, cars you've driven for more than 60,000 business miles. For these automobiles, you may claim only 11 cents a mile.

Caution: Sometimes you're not allowed to use the standard mileage rate and must write off actual expenses. The two instances: when you lease your car, and when you've claimed accelerated depreciation on your car in a previous year.

Actual Expenses

In most cases your actual expenses will exceed the standard mileage deduction. So you should opt to write off actual costs.

A portion of all the following expenses is deductible (the percentage you write off equals the percentage of your car's mileage that you attribute to business).

- Automobile club memberships
- Batteries
- Driver's license
- Gasoline and oil
- Insurance

- Lubrication and repairs
- Registration and other licensing fees
- Supplies, such as antifreeze
- Temporary rentals
- Washing and waxing

You also may write off tires with a life of less than one year. (You should depreciate tires that last longer and are purchased separately from the car.)

But you may not deduct on your personal return the cost of parking your car at or near your office. However, if your company provides you with parking, the value of this fringe benefit is not taxable to you. So your employer does not report it as income on your Form W-2.

Nor may you fully deduct interest on a car loan if you're an employee—even if you buy the car strictly for business. This interest is considered personal interest, which, thanks to tax reform, is only 40 percent deductible in 1988, 20 percent deductible in 1989, and 10 percent deductible in 1990. After 1990, personal interest isn't deductible at all. (See Chapter 4 for the rules on deducting personal interest.)

You also may depreciate your car in the same way you depreciate other personal property you use for business. If you're buying a car that will be used for business, you calculate your depreciation deduction based on the total purchase price of your car. If you're converting your family car into a business automobile, then you base depreciation deductions on the lower of the fair market value at the date you convert, or its original purchase price. In either case, you must multiply the depreciation amount times the percentage of your actual business use.

But note: A special cap applies to cars. The law limits depreciation deductions for business cars purchased after December 31, 1986, to $2,560 in the first year, $4,100 in the second year, $2,450 in the third year, and $1,475 in all remaining years.

Here's an example. On January 15, 1988, you purchase an automobile for $19,000. You start driving it—or, in IRS lingo, "place it in service"—that same day. In 1988 and 1989 you use the car for business 70 percent of the time. So your depreciation deductions for 1988 and 1989 are $1,792 (the $2,560 limitation times your 70 percent business use) and $2,870 (the $4,100 limitation times 70 percent).

Another wrinkle: If business use of your car falls below 50 percent, you must go back to the first year you depreciated the car and recompute your depreciation using the straight-line method. The difference is picked up in your current return as income. You're not permitted to use the more favorable accelerated depreciation. And the limits on these deductions apply regardless of which depreciation method you use.

Also, the sales tax you pay is no longer currently deductible. You may, however, add this cost to the purchase price of your car when it comes time to calculate your depreciation deduction.

Caution: If you take the standard mileage deduction in year one, then write off actual costs in year two, you must depreciate the car using the straight-line method—that is, you write off the same amount each year.

But if you deduct your actual costs from the start, you may depreciate your car using the accelerated method—that is, you write off more in the early years of ownership.

Tip: If you use the actual cost method, reimbursements that exceed your expenses always count as taxable income. But let's say if you use the standard mileage rate, the excess is tax-free income.

So if you can't itemize—or the 2 percent floor eliminates your miscellaneous deductions—stick with the standard mileage rate method.

Tip: Whether you write off your actual automobile expenses or claim the standard mileage rate, you may still deduct parking fees and tolls you pay when you travel on business. But you may not write off fines for violating traffic and parking laws.

SPECIAL RULES FOR LEASING   When Congress voted to cap depreciation deductions for business automobiles, it also imposed tough new restrictions on cars that you lease. And these rules apply whether you're an employer or employee.

The law still allows you to deduct that portion of your lease payment that is attributable to business. For example, if you use your leased car 90 percent for business, you may write off 90 percent of your payment.

But here's the rub. The law wants to put people who lease business automobiles on an equal footing, tax-wise, with those who purchase their business autos outright. So if you lease, the law requires you to add to your taxable income—or reduce your deduction by—an amount that is based on two separate calculations.

The first calculation—which you make every year—is based on the fair market value of your car and your business use. You determine the income amount using tables and formulas provided by the IRS. The lower a car's business use, the smaller the adjustment.

You do the second calculation only once in your car's lifetime—when your business use falls below 50 percent. You base the calculation on the remaining term of the lease. Again, you use tables and formulas provided by the IRS to compute the amount.

QUESTIONS AND ANSWERS

Q: My employer reimburses me 22.5 cents a mile for every business mile I travel. Is that amount reported as income on my W-2 form?

No, it isn't. Uncle Sam says that if you are reimbursed at the standard mileage rate by your employer, the amount isn't reported as income to you on your W-2 form.

Q: My employer reimburses me 22.5 cents a mile for every business mile I travel. But my actual costs are greater than the amount I receive. May I write off the difference?

When you file your tax return, you also file a Form 2106, "Employee Business Expenses." On that form you report your actual expenses. You also record any reimbursements you receive from your employer. If your actual expenses exceed the amount you're reimbursed, you deduct the difference as a miscellaneous expense—subject to the 2 percent floor.

Q: My company reimburses me a flat $100 a month for automobile expenses. I don't have to account to my employer for how I spend this money or how I use my automobile. How do I treat this $100 a month for tax purposes?

Your employer has no way of knowing whether you spent the $100 on "ordinary and necessary" business expenses. So, under the law, he must report this amount as income on your W-2 form. And your employer must withhold taxes—including FICA taxes—on your automobile stipend.

But all is not lost.

You may claim a deduction for your expenses as a miscellaneous itemized deduction, subject to the 2 percent floor.

Moreover, if your company has a documented reason for the amount of allowance it gives you, you may not be required to have taxes withheld. In this case you may deduct up to

$1,200—your $100 allowance times 12 months—above the line (see Chapter 3 for definition). You may write off any expenses in excess of that amount as a miscellaneous itemized deduction, which is subject to the 2 percent floor.

Q: Business use of my car added up to 70 percent last year. But this year my business use will fall to about 45 percent. Are there any tax consequences?

Unfortunately, if your business use falls below 50 percent, you have to "recapture" some of the depreciation deductions you claimed in the previous year.

Say you purchase a car in 1988 for $19,000 and you depreciate the car using the accelerated method, which allows you to claim larger write-offs in the early years of ownership. (See Chapter 18 for more information on depreciation.)

In 1989, however, your business use falls to 45 percent. The law says you must redepreciate the car using the straight-line method. With the straight-line method, you claim the same amount of depreciation each year you own the car.

This change in depreciation methods results in a lowering of your depreciation deduction for last year. So you must add to your taxable income in the current year the difference between your deductions under the straight-line and accelerated methods.

Q: If I use the actual cost method, what's the best way to keep the data in one place?

Many people jot down mileage in a small pocket notebook, then attach expense receipts to the pages with paper clips.

You may also purchase a mileage log. Most mileage logs include a place to list these expenses, so you can find them easily when you summarize your tax data.

Q: I keep a log to document my automobile expenses, and I find it a real headache. Is there any way to reduce my record keeping?

You could try a method known as sampling. But you may use it only if your percentage of business use remains consistent from month to month.

Here's an example to illustrate how sampling works. Say you have your own interior decorating business and operate out of an office in your home.

You use your automobile for local business travel: to visit the homes or offices of clients, to meet with suppliers and other subcontractors, and to pick up and deliver materials to your customers. You log no other business miles on your car.

You maintain a diary for the first three months of 1988, and it indicates that 75 percent of your use of your automobile was for your interior decorating business. Based on invoices from subcontractors and other paid bills, you can prove that your business continued at approximately the same pace for the rest of 1988.

If there are no other significant changes in your business operation in the last nine months of 1988, you may use the log that you maintain for the first three months to document your business use of 75 percent.

Another option: You could maintain a log for the first week of every month during 1988. If your invoices indicate that you did about the same volume of business during the other weeks of each month, your records—in the eyes of the IRS—would support your claim of using your car 75 percent for business each month.

Q: My company won't allow me to use my company car during off hours. Do I still need to maintain records, since I don't use the car personally?

If you have a company car but company rules don't allow you to use the car for personal reasons—or if you use it only to commute—then you're off the hook when it comes to record keeping. You don't have to keep a log.

CHAPTER 13

Making the Most of
Your Capital Gain

Long-term capital gains—the profit you realize when you sell an investment you've held for more than a year—used to receive favorable tax treatment. But not anymore.

The 1986 Tax Reform Act zapped the federal tax break.

You still have to separate long-term from short-term gains when filling out your tax form. But from now on—unless Congress and the new president change their minds—you pay taxes on both long- and short-term capital gains at the same rate as ordinary income.

And that's even worse than it sounds.

Here's why. Uncle Sam imposes an additional 5 percent tax on income that falls within certain ranges. On this income, you pay a 33 percent marginal tax rate—that is, your normal 28 percent rate *plus* the 5 percent surtax.

For 1988 these income ranges run from $71,900 to $171,090 for married couples filing joint returns, and surviving spouses; $61,650 to $145,630 for heads of household; $43,150 to $100,480 for single taxpayers; and $39,950 to $125,220 for married couples filing separate returns.

If you fall into one of these income categories, you'll pay a 33 percent tax on some of your long-term gains—much higher than the old maximum 20 percent capital gains rate. (See Chapter 2 for more information on the 5 percent surtax.)

Tip: If you acquired an asset before 1987, the rules require you to hold it only six months before it qualifies as a long-term gain.

Tip: A few states still tax long-term capital gains at a lower rate than short-term capital gains. Your tax adviser will know the rules in your state.

Caution: The less favorable tax treatment of long-term capital gains applies as well to installment sales—even if they took place before 1988.

Say you purchased rental property in 1970 for $60,000 and sold it in 1985 for $100,000. You decided to provide the full amount of the financing to your buyer. The new owners agreed to repay the loan over a ten-year period—that is, they make payments to you once a month for ten years.

Under the installment rules, you pay no taxes on your gain when you sell your property. Rather, you pay taxes on the income as you receive it—each year for ten years.

Suppose, in 1987, your gain from the sale added up to $5,000. You reported your profit and paid taxes at what was then the top capital gains rate—28 percent.

In 1988 your profit again amounts to $5,000, but you pay capital gains taxes at the going rate—as much as 33 percent if your income falls within the surtax range.

LOCKING IN LOWER RATES Back in 1986, when the tax rate for long-term capital gains rates was capped at 20 percent, many taxpayers decided they were better off selling their investments and reporting their profits that year. That way they were guaranteed to pay a tax of no more than 20 percent on their gains.

Now that you no longer have that option, is there anything you can do to reduce your capital gains tax rate? The answer depends on your personal tax situation. As you know, the 5 percent surcharge kicks in at $43,150 for single filers and at $71,900 for joint filers.

If you're not subject to the surcharge in 1988 but you will be in 1989, consider this strategy: Sell a stock or other security now to lock in the lower 28 percent rate on your gain to date. Then, if you believe it will continue to appreciate in the future, immediately repurchase the security.

Caution: The best tax strategy isn't always the best financial strategy. The additional brokerage charges you'll incur in the repurchase may wipe out the tax savings. Also, you'll want to watch out for "wash-sale" rules, covered later in this chapter.

WRITING OFF YOUR CAPITAL LOSSES Now you know the rules governing capital gains, but what about capital losses? Uncle Sam allows you to deduct up to $3,000 in capital losses from your ordinary income in any one year—and it makes no difference whether these are long-term or short-term losses.

In addition, Uncle Sam says, you may carry forward any

losses that you are unable to write off in the current year to future tax years.

Let's say, for instance, that you've accumulated net long-term capital losses of $10,000. This year you had $3,000 in short-term gains. You may use $3,000 of your long-term losses to offset the gain. And you still have $7,000 in long-term losses to carry forward into future tax years.

But there's a catch, of course. Even if you had zero or negative taxable income this year, and thus have no need to use your $3,000 capital loss deduction, you lose it anyway. The law deems that you have used your maximum annual capital loss write-off whether you do or not. The effect in this example is that you still may carry forward only $7,000 of capital losses into future tax years.

Caution: Legislation now before Congress would eliminate this rule. If it's adopted, the amount of capital losses you could carry forward would be capped at $3,000 or your taxable income, whichever is less. Your tax adviser will update you on the status of this legislation.

QUESTIONS AND ANSWERS

QUESTION: Do you think it's possible long-term capital gains will again get a preferential rate?

We don't have a crystal ball. But with the growing budget deficit, chances are there won't be a rate lower than 28 percent for long-term capital gains.

However, the Treasury Department is examining whether a reduction in the capital gains rate would actually increase federal tax receipts.

But if lawmakers and the new president raise tax rates, expect the capital gain rate to stay at a maximum of 28 percent. The result: Capital gains would again enjoy a preferential rate.

Q: I've heard about "wash sales." What is a wash sale and what is its significance for me?

You could be in for a large, and unexpected, tax bite if you plan to offset your capital gains with losses the IRS classifies in the "wash-sale" category.

Wash-sale rules are intended to prevent you from selling a stock at a loss, writing off the loss on your tax return, then immediately buying the stock back.

These regulations say that you may not take a loss if—within a period beginning 30 days before you sell your security and ending 30 days after that date (a period covering 61 days)—you've acquired or entered into a contract or option to acquire "substantially identical stock or securities."

Moreover, the Supreme Court has ruled that you may not take a loss if your spouse purchases identical securities.

Let's say on December 15, 1987, you bought 100 shares of XYZ Company stock for $1,000, and on December 22, 1987, you bought an additional 100 shares of $975. On January 6, 1988, you sold the 100 shares you purchased on December 22 for $900.

Since you bought 100 shares of the same stock within the period beginning 30 days before the date of the sale and ending 30 days after that date, you may not claim a loss on your return.

The rules don't apply, incidentally, if you received your stock or security through a gift, bequest, inheritance, or tax-free exchange.

Q: I hear there's a way to postpone paying taxes on my stock market investments until next year. How do I do it?

It's possible to nail down a 1988 paper profit on your stocks and have it taxed in 1989. In effect, you freeze a profit (or loss) and postpone the tax result by using a technique known as a "short sale."

For example, to fix the current paper profit in a block of stock, you go to your broker and tell him or her you want to arrange a short sale.

It works something like this. You own 100 shares of XYZ Corporation. The stockbroker allows you to borrow another 100 shares, using your existing shares as collateral. You then sell the borrowed shares, thus fixing your profit.

In January 1989 you don't owe the stockbroker money. You owe the broker shares. You deliver your original shares to the broker in repayment.

The result: The profit on the 1988 short sale becomes next year's taxable income. The maneuver can work beautifully purely as a tax move—but its viability depends more on the price movement of the block of stock.

Q: I have bought several tax-exempt bonds over the years at their par, or face, value. Because interest rates have fallen, these bonds are currently selling at a premium. If I sell my tax-exempts now, is my gain taxable?

It is. The interest paid on the bond is tax exempt, but any capital gain you realize is taxed just like the gain on the sale of a taxable security.

Caution: If you sell a bond, tax-exempt or not, for which you paid either more or less than face value, the price you paid may not be your basis in the bond for figuring gains or losses.

Rather, the price you paid for the bond may have to be adjusted mathematically so that by the time the bond matures, your basis in the bond is equal to the bond's face value. The rules here are complicated, so you should see your tax adviser. He or she will help you make these computations and determine which rules apply.

Q: I have purchased stock in the same company on three different occasions at three different prices. Now I want to sell just some of the stock. When I'm calculating my gain (or loss) for tax purposes, which of the three stock prices do I use in computing my basis?

Unless you can identify the specific shares you are selling by, say, certificate number or by virtue of having held them in different accounts, you must abide by the "ordering rule." It says that you are considered to be selling the stock in the order in which you bought it.

Q: I own stock in a company, and the stock recently split. How long do I have to hold the new stock before it qualifies as a long-term capital gain?

You calculate your holding period—for the capital gain purposes—from the date you originally bought the stock, not from the time the stock split.

And this same rule holds true for companies that pay dividends in the form of additional shares. The holding period for the new shares is the same as for the old shares.

What about dividend reinvestment plans that allow you to use your cash dividends to purchase additional shares of stock, sometimes at a discount?

Another rule applies. The holding period for stock purchased through these plans begins on the date you purchase the new shares.

Q: I loaned money to a friend of mine to start a business. She's filed for bankruptcy, and I'm not going to get my money back. May I write off this bad debt?

Uncle Sam says that you may deduct this amount as a short-term capital loss on your tax return—as long as it is truly uncollectible.

Q: I invested in a small company that went belly-up. The company's stock was classified as "small business stock." How is my loss treated for tax purposes?

Congress wants you to invest in small companies, and it's willing to share the risk with you. It says that you may deduct from your ordinary income losses of up to $50,000 ($100,000 if you're married and file a joint return). This amount has no bearing on your other capital losses.

CHAPTER 14

Tax Rules You Need to Know When You Sell Your Home

Though we usually think of homes as—well, homes—they're also investments. And, as such, they're subject to a number of tax consequences.

Overall, though, the tax laws are kind to homeowners. The reason: the long-standing philosophy of the country's lawmakers that people who own homes deserve some sort of tax protection.

We ran through the rules governing mortgage interest deductions in Chapter 4. In this chapter we'll cover the tax rules that apply to that most complicated of transactions—the sale of your home.

FOR SALE If you sell your house or condominium at a profit, you defer paying taxes on the gain from the sale as long as you meet two conditions:

• You buy or build and occupy a new principal residence within 24 months before or after the date you complete the sale of your old home
• You buy or build and occupy that new house or condominium for an amount that equals at least the "adjusted selling price" of your old home

What is the adjusted selling price? Uncle Sam defines it as the amount you pocket from the sale—that is, the sales price minus any selling costs—less the expenses you incur in fixing up your home and getting it ready to sell.

Ordinarily, of course, you gain no tax benefit when you fix up your personal residence. Painting and wallpapering, for example, aren't currently deductible. And they don't directly reduce your gain when you sell, either.

But when you sell your home, these expenses do enter the picture. How? They reduce your adjusted sales price, meaning the amount you must reinvest in a new home to defer tax on your gain from your old home.

The rules say you may not deduct these expenses on your return. Moreover, the work must be for repair and maintenance—not for improvements, a distinction we'll explain shortly. Finally, you must do the fixing up during the 90 days before you sign the contract to sell your house, and you must pay for your repairs within 30 days after the sale.

But what about selling expenses, such as real estate commissions? Unlike fixing-up costs, these expenses actually reduce the gain on your home—whether you get to defer the gain or not. (We'll get to selling costs and how you should compute your gain later.)

And keep this point in mind. Postponement of the gain applies only to the sale of your principal residence. A vacation cottage—or any second home—doesn't qualify. But a condominium, a co-op, or even a houseboat, fits the bill as long as you make it your principal residence.

The key point is not the type of dwelling you sell, but whether you make it your primary home. Beware, however, that ownership alone doesn't make a house your principal residence. You and your family must actually live in the house for it to qualify.

The amount of time you spend in your home doesn't matter all that much—Uncle Sam imposes no set limits on how long you must occupy your home for it to qualify as your primary residence. But use common sense. Moving your furniture into a house and then leaving immediately to spend the year in Europe won't satisfy the IRS.

So far, rolling over the gain from your old home to a new one sounds simple. It can be—but often there are complicating factors.

Here's an example. You are an up-and-coming executive transferred to another division of your corporation in another city. You put your home up for sale, and you sign a contract to purchase a house for a slightly higher price in a suburb of the new city. You figure that you'll sell your old house at about the same time that you are scheduled to move into your new house.

But it doesn't quite work out that way. The housing marketing in your old neighborhood is depressed, and, although several buyers are interested in your property, you have no firm offers.

You decide to rent your house until you find a buyer. The rental agreement includes an option to buy, but your tenant never exercises the option. It takes you a year to locate a buyer.

Here's how the situation gets sticky. The rules say that you may defer the gain on the sale of a house only if it's your principal residence *at the time of the sale*. So does that mean your old home is no longer considered your principal residence, since it is occupied by a tenant at the time you sell it?

Well, not really. The tax courts have ruled that temporarily renting out your old house because of a depressed real estate market won't prevent you from deferring your gain. So in this case you don't have to actually occupy the house at the time of the sale.

And you get another break as well. Not only may you consider your house as a principal residence for the purpose of deferring your gain, but you may also treat the property as rental real estate—and claim operating expenses and even depreciation deductions for the period you rent it. So in this situation you're way ahead.

But what if the new house you buy costs less than the adjusted selling price of your old one?

Consider this example. You are fifty-two years old and your spouse is fifty. You commute every day from your home in Connecticut to your job in New York. Weary of your ninety-minute trek into Manhattan, you suggest that you sell your ten-room house and purchase a small condominium near your midtown office.

Your spouse agrees, and you put your home on the market. A buyer offers $610,000. You're delighted, since you purchased the house twenty years earlier for $150,000.

You sign a contract and pay the real estate agent a 6 percent commission, or $36,600. Since you have no remaining mortgage and no other selling expenses, you collect $573,400 from the sale.

All told, your gain amounts to $423,400—$573,400 less the $150,000 cost of your home. You begin looking for a condominium but find nothing you like.

So you decide to temporarily rent an apartment in midtown Manhattan. A year later you locate the perfect condo. Its price: $550,000, or $23,400 less than the $573,400 you pocketed from the sale of your home in Connecticut. You move into the condo immediately.

What are the tax consequences?

Since you did not reinvest all of the proceeds from the sale of your previous house, you must report on your federal tax return the difference in price between what you sold your old house for and what you paid for your new one—in this case, $23,400. But you still get to defer $400,000 of the gain from the sale of your old house ($423,400 less the $23,400 you do have to report).

If you had paid for your condo an amount equal to or greater than the adjusted selling price of your previous home, you would defer paying tax on all your $423,400 profit.

Still another complication in the law involves taxpayers who are building new homes. Say you hire an architect or a contractor to build a house, or you contract the work yourself. Ready or not, you must move into your new home within 24 months after the sale of your old home. Otherwise, you pay taxes on your gain.

What's more, the house must be substantially complete when you move in. You can't pitch a tent on the foundation and claim you occupy your new home. The IRS is strict on this point—despite the house-building delays people suffer—and the tax courts have backed it up.

Tip: Include a clause in your construction contract that calls for your contractor to pay any taxes you owe if construction is delayed beyond the 24-month limit.

HOW TO CALCULATE YOUR GAIN   Let's say your new home does cost less than the amount you collect when you sell your old house. Or suppose you don't buy a new residence at all but choose to rent.

In these cases, some or all of any gain you pocket is taxes. So, clearly, you should do everything you can to keep your taxable gain as low as possible.

Let's look at some strategies you should consider.

To begin with, you need to know how to determine the actual profit and the taxable gain or loss on the sale of your home. The calculation is simple.

You just subtract your basis—the cost of your house plus improvements (but not fixing-up expenses)—from your selling price—less, of course, your selling expenses.

Now, to maximize your tax savings, be sure to include every item that increases your basis and to subtract all legitimate adjustments from your sales proceeds.

And note: You may use some of the costs you ran up when

you bought your home—and while you owned it—to slash your taxable profit when you later sell.

Here are some expenses you may include.

Purchasing Costs

You should add to your house's original cost any of the following fees you shelled out when you bought your home: appraisal fees, attorneys' fees, costs of removing any cloud on the title, costs for title search and insurance, fees for the recording of the deed and mortgage, late closing charge, and survey expenses.

Improvements

Also add to your costs all amounts you paid for improvements. What counts as an improvement? Anything that adds to your home's value or appreciably prolongs its life. (You'll find a checklist of these items at the end of this chapter.)

Note, though: You may not increase the basis by the cost of ordinary repairs and maintenance designed to keep up the building and grounds.

What counts as a repair? Common examples include repainting inside or out, fixing the gutters or floors, mending leaks, replastering, or replacing broken windowpanes.

Now let's look at an example of how you might figure your taxable gain. Let's say the original cost of your home was $50,000. And you had purchasing expenses of $2,000. Over the years you added a new room for $9,000 and installed central air conditioning and heating for $3,000.

Finally, you sell the old homestead for $90,000. But your broker's commission and other selling expenses total $5,000.

Is your gain $40,000 (your $90,000 sales price less your $50,000 cost)? Definitely not. As we've seen, to determine your gain, you add your purchasing expenses and the cost of improvements to your basis, and you subtract your selling expenses from the sales proceeds.

So in our example, your cost basis comes to $64,000 (your $50,000 original cost plus $14,000 in improvements and purchasing expenses).

The amount you collect in cash after you subtract your selling expenses totals $85,000 (your $90,000 sales price less $5,000 in selling costs). So your gain comes to only $21,000 ($85,000 less $64,000).

The one caveat: You must be prepared to substantiate your expenses. And doing so requires accurate and careful record keeping. So keep detailed records of all your home-related expenses.

PUT OFF TODAY WHAT YOU CAN PAY TOMORROW

Let's go back to the example we just gave.

You pay no tax on your $21,000 profit as long as you buy a new house costing $85,000 or more—or at least you don't pay any tax now.

Say you buy a new house for $86,000. Your purchasing costs add up to $4,000. Your basis in your new home is $90,000 ($86,000 plus $4,000). Right?

Wrong. Uncle Sam says you must reduce your basis in your new house by the amount of gain from your old house that you rolled over, or deferred.

Your basis in your new home then comes to $69,000—that is, $86,000 plus $4,000 minus the $21,000 gain you rolled over.

Now, let's say, it's a year later and you decide to tour the world for two years. You sell your house for $90,000, but you don't buy a new one.

The law says you must report on your tax return the difference between the selling price—$90,000—and your basis in your home—$69,000. And your gain—$21,000—is taxable now because you didn't buy a new home.

But what if you had purchased another house? You're still in trouble. Under the rules, you may roll over your gain from the sale of a house only once every two years—unless you take a new job in another location or are transferred as part of your old job.

Here's another example. You sell your old house on January 15, 1989, at a $10,000 profit. Then you buy a new one on February 15. The cost of your new home tops the amount you received for your old house.

Then you discover oil in the backyard of your new home. So, on March 15 you sell the second house at a hefty profit. And, finally, on April 15 you move into yet another, even more expensive home. Under the rules, you may defer only the $10,000 gain from your original home.

Why? The rollover break doesn't apply to the sale of your second home, because it was purchased and sold within two years of the sale of your original home. Instead you must report and pay taxes on the gain from the March 15 sale of the house with the gusher in the backyard. And you reduce the basis of your last home—the one you bought on April 15—by the $10,000 gain you deferred on the sale of your first one.

TIMING YOUR SALE   When Congress adopted the 1986 Tax Reform Act, it zapped favorable tax treatment of long-term capital gains. (See Chapter 13 for more information on capital gains.) And that's bad news for many homeowners.

Here's why. Nowadays, if you sell your house for a profit and don't purchase another home to replace it, your gain is taxed at the same rate as ordinary income—potentially as high as 33 percent.

Our advice: If you plan to sell your home and not purchase a replacement residence, identify your tax rate for 1988. Then identify your tax rate for 1989.

If your tax rate is lower in 1988, sell in 1988. What if your tax rate is the same? It makes no difference—taxwise, at least—when you sell your home.

WAITING UNTIL YOU'RE OLDER   Say you're a sixty-four-year-old widow. You owe no money on your eight-room house, since you paid off the entire purchase price of $50,000 years ago.

Tired of property taxes and the expense of maintaining your large home, you decide to sell the house and move into an apartment building near your daughter. You contact a real estate agent and learn that the property—which you bought thirty years previously—is now worth $170,000. You place it on the market at that price.

What is the tax consequence for you? The answer, simply stated, is none. Under the law, you owe no tax as a result of selling your home—even though your gain is $120,000.

And it doesn't matter to the IRS whether you use the proceeds from the sale to buy another house, place the entire amount in the bank, or stuff your gains into a jar. You owe no taxes.

Why? Congress voted to allow older taxpayers who sell their principal residence to pocket the profit tax free—if they meet four conditions. The conditions are as follows:

• The tax-free profit on the sale of your house may not top $125,000.

This ceiling applies to a single person or a married couple filing jointly. In the case of a married couple filing separately, the limit is $62,500 per spouse. Any profit on your house above $125,000 is taxed as a capital gain.

• You must be fifty-five years of age or older before the date of sale.

It is not enough to reach age fifty-five during the year of the sale. You must turn that age before the day of the sale. But the IRS carves out one exception to this rule. If you turn fifty-five on the exact date of sale, happy birthday: You also qualify for the break. That's because the IRS says, for purposes of the exclusion, you turn fifty-five not on the day you were born but on the day before your birthday.

The rules treat a married couple filing a joint return as one person. So a couple qualifies for the tax break if only one spouse is age fifty-five before the sale.

Another important point: You may exclude a profit on the sale of a house from your taxable income only if you didn't previously take advantage of this break. The $125,000 exclusion is a once-in-a-lifetime offer.

What happens if you remarry? Neither you nor your new spouse may claim the exclusion if either of you took it previously.

Tip: Don't allow your buyer to take possession of your house before you turn age fifty-five. Sometimes, simply taking possessions constitutes a sale for tax purposes—even though title has not actually changed hands.

• You own and live in the same house and maintain it as your principal residence for at least three of the five years immediately before the sale.

But the house doesn't have to be your principal residence at the time of the sale. Under the rules, up to two years may elapse between the time you move out and the sale takes place—as long as you occupied it for the previous three years.

• You tell the IRS that you are making use of the exclusion by filing a tax form.

You must inform the IRS of the sale of your principal residence and your decision to make use of this part of the law. The IRS calls filing this form "making a formal election," and it is the government's way of making sure you don't capture the break more than once. The required "formal election" actually is a government-printed, government-provided form telling the IRS when you sold your home and how much profit you made.

If you want to complete the form yourself, just stop by or

telephone your local IRS office for a copy. (Ask for Form 2119, "Sale or Exchange of Principal Residence.") The IRS will also provide instructions on how to prepare the form and will offer assistance if you need it.

The important point to keep in mind: Plan carefully for your use of this tax break. It is far too valuable to waste. Here is an example of how you may lose part of your benefits.

Say in early 1962 you bought a house for $30,000. By 1988 you are older than age fifty-five. And you and your spouse decide to sell your house. You plan to invest the tax-free profit in securities, then move to the Florida vacation cottage you purchased some years earlier.

A willing buyer pays $130,000 for the old homestead. To figure your profit, you subtract the original cost of the house—$30,000—and a 6 percent real estate agent's commission—$7,800. The result: $92,200. You notify the IRS that you intend to make use of the one-time, age-fifty-five, home-sale exclusion.

You invest your $92,200 and move south.

So far so good—until you think about your situation a little more carefully. You used only $92,200 of the amount of gain you're allowed to exclude—$125,000—on the sale. And the difference between the amount you use and the amount allowed—$32,800—is gone forever. Remember: The law lets you make use of this exclusion only once.

This provision is fine if you can exclude the maximum amount you're allowed or close to it. But you can't exclude the difference later on.

If you could have waited a year or two before you sold your house, you might have been better off. By then the housing market might have become stronger and you could have gotten a better price and been able to take better advantage of this once-in-a-lifetime tax break.

Tip: Here's some advice for people who own more than one home. It usually doesn't make sense to cash in on the $125,000 exclusion if you can make better use of it later.

Say, for example, that you just sold your home and are retiring to your vacation house in the mountains of North Carolina. Your vacation home has appreciated more in value than the house you just sold.

Why not wait to claim the $125,000 exclusion until you sell your North Carolina property? That way you can take better advantage of the exclusion.

Tip: You can cash in on a really impressive tax-free parlay. How? Combine the $125,000 exclusion and the sale-and-replacement break.

And doing so is a big break for the home seller who's "buying down"—for example, a retiree who's selling his or her big home and buying a smaller one.

By combining the exclusion and the rollover, you may collect more than $125,000 in profit and buy a much less expensive home without paying one dime in taxes.

Here's how. Say you paid $165,000 for your house in 1977, then, ten years later, you sold it for $380,000. You pocketed a hefty $215,000 profit. And you opted for the one-time exclusion. So $125,000 of your $215,000 gain is tax free to you—forever.

Now you want to purchase a house of equal value to your old one, so you'll qualify for the sale-and-replacement break.

But wait: When it comes time to calculate how much you must spend on a new home, the law allows you to subtract the amount of your exclusion—$125,000—from the selling price of your old home—$380,000. So you need to spend only $255,000 for a new house—not $380,000.

As long as your new house costs $255,000 or more, you defer paying taxes on your remaining gain of $90,000. And you reduce the basis of your new house by only the $90,000 gain that you don't pay taxes on now.

QUESTIONS AND ANSWERS

QUESTION: We bought a new home, but we're holding on to our old one and plan to rent it. What depreciation period do we use?

The length of time over which you depreciate your house depends on two factors: when you purchased your home, and when you placed it in service as rental property.

If you bought your house after 1980 and you began renting in 1987 or later, you depreciate it over 27½ years. But if you bought it before 1980 and began renting it after 1980, you must follow the depreciation rules in place at the time of your purchase.

Q: We sold our old house, which we bought for $100,000, for $125,000. We bought a new one for $100,000, then six months later spent $50,000 making improvements (we remodeled the kitchen and both bathrooms). How much of the $25,000 gain do we include in our tax return?

You might think that you have to include the entire $25,000 on your return, since the amount you paid for your new house is less than the selling price of your old home. Not so.

The law gives you a break. You may add to the cost of your new house the amount you spend on improvements within 24 months before or after the sale of your old home.

So your taxable gain equals zero. Here's why: The $100,000 you paid for your new house plus the $50,000 you spent on improvements is greater than the $25,000 you collected for your old house.

Tip: If you plan on making improvements to your new home, do so within 24 months before or after the sale of the old one. Acting fast is particularly important if, as in this case, the cost of your new home is less than the selling price of your old one.

Q: The real estate market in our area is really depressed. We had to sell our house at a loss. May I claim this loss on my tax return?

You may not deduct a loss from selling a personal residence. But you do get a write-off for a loss when you've converted a home to rental property. The reason: Your home is no longer considered your personal residence—rather, it now qualifies as business property. The deduction is limited, however, and taking advantage of it is complicated. So check with your tax adviser.

Converting a personal residence into rental property has another plus. You may also deduct operating expenses and depreciation during the rental period, as well as any loss when you eventually sell. You should know, however, that depreciation is not the big tax saver it once was. (See Chapter 16 for more on depreciating real estate.)

Tip: If you have to sell a home in a depressed market and it looks as if you're going to take a loss, rent out your house until conditions improve. That way you've converted your house to a rental and will be able to deduct your loss when you eventually sell.

Q: We sold our old home. But we won't buy a new one before we file our next tax return. Do we have to notify the IRS of the sale?

Attach Form 2119 to your return, showing how you figured your gain. Then, on a separate piece of paper attached to Form 2119, write down the date you sold your old residence, the sales price, and your basis in the house. Also state that you intend to acquire a new residence within the required 24 months. Once you replace your home, let the IRS know in writing on another Form 2119.

But what if you decide not to buy another house or the 24-month period has passed? In these cases you report your taxable gain for the year of your sale on Form 1040X (an amended 1040), to which you attach a Schedule D (to report capital gains and losses) and a new Form 2119.

Q: How does the IRS know that I sold my house?

The 1986 Tax Reform Act makes it easier for the IRS to uncover unreported profits by sellers of residential real estate. The reason: The law requires that real estate sales be reported to the IRS on Form 1099-S.

As the rules are presently written, this reporting requirement applies only to the sale of residential real estate of four or fewer units. But the IRS plans to change this rule by expanding the reporting requirements to include additional real estate transactions.

For now, the rule applies to any sale of a single house, town house, condominium unit, duplex, triplex, or fourplex, as well as a co-op.

Who does the reporting? Usually the person listed as the settlement agent on a settlement statement, or the person who prepares the settlement or closing statement.

If there is no statement, responsibility passes in descending order to: the buyer's attorney, the seller's attorney, the title company, the mortgage lender, the seller's broker, the buyer's broker, and finally, the buyer. Or both the buyer and the seller may designate someone to file Form 1099-S with the IRS.

Whoever the person is, he or she must report the total amount—with no reduction for selling expenses—received by the seller. And he or she must list the seller's name, address, and Social Security number, as well as the closing date of the sale and the address of the property sold.

The information must be submitted to the IRS by February 28 following the year of the closing. And a copy must also be sent to the seller by January 31 following the year of closing.

Q: Who pays for the cost of preparing this 1099-S? Will I, as the home buyer, have to pay?

Not if Congress has its way. Proposed legislation prohibits reporting costs being charged to buyers. Rather, the person responsible for filing the 1099 will have to pay.

Q: I don't own a house. I own a condo. Do the same rules apply?

First, a critical distinction: A condominium owner owns his or her residence outright, while a cooperative apartment is owned by a corporation in which the resident owns stock. Stock ownership entitles the co-op "owner" to the exclusive right to lease his or her apartment. But whether you own a condo or a co-op, you get the same tax treatment as owners of single-family homes.

You may deduct mortgage interest and taxes. Of course, if you're a condo owner, you—like the owner of a house—pay your interest and taxes directly. If you're a co-op shareholder, you pay a portion of the corporation's interest and taxes, based on the number of shares you own.

And you may deduct the portion of your co-op payment that is allocated to the corporation's interest and taxes. (Of course, your co-op or condo interest must meet the tests for deductibility. See Chapter 4 for more on interest deductions.)

When it comes time to sell, your cost is increased by the amount you spend for improvements—again, just as if you owned a house. Remember, though, to include your share of maintenance charges or special assessments that your association spends on improvements for the benefit of all the condos or co-ops in your building.

Q: I bought a washer five years ago and added its cost ($200) to my basis in the house. Now the washer is kaput. I've bought a new one for $350. Do I also add its cost to my basis?

Uncle Sam won't allow you to increase your basis by the purchase price of both machines. He says you must subtract the amount you paid for the first washer, $200, from your basis. Then you may add the price of the new machine—$350.

So your basis in your home increases by $150 at the time you purchase the second machine—that is, the difference between the purchase prices of the first and second machines.

Checklist of Improvements Uncle Sam defines an improvement as anything that adds to the value of your home or appreciably prolongs its life. Here's a checklist of what counts as an improvement.

- Additional acreage
- Additional rooms
- Air cleaner
- Air-conditioning
- Alarm system
- Aluminum siding
- Attic fan
- Attic improvement (converting it into living space)
- Awnings

- Basketball goalpost
- Bathroom addition
- Bathtub
- Bathtub enclosure
- Bathtub sliding doors
- Beams (decorative)
- Bird bath
- Boiler
- Bookcases
- Breezeway
- Built-in furniture
- Burglar alarm system

- Barbecue grill
- Baseboard heating
- Basement improvement (converting it into living space)

- Cabana
- Cabinets
- Carpeting
- Caulking

- Ceilings (acoustical)
- Chimes (door)
- Chimney
- Circuit breakers
- Circulating system
- Closets and closet organizers
- Clothes dryer
- Cold water pipes
- Concrete walks
- Cooling equipment
- Copper tubing
- Cornice
- Countertops
- Cupboards
- Curtains

- Electrical heat
- Electrical outlets
- Electrical wiring
- Electronic air filter
- Exhaust fans

- Fences
- Fire alarm system
- Fireplace
- Fireplace mantel
- Fixtures (lighting and plumbing)
- Flagstone walks
- Flooring (wood, tile, and so on)
- Food freezer
- Furnace (replacement)
- Furnace filter system
- Fuse boxes

- Deck
- Dehumidifier
- Dishwasher (built-in)
- Doors
- Doorbells
- Dormers
- Drain boards
- Drainpipes
- Drainage system
- Drapes
- Driveway (paving or blacktopping)
- Dry wells
- Ducts

- Garage
- Garage door
- Garage door opener
- Garbage disposal systems
- Garden and grounds
- Gates
- Glass enclosure
- Grading

- Grease traps
- Greenhouse
- Grills, air ducts
- Gutters

- Hamper
- Hardware
  (fixtures and locks)
- Heat ducts
- Heat pumps
- Heating system
- Hedges
- Hot tub
- Hot water heater
- Hot water pipes
- House numbers
- Humidifier
  (furnace)
- Humidistat

- Inside walls (altering)
- Insulation
- Intercommunication
  system

- Kitchen

- Lamp post
- Landscaping
- Laundry equipment
- Lawn sprinkling
  system
- Lighting fixtures
- Lightning rods
- Linen chute
- Linoleum
- Locks (door)

- Mailbox
- Medicine cabinet
- Mirrors

- Outdoor lighting
- Ovens

- Paneling
- Partitions
- Pathways
- Patio
- Play yard
- Plumbing
- Porch
- Pumps

- Racks (garage)
- Radiator covers
- Radiators and valves
- Railings
- Range (gas or electric)
- Range hood
- Refrigerator
- Retaining walls
- Roofing
- Room dividers

- Solar room
- Space heater
- Stairs
- Steam room
- Steps
- Storm doors
- Sump pump
- Supply cabinets
- Survey (property)
- Swimming pool
- Switch plates

- Screen doors
- Screens
- Security system
- Septic system
- Sewer assessment
- Sewers
- Shades
- Shed
- Shelves (built-in)
- Shower controls
- Shower doors
- Showers
- Shutters
- Shrubs
- Sidewalks
- Siding
- Sinks
- Skylights
- Smoke detector
- Softwater system
- Solar heating unit

- Telephone outlets
- Television antenna
- Termite-proofing
- Terraces
- Thermostat
- Tiles
- Toilets
- Topsoil
- Towel racks
- Trees
- Trellises

- Vacuuming system
- Vanity
- Venetian blinds
- Vent pipe

- Walks
- Wall coverings
- Washer
- Weather stripping

CHAPTER 15

Answers to Questions about Home Office Deductions

Changing life-styles, along with inexpensive computers and communication technologies, such as modems, make it easier for people to go to work without ever leaving home.

But changing tax laws make it harder for people to claim deductions for home office expenses. Let's take a look at the rules governing these deductions.

RULES ON HOME OFFICE DEDUCTIONS If you work at home—and your office qualifies—you may deduct the costs of operating and maintaining that portion of your home you use for business.

If you own your home, you may write off a portion of your operating expenses, such as utilities, and you may depreciate that part of your home that you use as an office.

If you rent your house, you may deduct part of your rent, in addition to your operating expenses for the office portion of your home.

But the qualifying rules are stringent. You must use whatever space you designate as your home office regularly and exclusively as your principal place of business. Or you must use it regularly and exclusively as a place where you meet with customers, patients, or clients—if meeting with clients is a normal part of your business.

Tip: A home office you use for a *second* business may qualify for a deduction. Say, for instance, that you teach in the public schools but also sell vitamins door to door in the evenings. You use your den regularly and exclusively to run your business—

that is, manage the books, order the vitamins, make phone calls, and so on. So you may take the write-off.

A home office that you use exclusively to manage your own investment portfolio, however, does not qualify for a write-off. Managing your personal investments may be how you make your money, but it is not your trade or profession.

You don't need to maintain an office in a separate room to qualify for a write-off. You need only use some separately identifiable space exclusively and regularly for business.

What happens if you maintain your office in a separate structure—a carriage house, for instance? Then the rules are less strict.

In this case you may claim a deduction if you use the structure regularly and exclusively in your trade or business. In other words, the building doesn't have to be your principal place of business.

Another important rule: If you are employed by someone else, you must maintain your home office for the convenience of your employer—or you don't get a write-off.

What do these rules mean to you? Say you're an attorney with a downtown firm. You sometimes use your den to catch up on your reading and to occasionally meet with clients. Does your den qualify as a home office?

No, and here's why. You don't use it regularly and exclusively to conduct your law business. And it's not your principal place of business. Your principal place of business is your downtown office. Also, you use it only occasionally to meet clients—not regularly.

Now, let's say that you're a typist employed by a large company to perform word processing. The company requires you to work at home full-time. You set up shop in what used to be your child's nursery.

You've already jumped one hurdle—the office is for the convenience of your employer. Now you have only one more hurdle to go over.

If you use your office exclusively as your principal place of business—that is, you don't use it as a den, say, during the evening—you're entitled to deduct the appropriate costs. (See Chapter 8 for more information on rules governing deductions for employee business expenses.)

Tip: If you're audited, the IRS may ask you to prove that you maintain your office for the convenience of your employer.

Protect yourself. Ask your employer to write you a letter specifying that your home office is maintained at his or her request.

In the past some taxpayers used another part of the tax law to bypass the requirement that a home office serve as their principal place of business.

They would lease a part of their home to their employer. Then they would deduct the costs associated with the leased space—but they wouldn't use the home office rules to justify their write-offs.

Rather, they used the section of the tax law that allowed them to deduct expenses for rented space. The 1986 tax law specifically forbids this practice.

Here's why. Congress worried that employees would get around the restrictions on home office deductions by arranging to have a portion of their salary paid in rent. And the legislators didn't like these sham transactions one bit.

Renting a portion of your home to your employer may still provide tax benefits, even though you may not deduct your expenses.

Say, for example, that you rack up passive losses from an investment in a limited partnership. The rules say that you may deduce passive losses only from your passive income. Rental activities are always considered passive, so you can generate passive income by renting your home office. (See Chapter 19 for more on passive losses.)

Just remember you must charge a fair and reasonable rent, you should have a written lease, and you should use the rented space exclusively for business.

FIGURING THE DEDUCTION   The reformed law also imposes a stricter limit on the total amount of home office expenses you may deduct. It says that you may not use the cost of maintaining a home office to create or increase a loss from your business and therefore reduce your other, unrelated income.

Specifically, the law says that you must first reduce your gross business income by the amount of your direct expenses—all expenses but the home office costs. Then, it says, your deduction for home office expenses may not exceed this amount.

Here's an example. As an accountant, just out of school, you decide to work out of a basement office in your St. Louis home. In your first year you earn $20,000 in client fees.

The expenses for your part-time secretary, phone answering service, stationery, and so on—eveyrthing but the home office expenses we noted at the beginning of this chapter—come to $12,000. So your net income, before deducting home office expenses, is $8,000 ($20,000 in income minus $12,000 in direct expenses).

From this amount you subtract your home office expenses in the following order: interest and taxes, operating expenses, and depreciation.

The interest and taxes on that part of your home you use for your office add up to $4,000. So you subtract $4,000 from your $8,000 of net income to get $4,000.

Operating expenses, such as utilities, come to $2,000. So you subtract $2,000 from the remaining $4,000 to get $2,000.

Your depreciation expense totals $3,000. Now, you subtract $3,000 from your remaining income of $2,000 to get a loss of $1,000.

But you may not use these expenses to reduce your taxable income below zero. So $1,000 of depreciation is disallowed for that year.

Here's a break, though. You may carry this unused office expense deduction forward to offset your business income in future years.

Assume that in the second year of your accounting practice you earn $30,000 in fees, rack up $10,000 in direct expenses for telephone, secretarial help, and so forth, and have home office expenses of $7,000.

First you calculate your net income by reducing your gross income by your direct expenses—$30,000 minus $10,000, or $20,000. From this $20,000 you may deduct your home office expenses of $8,000 ($7,000 in current expenses plus $1,000 in expenses you've carried forward from previous years)—again, as long as they do not lower your business income to less than zero.

In this case you may deduct the entire $8,000, giving you taxable income in your second year of only $12,000.

Tip: Don't worry about deducting the portion of your mortgage interest and property taxes attributable to your home office. If your home office deduction is limited, you may write off each year—as an itemized deduction—any excess mortgage interest and property taxes. (See Chapter 4 for more on mortgage interest.)

Say your net income before you deduct your home office expenses adds up to $8,000. Say, too, that interest and taxes attributable to your home office come to $10,000. Under the rules, you may not use home office expense deductions to reduce your net income below zero.

So you would write off $8,000 as home office expenses—that is, the amount of your expenses equal to your net income before you deduct your home office costs.

Then you would write off the remaining $2,000 of interest and taxes as itemized deductions. You may not write off any other home office costs—utilities, maintenance, and so on—since you may not reduce your net income to less than zero.

Caution: If you're audited, expect Uncle Sam to ask you to prove that you actually spent the amount you claimed for your home office. Maintain documentation of all your expenditures—utility bills, cancelled checks, and so on.

QUESTIONS AND ANSWERS

Question: I am a physician, and I maintain an office downtown. I don't use my home office to meet with patients. But I do telephone patients from my home office in the evening. And I do use the office exclusively for business. Am I entitled to a write-off?

Sorry. Uncle Sam won't allow you to take a deduction. The reason: Your home office isn't your principal place of business. Also, you don't meet there with patients face-to-face (phone calls don't count).

Q: I'm a musician, and I'm employed by an orchestra. I practice in our spare bedroom, because there's no place to practice at Symphony Hall. May I claim a deduction?

In most cases your employer's principal place of business is your principal place of business. But you're an exception to this rule.

Because your employer did not provide you with practice space, and practicing is essential to maintaining your skills, you're entitled to a write-off. The only catch: You must use your spare bedroom regularly and exclusively as a practice room.

Q: I maintain an office in my eight-room home. Do I write off one eighth of the expense of maintaining my home?

You may, if all eight rooms are approximately the same size. Otherwise, you must calculate the percentage of floor space your home office occupies.

Q: I operate a day-care center and use the basement of my home exclusively for this purpose. May I claim a home office deduction?

Yes. You're also entitled to a write-off if you use your home regularly to provide day care for children or people who are elderly or handicapped. But you must operate a licensed facility. And, when it comes time to calculate your deduction, you must take into account the amount of space your day-care operation occupies.

Say you use 30 percent of the floor space of your home for day care. You're entitled to write off 30 percent of the expense of operating your home. You may deduct 30 percent of your heating bills, 30 percent of your cooling bills, 30 percent of your home insurance bills, and so on.

Congress carved out an exception to the exclusively-for-business rules for day-care-center operators. If, for instance, you use your living room and kitchen as a day-care center only during the day, you may still claim a home office deduction.

You're subject to the same rules as the day-care center operator above—plus one other rule. You must take into account how much time you use your home for day care and how much as a residence. And you deduct only those costs attributable to the day care.

Here's how it works. Say that you use 30 percent of your floor space for day care. And your business uses this space 10 hours a day Monday through Friday and 6 hours on Saturday—for a total of 56 hours each week.

During the remaining 112 hours your family uses the space. Under the rules, you may write off 10 percent of the cost of operating and maintaining your home—that is, 30 percent of your floor space times the 33 percent of time you use the house for your day-care business.

Q: Where on my tax return do I claim a deduction for my home office?

If you're self-employed, write off your home office on Schedule C of your Form 1040. If you're employed by someone else, claim your home office on Schedule A, with Form 2106 attached, as a miscellaneous itemized deduction—subject to the 2 percent floor. That is, you write off only those expenses that, when added with other miscellaneous expenses, top 2 percent of your adjusted gross income. (See Chapter 8 for the details on how to write off miscellaneous deductions.)

Q: I claimed a home office deduction for the last ten years I'm planning on selling my house. Are there any tax implications?

If you claim a home office deduction and plan to sell your home, there may be tax implications at the time of the sale. It depends on whether you're entitled to claim a home office deduction in the year you sell your home. And the key word here is "entitled."

If you're not entitled to claim a write-off that year, you may roll over the entire gain from your house into another home and defer paying taxes on your profit.

But what happens if you satisfy all the rules and you're entitled to claim a home office deduction in the year you sell your house? You're taxed on that portion of your gain attributable to the part of your home you used as a home office.

Say, for example, that the cost of your house plus improvements is $125,000, and you sell it for $150,000. From the time you purchased your home until you sold it, you used 10 percent of the floor space in your house as a home office.

So you allocated $12,500 of the cost of your home to your home office. Over the years you claimed depreciation deductions of $5,000.

The net gain on the sale of your house is $30,000 ($150,000 less your cost of $125,000 reduced by depreciation of $5,000).

Uncle Sam says you may roll over a portion of this gain, tax free, into a new house. But, since you were entitled to a home office deduction in the year you sold your house, the portion of your gain allocable to your home office is taxable.

Here's how to calculate this taxable gain.

You allocate the sales proceeds between the office and nonoffice portions of your home. Remember, you allocated 10 percent of the cost of your house to your home office. So you use this same 10 percent to allocate the proceeds from the sale of your home. That is, you allocate $15,000 of your sales price to your home office (10 percent times $150,000).

Your taxable gain on the sale comes to $7,500 ($15,000 less $12,500 cost reduced by $5,000 depreciation). And you may roll over the remaining $22,500 of your gain into a new house. (See Chapter 14 for more information on the tax implications of home ownership.)

Tip: If you're planning to sell your home, put pencil to paper to decide what's worth more to you in the tax department:

  • Claiming a home office deduction in the year you sell your house, or
  • Rolling over that portion of your gain on the sale attributable to your home office

If postponing the gain gets you more, violate the home office rules. For example, don't use your home office exclusively for business.

That way, you're not entitled to claim a home office deduction in the year of the sale. You lose the write-off, but you get to postpone the gain on that portion of your house.

Another important rule: If you claim a depreciation deduction for a home office, you must adjust your basis—that is, the cost of your home plus improvements. When you sell your house, you calculate your gain by subtracting your basis, reduced by the amount of depreciation you claimed, from the amount you receive.

CHAPTER 16

It Still Pays to Invest in Real Estate

In days gone by, an investment in real estate could produce significant benefits. First, your property might appreciate in value. And second, it might put some extra cash in your pocket. But even if you reaped neither of these benefits, you were bound to collect generous tax breaks.

Today these tax benefits are not quite as lavish. But in 1988 and beyond, the law still allows you to write off many of the costs of owning real estate. Here's the lowdown.

TIMING IS EVERYTHING The biggest break you get from rental property: Uncle Sam helps you recoup the cost of your investment by letting you deduct a portion of your purchase price each year. This gradual write-off—known as depreciation—compensates you for the effects on your property of corrosion, wear and tear, and decay.

But there's one restriction. Since, as far as the law is concerned, land does not decay, you may write off only the cost of buildings.

Before the 1986 Tax Reform Act, you could deduct the cost of your rental property—whether residential or commercial—over 19 years. Now, however, you must write off the cost of residential rental property over 27½ years and commercial property over 31½ years.

The result: A less generous write-off each year.

Also, you now must use the straight-line method of depreciation—that is, you must write off the same amount each year. Under the old rules, you could opt for accelerated depreciation and collect greater benefits in the earlier years you owned the property.

AT YOUR SERVICE The law says you may begin taking depreciation deductions once your property is "placed in service," but not before. This bit of IRS jargon simply means that your building is on the rental market or ready for its intended use.

And the law says you must abide by its so-called mid-month convention. This rule, which goes for both residential and commercial investments, means that you figure your first year's depreciation deduction from the middle of the month in which you place your property in service. The mid-month convention applies even if you place your property in service on the first day of the month.

Here's an example of how you'd figure your depreciation deductions. Say you and a colleague buy a small office complex on August 1, 1988, in a nearby suburban development. The property costs you $500,000—$400,000 for the building and $100,000 for the land.

You spruce up your property and put it on the rental market on September 1, 1988. How much may you now write off on your 1988 tax return?

Even though the complex was placed in service on September 1, the mid-month convention says the property is placed in service on September 15. So in 1988 you may deduct 3½ months in depreciation write-offs, or $3,704. Here's how it adds up.

You take the cost of your building, $400,000, and divide it by 31½ years, the number of years over which you must depreciate commercial property. Then you divide the result—$12,698—by 12 months and multiply by 3½ months.

While the mid-month convention may seem unfair, it can actually work to your advantage. The reason: You're entitled to a half month's depreciation no matter when during the month you place your property in service—even if, in the above example, it's September 30.

And you have another option. You may depreciate your property over 40 years, rather than the usual 27½ for residential property or 31½ years for commercial property.

Why would you want to? It's true, you get to write off less each year when you use the 40-year method. But here's the advantage.

If you are subject to the alternative minimum tax (AMT) you may end up saving money. The AMT is a tax paid by those who, by taking advantage of the tax code, would end up paying little or no regular tax despite their high incomes.

Usually, the more deductions—and that includes depreciation write-offs—you take, the more likely you are to face the AMT, which is a flat tax of 21 percent.

When you use the 40-year method, you don't have to add back to your income the difference between the depreciation write-offs you took over 27½ or 31½ years and those you took over 40 years when it comes time to figure your AMT liability. (For more on the AMT, see Chapter 20.)

PASSIVE AGGRESSIVE   Homeowners may deduct only the interest on their principal residence and the one other house, a vacation cottage, for example. But people who invest in rental real estate may write off mortgage interest—as well as their other rental expenses—on all their investment properties, theoretically at least. In reality, the law imposes a number of restrictions.

The first important rule: You may deduct so-called passive losses only from passive income. And, alas, income from rental property qualifies as passive income. (Income from limited partnerships also counts as passive income—though income from dividends and interest does not.)

This rule means that expenses you pile up when you rent property—mortgage interest, depreciation, utility bills, insurance, repair costs, and so on—are deductible only against your income from passive investments.

The law, however, does allow a phase-in period for this new rule limiting passive loss deductions. If you made your rental investment before October 23, 1986, and you placed the building in service by December 31, 1986, you still may deduct a portion of your losses from your regular income until 1990.

Under the 1986 Tax Reform Act's phase-in rules, you may write off from your regular income:

- 40 percent of net passive rental losses in 1988
- 20 percent in 1989
- 10 percent in 1990

But if you bought your rental property after October 22, 1986, you may deduct your losses only from your passive income. If you report no passive income, you may not write off your rental losses at all.

You may, however, carry forward any passive losses you can't use currently, and deduct them in future years—as long as you have enough passive income in those years. When you sell your property, you get to deduct any remaining losses from your gain.

These rules are strict, but don't despair.

Fortunately there are several exceptions—designed to help the "moderate-income" taxpayer get around the passive loss rules.

The exceptions: You may deduct rental losses of up to $25,000 from your regular income under two conditions:

- You meet certain income guidelines
- You actively participate in the operation of your rental property

Let's look at the income guidelines first.

NOT-SO-RICH MAY BE BETTER   As long as your adjusted gross income (AGI) is $100,000 or less—figured before you subtract any rental or passive losses—you may deduct from your ordinary income up to $25,000 in rental losses from residential or commercial property.

But you lose the deduction for part of the loss if your income falls between $100,000 and $150,000. In this case, you must reduce the $25,000 limit by 50 percent of the amount by which your AGI exceeds $100,000.

Let's say your AGI comes to $140,000—that is, it tops $100,000 by $40,000. So you multiply 50 percent times $40,000 and subtract the result—$20,000—from $25,000.

You may deduct $5,000 in rental losses from your regular income—as long as you meet the second major condition, the active participation rule.

How do you combine the AGI limits with the phase-in period? Here's an example to illustrate.

Say you acquired an apartment building in 1985, and you manage the property yourself. It's time to file your 1988 return. Your AGI adds up to less than $100,000 in 1988. You record a loss of $30,000 from the building. You report no other passive income or losses.

You may write off the first $25,000 in rental losses from your ordinary income. And you may deduct 65 percent of your remaining loss—$5,000 times 65 percent, or $3,250. Your total write-off: $28,250. The remaining loss of $1,750 is carried forward and can be used to offset passive income in future years.

GET ACTIVE   How does the IRS define active participation? As long as you make significant and bona fide management decisions—and own at least a 10 percent stake in the property—you are an active participant.

The management decisions that count: deciding on rental terms, approving tenants, and approving major expenditures. And, the IRS says, as long as you make these decisions, it's fine to use a rental agent to execute them for you.

If you don't meet the active participation test, though, you may deduct your rental losses only from income from your other passive investments.

EXCEPTIONS TO THE RULE   As we've seen, rental property is a passive investment, although Uncle Sam gives you a break if you actively participate in the management of the property.

But, as always, there are exceptions to this rule.

Here are three tests you need to know about. (If you're renting property in connection with another business, see your tax adviser for the other exceptions that may apply to you.)

If you meet one of these three narrow tests, your rental property isn't automatically deemed passive by Uncle Sam. Instead, you must determine if your investment is passive by running through the rules outlined in Chapter 19.

Exception 1—The average rental period of your property is seven days or less

You determine the average rental period by dividing the total number of days you've rented the property by the number of rental periods. Uncle Sam defines a rental period as a period during which a customer has a continuous or recurring right to use the property.

This exception exempts most hotels and motels from the rental property rules, but it also traps owners of vacation homes. Here's an example.

Say you own an interest in a beach house that's not considered a residence. The average rental period of the house is less than seven days, and you actively participate in the management of the property.

Under the exception we just outlined, your beach house isn't rental property. That means you may not take advantage of the $25,000 rental-loss provision.

But you still may be able to write off your losses if you materially participate in the management of the property. (For more on deducting these amounts, see Chapter 19. For the rules on vacation homes, see Chapter 17.)

Exception 2—The property isn't rental property if the average rental period is 30 days or less and if you or someone you hire provides "significant personal services" to your rental customers

Say you operate a bed-and-breakfast and the average rental period is 15 days. You hire someone to manage the inn on a day-to-day basis. This person prepares meals, cleans the rooms, and so on. Under this exception, the property isn't rental property.

Caution: In the eyes of the IRS, "significant personal service" doesn't include routine repair, maintenance, security, and trash collection.

Exception 3—Property you provide free of charge to a partnership or S corporation isn't rental property if you own an interest in that partnership or S corporation

Say, for example, that you own a building and you make it available for use—without charge—to an S corporation that you own and run.

The rules won't allow you to treat the building as rental property in order to take advantage of the $25,000 rental-loss provision. Instead, you follow the material participation test under the passive loss rules to determine how much, if any, of your loss is deductible.

What if you charge the S corporation, in which you materially participate, rent on the building? The IRS says that income from this rental is treated as nonpassive income, while losses from this property are treated as passive.

What's the bottom line?

You must look closely at the way you rent your real estate. And if you have any questions about which rules apply to you, seek help from your tax adviser.

TO YOUR CREDIT   If you're looking for tax benefits, consider these two classes of property—older buildings and low-income housing projects. Both provide tax credits to investors.

There are some restrictions, which we get to in a minute, on how you may use these credits. First, though, let's look at how these credits work, starting with the rehabilitation credit.

THE LURE OF THE OLD   The rehabilitation tax credit dates back to 1976 and is intended to encourage the preservation of historic buildings and other older structures.

The credit totals: 10 percent of the amount you spend to fix up a building built before 1936, or 20 percent of the amount you spend rehabilitating a designated certified historic structure (CHS). (Your local historical society or an office of the U.S. Department of the Interior can provide you with the guidelines on certified historic structures.)

Let's say you buy a hundred-year-old cookie manufacturing plant. And the building is a CHS. You spend $50,000 converting it into offices to house your law firm. You may collect a 20 percent credit, or $10,000.

But note: Congress granted the credit to encourage people to preserve older buildings, not to demolish them. So to collect it, you must follow certain rules. You must keep at least 50 percent of the building's external walls as external walls: That is, you can't place new walls around more than half the old external walls.

Two more rules you must follow:

• You must preserve at least 75 percent of the existing external walls either as internal or external walls.

• You must keep at least 75 percent of the existing internal structural framework. So if you gut the inside of your building, you're out of luck.

The tax law specifically exempts certified historic structures from the external and internal wall retention requirements. As a practical matter, however, the Secretary of the Interior usually won't certify a structure as a CHS unless you keep at least 75 percent of the existing external walls as external walls.

And the legislators imposed one more regulation. You may pocket your credit only if the amount you spend rehabilitating the building tops $5,000 or the "adjusted basis" of the building, whichever is greater.

The adjusted basis is usually the amount you pay for the structure less the deductions you take for depreciation. So if you buy a building for $100,000 and write off $20,000 in depreciation, your adjusted basis comes to $80,000. And you must spend at least this amount to renovate the structure.

One final wrinkle: When it comes time to figure your future depreciation write-offs, you must subtract the amount of the credit you take from the amount you're depreciating.

Let's say you own a non-CHS building built before 1936 with an adjusted basis (not including the cost of the land) of $80,000. And you spend $180,000 fixing it up.

Since the building is not a CHS, you may take a credit of

$18,000 (10 percent of $180,000). But you have to figure your future depreciation deductions on an adjusted basis of $242,000— that is, $80,000 plus $180,000 minus your credit of $18,000.

LOW-INCOME HOUSING CREDIT Enacted in 1986, the low-income housing credit constitutes one of the few tax breaks left after tax reform. The amount of the credit depends on the type of housing involved in the project and when you place the building or buildings in service.

You get a higher credit if you construct new housing or rehabilitate existing structures. You get a lower credit for existing housing that you don't rehabilitate and for new housing that you construct with the help of federal subsidies.

The amount of the credit for both categories of property is computed by the Treasury Department each month and published in the Internal Revenue Bulletin. Your tax adviser or local IRS office will help you determine which credit applies in your situation.

The table below summarizes the credit percentages announced prior to publication for 1988.

1988 LOW-INCOME HOUSING CREDITS

Month	New or Rehabilitated Property	Existing or Subsidized Property
January	9.15%	3.92%
February	9.12%	3.91%
March	8.99%	3.85%
April	8.96%	3.84%
May	9.04%	3.87%
June	9.13%	3.91%
July	9.17%	3.93%
August	9.14%	3.92%
September	9.19%	3.94%

To compute the credit, multiply the percentage in effect for the month in which you place the property in service by the "qualified basis" of the property. In most cases the qualified basis is the cost of the building plus any improvements or additions you make prior to the end of the year in which you place the structure in service.

The qualified basis is reduced if the entire building isn't used as low-income housing. How do you calculate the reduced basis?

Multiply the total basis by the smaller of these two fractions: One is the percentage of low-income units in the building to total residential rental units (whether occupied or not). The other is the percentage of floor space of low-income units to total available rental floor space.

Once computed, you subtract the amount of the credit from your tax bill each year for 10 years.

To qualify for the credit, Uncle Sam requires that you spend more than $2,000 per housing unit. And the housing must remain as low-income rental property for 15 years. If it doesn't, the government takes back some of the tax benefits you pocketed.

In addition, the housing must be open to tenants after December 31, 1986, and before January 1, 1990. The tenants must meet stringent income requirements.

And the occupants must not be transients—that is, you don't get the credit for dormitories, nursing homes, hospitals, and similar facilities.

MORE RULES   In the old days Uncle Sam set very few limits on the amount of rehabilitation credits you could claim. But the 1986 Tax Reform Act imposed ceilings.

Each year you may offset the tax on your passive income and no more than $25,000 of your ordinary income—wages or interest, for example—with the rehabilitation or low-income housing credits. You don't even have to actively participate in managing the property. You could, for instance, be a limited partner.

Before we see how this $25,000 limit works, a critical reminder. As we saw in Chapter 1, a deduction reduces your taxes by the amount of your marginal tax rate. If you're in the 28 percent bracket, for example, a deduction of $100 cuts your taxes by $28. But a credit slashes the taxes you pay dollar for dollar—that is, a tax credit of $100 reduces your tax bill by $100.

Now, let's return to the $25,000 ceiling.

The law says you may claim up to the rehabilitation or low-income housing "tax credit equivalent" of a $25,000 deduction without being an active participant in the venture. So you may not, alas, take up to $25,000 off your tax bill.

What you may do is take a credit that reduces the taxes you owe by the same amount as a $25,000 tax deduction would. So if your marginal rate is 28 percent, the credit equivalent of a $25,000 deduction comes to $7,000 ($25,000 times 28 percent). There's one other important rule if you invest in older structures or low-income housing. The $25,000 credit equivalent phases out as your income rises.

But—and here's the good news—it does not phase out until your AGI tops $200,000. After that point you must reduce the $25,000 by 50 percent of the amount by which your AGI exceeds $200,000. And then you must convert this amount to a credit equivalent. So you get no benefit from the $25,000 credit equivalent once your AGI reaches $250,000.

What if you claim *both* the rehabilitation and low-income housing credits? You still may offset taxes on only up to $25,000 of your ordinary income—not $50,000.

And here's one more limit you should know. Both the rehabilitation and low-income housing credits are classified as general business credits. And you may claim, in general, business credits no more than $25,000 plus 75 percent of any tax you owe over $25,000.

The ceilings imposed on the amount of rehabilitation and low-income housing credits you may claim make these credits much less attractive as tax-saving devices. That's one reason the National Trust for Historic Preservation, a federal agency, reports that applications to qualify for the rehabilitation credit have plummeted to about 150 a month—from an earlier rate of 270 a month—since the Tax Reform Act took effect.

But note: Investing in older buildings and low-income housing is the only real estate rental activity left for which you may collect at least some tax breaks without actively participating.

QUESTIONS AND ANSWERS

QUESTION: I own some rental property that I actively participate in managing. Now I'm thinking about investing as a limited partner in a rehabilitation deal. May I claim both losses up to $25,000 from my rental property and the credit equivalent of $25,000 from the rehabilitation partnership?

Unfortunately, the answer is no. You may deduct from your ordinary income no more than $25,000 a year in *combined* losses from rental real estate and credit equivalents.

How do you calculate how much you may write off?

Here's an example. Say you report a $25,000 loss from an apartment building you manage yourself. You post a loss of $5,000 from an oil and gas limited partnership. But you record a $15,000 gain from a research and development limited partnership.

The rules require you to first count up all your losses from rental properties in which you actively participate—in your case the total comes to $25,000. Then you add up any profits, and subtract your losses from your profits. You post no profits. So you're left with a $25,000 loss.

Next you add up your gains from passive investments—$15,000 in your case. Then you subtract your losses from passive activities—$5,000. The result, $10,000, is your net passive income.

Now subtract your $25,000 of rental losses from your $10,000 of passive income. The result, $15,000, is the amount you may write off on your return as a rental loss.

But remember: You may deduct rental losses up to $25,000. So if you also invest in a rehabilitation partnership, for instance, you may write off as much as $10,000 in credit equivalents.

Q: I'm in the situation you describe above. But I've exhausted the $25,000 limit and still have losses and credit equivalents left. What do I do?

You may carry these losses and credit equivalents forward for use in future years. But, even then, you're subject to all the limits we described earlier, including the $25,000 ceiling on rental losses.

Q: I subtracted my passive losses from my passive income and I came out $23,000 in the red. I also have a loss of $2,000 from my rental property in which I actively participate. May I deduct this entire $25,000 loss from my regular income?

Alas, no. The rules say you may deduct passive losses only from passive income. You subtracted your passive losses from your passive income and you're still $23,000 in the red.

But the news is not all bad. You may carry forward this loss to future years. And you may deduct your $2,000 rental loss—as long as your AGI falls within the limits we've described.

CHAPTER 17

Getting the Most
from Your Vacation Home

So what do you want from your vacation home?

A place you and the family can use whenever you like? A place that you know you can always escape to? Or is your primary consideration keeping the costs down?

If getting away from the madding crowd is uppermost on your mind, then tax expense is a secondary consideration and shouldn't interfere with your choice.

But in either case you ought to know the rules so that when you make the choice, it's an informed one. An unexpected tax bill can make an ugly end to a vacation.

The tax treatment of a second home varies, depending on how you use your retreat. Is it strictly for personal use? Do you rent it? To whom? And for how long?

The information you'll find in this chapter will help you decide—at least from a tax perspective—how best to use your vacation home.

WHAT IS A VACATION HOME? As far as the IRS is concerned, your second home is either a vacation home that you and your family use personally, rental property, or some combination of the two. How Uncle Sam treats the house depends on which of these classifications it falls into.

We cover the details in the sections just ahead, but here is an overview of the tax differences among these three categories.

A *vacation home* that you use personally gets the same tax treatment as your first home—even if you rent the property to others for as much as 14 days a year.

You may write off your mortgage interest and property taxes, but you may not deduct other expenses, such as repairs and utilities. And the same restrictions that apply to the deductibility of mortgage interest on your first home apply to the second. (Chapter 4 explains these rules.)

The other good news about a vacation home is this: If you rent out your home for less than 15 days, the rental income you collect is tax free.

Rental property is very different. You get income from renting the property, and you may deduct most of the expenses that you run up—utilities and repairs, for instance—from that income. You may also depreciate the property—write off a portion of its cost each year.

Moreover, you may deduct property taxes and mortgage interest expenses. A good deal, you say. And you're right—up to a point.

The total amount of the loss you take on rental property may be limited. How limited depends on your total income and on whether you are an "active" or "passive" investor in the property, as defined by the tax code. (We explain these rules later in this chapter.)

Combination property gets different treatment, depending on how much rental use and how much personal use your vacation hideaway gets. Just one day one way or the other, as you will see when we get to the details, can make a big difference in your tax bill.

DEFINING THE DIFFERENCE   Since, for tax purposes, the differences between a personal vacation home and rental property are so great, the tax code is very precise about which is which. If you intend to rent your second home and take advantage of the tax deductions that renting brings you, these distinctions are important to you.

The tax law says that you may classify your second home as rental property as long as you do not occupy it yourself for more than 14 days in the year or for more than 10 percent of the total number of days that it is rented at fair market value, whichever is greater.

If, in other words, you rent your second home at the going rate for 300 days, you could use it yourself for as many as 30 days and it would still qualify as rental property.

What happens if you occupy it for 31 days? You may still

claim a write-off for mortgage interest and taxes, but you are limited on the deductions you may take for operating expenses and depreciation.

Uncle Sam is quite strict about what he considers personal use. You've used your home for personal purposes—in his view—if on any part of any day your vacation home is occupied by you or any of the following people:

• A person who has an equity stake in the property
• A spouse or blood relative (meaning your parents, children, siblings, and grandparents)
• A person with whom you have a barter arrangement that allows you to use another dwelling
• A person to whom the vacation home is not rented at "fair market value"—which, according to the law, is the going rate for other, similar homes in the area

And take care: Even if you charge a relative—or someone with an equity interest in the property—a fair rent, the IRS still considers this personal use.

Say, for instance, you own a vacation home in upstate New York. You rent it to your sister—a relative—for the going rate, $1,500 for 10 days.

Next, as part of a barter agreement, you allow your friend Bob to occupy your vacation home for 11 days. In exchange, you use his home in California for 8 days.

Finally, you rent your vacation home to your father's boss for 10 days and charge the man only half the fair market rental.

How many of these days are personal days? By the IRS rules, all 31 count as personal use. What, by the way, constitutes a day? When you're counting, do it the way hotels do—by the 24-hour period.

Say you occupy your vacation home from Saturday afternoon through the following Saturday morning. For IRS purposes you've used your house for 7 days—even though you were on the premises for part of 8 calendar days.

The law does contain one exception to the general rule on renting to relatives. Let's say you rent your property at fair market value to a relative who uses the house as a principal residence—a condo for your parents, for instance. The IRS does not consider this use personal use.

MAINTENANCE AND REPAIR VISITS   Anyone who owns vacation homes knows that they require repairs and maintenance.

If you stay at the house while doing the repairs, does the IRS count these as personal use days? Not if your "principal purpose" in staying there is to make repairs or perform maintenance chores.

Say, for example, that you own a mountain cabin that you rent during the winter. You and your spouse arrive at the cabin late Thursday evening. The point of the trip: to prepare the cabin for the rental season. But the two of you are tired.

So you enjoy dinner by the fire, then turn in early to get plenty of rest for the days ahead. You work on the cabin all day Friday and Saturday. Your spouse helps for a few hours each day, but spends most of the time catching up on paperwork.

By Saturday evening the work is done. You spend the rest of the evening relaxing, then head home shortly before noon on Sunday.

Since the principal purpose of your trip was for maintenance, none of these days are counted as personal days. They're all maintenance days.

But take care: In an audit, the IRS will probe to make sure your "principal purpose" was indeed repair and maintenance.

An auditor will look at the frequency with which you did your chores, the amount of time you spent on these activities, and the presence and activities of friends. If the auditor sees that you claim to spend most of your time at your home doing maintenance— but you always bring along companions—he or she may argue that your activities are not on the up and up. And the IRS might count those days as personal use, which may result in a loss of deductions.

Tip: Keep a log of your repair and maintenance days. Write down when you arrive, how much time you spend on various tasks, and what kind of work you perform. That way you can prove how you spent your time should Uncle Sam ever question you.

RENTAL PROPERTY   What's rental property worth to you in the tax department? Probably a lot of deductions. Let's take a look.

Advertising and Commissions

Say you own a mountain cabin in West Virginia. And you enlist the help of a local real estate agent to keep the property occupied. Each time he signs someone up to rent your cabin, you pay him a commission.

Under the rules, you may deduct these commissions directly from your rental income. You may also write off advertising expenses.

Mortgage Interest and Property Taxes

You may deduct state and local property taxes that are assessed on your rental property. And you may write off mortgage interest. (Of course, these same costs are deductible even if your vacation home doesn't qualify as rental property—that is, you use it as a personal residence.)

See Chapter 4 for more on writing off interest expenses. See Chapter 7 for more on deducting state and local taxes.

Operating Expenses

Deductible operating costs include utilities, maintenance, insurance, and any other expenses, such as professional fees and repairs. You may also write off any supplies—a receipt book, for example—that are normally deductible for profit-oriented activities.

Depreciation

You probably can reduce your taxes by depreciating your vacation home. If you started renting your house before 1987, you may write it off using the depreciation rules that were in effect before the 1986 tax reform bill took effect.

If you began renting it after 1986, however, you must abide by the new, less generous rules. These rules require you to depreciate your house over a 27½-year period.

See Chapter 18 for the details on depreciation.

Of course, you don't get a deduction without incurring an expense, and as people who own them know, maintaining property that you rent out *is* expensive.

So don't be surprised if at the end of the year you show a loss. Uncle Sam will share this loss with you. But how much he'll share depends, in part, on your income. As it goes up, the amount of loss you claim on rental property may go down.

If your adjusted gross income (AGI) is less than $100,000, you may deduct as much as $25,000 in rental losses from your vacation home—unless your vacation home is a houseboat or trailer. In these cases the passive loss rules apply—that is, you may deduct your losses only from your passive income. (See Chapter 19 for more on the passive loss rules.) The same limit applies to single taxpayers and married couples filing jointly. Married couples filing separately must cut these levels in half.

If your AGI tops $100,000, however, you must reduce the $25,000 cap by 50 percent of the amount that your AGI exceeds $100,000.

Say that your adjusted gross income in 1988 was $110,000. You took in $20,000 in rent from your cottage on the beach, but taxes, interest, operating expenses, and depreciation came to $50,000. In other words, you lost $30,000 on your cottage. You can't claim it all.

The maximum loss anyone may claim is $25,000. You, however, may not even claim that much because your AGI exceeds $100,000. The most you may take off your taxable income is $20,000 ($25,000 minus 50 percent of the $10,000 by which your AGI exceeds $100,000).

What happens to the remaining $10,000 loss? Uncle Sam considers it a passive loss subject to the passive loss rules.

Caution: The $25,000 limit on losses applies cumulatively to all your rental property—not just your vacation home. No matter how much rental buildings you own, the loss you claim may not exceed $25,000—total. (See Chapter 16 for more on rental real estate.)

ACTIVE AND PASSIVE LOSSES   There's another condition you have to meet before you may claim rental losses against your taxable income. You and/or your spouse must be what the tax law calls an "active participant" in the rental operations. Otherwise, you're subject to the passive loss rules.

You actively participate if you and/or your spouse:

• Have at least a 10 percent ownership stake in the vacation home

• And are involved in management decisions in a significant and bona fide way

The management decisions that count, as far as the IRS is concerned, include approving tenants, establishing rental terms, and approving expenditures. If you make these major decisions, the IRS doesn't care if you use a rental agent to implement them for you.

If you don't "actively participate" in the management, however, you don't get the $25,000 loss allowance.

Passive investors in rental property may deduct rental losses, but only against income generated by other passive investments—limited partnerships, for instance. If you have no income from other passive investments, you have to postpone claiming your deductions from the vacation home that you operate as rental property until you do have passive income or dispose of the property. (For more information on this rule, see Chapter 19.)

MIXED USE—ALLOCATING EXPENSES   Remember, there are two categories of mixed use. In the first you may make personal use of your vacation home within the 14-day or 10 percent limits and still claim most of the deductions you would get for rental property.

If your use falls into this category, your property—in the eyes of the IRS—is not a personal residence. Therefore, you may not write off the mortgage interest allocated to your personal use. The IRS treats the interest as personal interest expense—the same as credit card interest, for instance. (Personal interest expense is partially deductible through 1990. See Chapter 4 for more information on interest deductions.)

Also, if you use your home primarily as rental property, you're subject to the passive loss rules. And you may deduct passive losses only from passive income. Though, as we've seen, you may deduct up to $25,000 in rental losses as long as your AGI is within the limits.

Property taxes, of course, are fully deductible.

In the second mixed-use category, your personal use of the house exceeds 14 days or the 10 percent limit, and the tax treatment your house receives is substantially different.

The portion of your interest, taxes, and expenses allocated to rental use are only deductible against rental income. In other words, if your second home falls into this category and you post a loss from renting the house, too bad. You may not write off that loss currently against your other taxable income. But you may write off any excess mortgage interest and taxes as itemized deductions. And, of course, you may deduct the personal portion of interest and taxes.

One other wrinkle: You must deduct your expenses in a certain order. First, you may write off advertising and commission charges; then property taxes and mortgage interest; next, your operating expenses; and finally, depreciation.

Why is the order important? Uncle Sam is forcing you to write off first against rental income the expenses that you are allowed to deduct in any case (with the exception of advertising and commissions). And only if you still have rental income left over after these deductions are made may you write off your other expenses.

Tip: You may carry forward to future tax years any expenses you may not deduct currently—subject to all the limits we've described, of course.

Caution: If you own a third home and use it as both a residence and rental property, different rules apply. The portion of your mortgage interest allocated to personal use isn't deductible as mortgage interest, because the IRS only lets you treat two homes as personal residences. Rather, the interest allocated to personal use is treated as personal interest and is only partially deductible through 1990 (see Chapter 4 for the details). Interest allocated to the rental use is deductible to the extent of rental income—less advertising, commission charges, and taxes, as discussed above.

No matter which mixed-use category your second home falls into, you must allocate expenses. Be careful. This rule holds true even if you use your home yourself just one day of the year—New Year's Day, say, or the Fourth of July. You now must allocate one day's worth of your vacation home's total expenses to personal use.

The allocation formula, however, is simple. Here's how it works. Calculate the number of days you actually rented your property at a fair market value. Call this number X.

Then figure the number of days you used the property for any other purpose. Don't count days it was standing vacant, and don't count any repair or maintenance days. Call the resulting number Y.

You allocate expenses by multiplying your total expenses (including property taxes and mortgage interest) for the year by the fraction X divided by the sum of X plus Y. The product of that multiplication is the amount that you may allocate to rental use.

WHAT A DIFFERENCE A DAY MAKES   Now let's use a couple of examples to see how to figure the allocation of expenses. The examples also show the big difference just one additional day of personal use can make in the tax cost of owning your second home.

Assume the following facts: Your principal residence is in Connecticut, and you also own a vacation home in New Mexico, which you actively participate in renting.

You take out a mortgage to buy the home in New Mexico, and the interest expense totals $4,000, taxes are $2,000, operating expenses (utilities and maintenance) equal $2,000, and depreciation comes to $5,000. You realize rental income in 1988 of $7,500—after you subtract commissions—for the year, and your adjusted gross income is $80,000.

Example A

You rent the house at a fair rental value for 126 days. You use it for family vacations for 14 days, and you spend 4 days there to take care of repairs and maintenance.

The IRS figures you used the house for 140 days (126 rental and 14 personal). The 4 days you spent on repair and maintenance are not included in your total use days.

You may allocate 90 percent—that is, 126 divided by 140—of the costs associated with the house to its rental use.

Since you used the house yourself for only 14 days, and since your AGI is $80,000, the rules allow you to claim a loss up to $25,000. (Any remaining loss is subject to the general passive loss rules.) You compute rental income and expenses as follows:

- Total rental income: $7,500
- 90 percent of taxes: $1,800
- 90 percent of mortgage interest: $3,600
- 90 percent of operating expenses: $1,800
- 90 percent of depreciation: $4,500
- The result: A rental loss of $4,200

You may also write off the other 10 percent of your property taxes, or $200. The remaining interest, however—the part allocated to personal use—is classified as personal interest. And in 1988 only 40 percent is deductible, or $160. So, in total, you have deductions against your normal taxable income of $4,560— $4,200 plus $200 plus $160.

Example B

Let's say, though, that you increase your use of the house by just one day, bringing your personal use to 15 days for the year.

Since 15 days exceeds the maximum 14-day limit and is more than 10 percent of the total rental days (126 days), your vacation home is now classified as a residence.

So your deductions for costs allocated to rental use—that is, 126 divided by 141, or 89 percent—may not exceed the rental income you received. And you must write off expenses allocated to rental use in the following order:

- Commissions and advertising
- Property taxes and mortgage interest
- Operating expenses
- Depreciation

On the plus side, the IRS counts the portion of mortgage interest you allocate to your personal use of your home as deductible—just like the interest expense on your principal residence. You may write this amount off on your personal return.

So, in this instance, rental income and expenses are as follows:

- Total rental income: $7,500
- 89 percent of taxes and interest: $5,340
- 89 percent of operating expenses: $1,780 (not limited since the $7,500 rental income exceeds the interest and taxes by $2,160)
- 89 percent of depreciation: $4,450 in reality, but limited to just $380, since that is the amount by which rental income ($7,500) tops interest, taxes, and operating expenses ($7,120)

The result: You had a loss of $4,070, but you aren't able to claim it currently. The reason: Your expenses cannot exceed your rental income. You may, however, still deduct the remaining 11 percent of property taxes and interest—or $660.

As you can see, using your house more than the maximum days allowed can cause your taxes to rise sharply. That extra day's use in our example cost you $3,900 in deductions (the difference between the $4,560 in deductions you got in Example A and the $660 in Example B). But remember, you may carry forward the excess not currently deductible—in this case, $4,070—to future tax years.

There's an alternative method for allocating taxes and mortgage interest—approved by the courts, but not the IRS—that you may use. Sometimes it works to your benefit.

How? It reduces the amount of interest and taxes allocated to the rental portion, giving you room to use more of your other expenses as deductions against rental income.

Under the alternative method, you divide the number of rental days by the total number of days in the year. You use the resulting percentage to determine the portion of mortgage interest and property taxes that you write off against rental income.

The percentage you calculate under the alternative method is usually smaller than the percentage you figured earlier. That's because the earlier method required you to divide the number of rental days by the number of days the property was actually in use.

So the alternative method usually results in greater savings. But to be sure, you have to perform both calculations with your own numbers and compare the results.

Remember, though, this alternative method applies only to the allocation of interest and taxes, not to any other expenses.

Here's an example. We assume the same facts as in Example B, but we allocate interest and taxes using this alternative method.

• Gross rental income: $7,500
• Taxes and interest: $2,071 (allocated based on the ratio of rental days to total days in the year—that is, 126 divided by 365, times $6,000)
• Limit on other deductions: $5,429 ($7,500 minus $2,071)
• Operating expenses: $1,780 (89 percent times $2,000)
• Depreciation: limited to the lesser of $4,450 (89 percent times $5,000) or $3,649 ($5,429 minus $1,780)
• Rental income or loss: zero
• Remaining taxes and interest deductible as an itemized deduction: 239/365 times $6,000, or $3,929

In this situation the alternative method works out much better for you. It gives you $3,929 in tax and interest deductions—compared to $660 using the other method.

QUESTIONS AND ANSWERS

QUESTION: In addition to my principal residence, I own a small houseboat. Does my boat count as a vacation home?

Uncle Sam is quite liberal when it comes to defining a vacation home. It doesn't much matter if you have an A-frame in the woods or a town house in the city.

Any dwelling unit, even a boat or house trailer, that contains basic living accommodations—kitchen, bathroom, and sleeping space—qualifies as a vacation home. So if your boat is equipped with a bunk, a head, and a galley, you're all set.

Caution: The $25,000 rental exception only applies to real estate—a boat is not real estate, even if you do use it as a vacation home.

Q: I own three homes. May I deduct mortgage interest on all of them?

Sorry, you're out of luck as far as the tax laws are concerned. If you have three or more homes, you may claim the mortgage interest deduction on only two of them—your principal residence and one other. You decide which one—and you may change your mind from year to year.

The mortgage interest on other homes gets the same tax treatment as interest on personal loans, provided you use the mortgage money to buy or improve the house.

Otherwise, the interest is classified by how you use the money. For example, if your mortgage proceeds go to purchase common stock, the interest is investment interest. (See Chapter 4 for more information on how to write off interest.)

Tip: You'll want to put pencil to paper to figure out which house—in addition to your principal residence—you should designate as your second home in order to collect the maximum interest deductions.

Q: I rent my second home only 10 days each year. The rest of the time my family and I use it personally. What rules apply to my situation?

There's good news and bad news. On the plus side, if you rent your second home for 14 days or less during the year, the rental income is yours tax free.

The tradeoff is that the only deductions you get to take are for mortgage interest and property taxes—no maintenance or repair costs and no depreciation.

But this could be a really good deal if your second home is in a location that commands sky-high rents for a very short period of time—the host city for a national political convention, for example. Rent it out for less than 15 days and enjoy the income—tax free.

Q: I own a condo—part of a 200-unit complex—in Denver. It's a full-service building, with a housekeeping staff and a switchboard. Each year I put my unit in a pool that rents the condos by the week. A team of my employees hired by our management group takes care of advertising, renting, and maintaining the units. And I limit my personal use of my condo to 14 days. What rules apply to my situation?

Unfortunately, the news is bad. Uncle Sam doesn't consider your condo a rental unit for the purpose of the $25,000 rental exception to the passive loss rules. Hard as it is to believe, he looks upon your condo as a hotel or motel.

Why? You rent your unit to "transients"—that is, people who stay in a place for less than 30 days. Moreover, your association provides "significant services," among them maid service and a telephone switchboard.

But even if your condo did qualify as a rental unit, you would fail the "active participation" test. The reason: Your management group runs the rental operation and makes the final decisions.

So you are only a "passive" investor. And any loss you post is subject to the passive loss rules—that is, you may deduct these losses only against passive income. (See Chapter 16 for more information when and how to write off rental losses.)

CHAPTER 18

What You Need to Know about Depreciation

Some parts of the tax code adhere to a consistent logic. Understand the logic and you've mastered the rules. Unfortunately, the rules governing depreciation are not one of those parts.

And yet depreciation is one of the most important techniques of business finance. So, complex or not, depreciation rules are something that anyone with business property—including rental property—must understand. Ignorance here can be costly.

In this chapter we'll cover depreciation procedures. We'll point out where they are different from those under earlier law. And we'll suggest strategies you can use to make the depreciation rules work for you.

PROPERTY CLASSES First, a key definition: The tax code refers to "personal property" when it is talking about depreciable business assets other than real estate. We use the same term in this book, even though there's nothing very personal about the property we're discussing. (We show you how to depreciate real property—real estate—in Chapter 16.)

The law assigns personal property—both new and used—to one of six classes. These classes really describe "recovery" periods—that is, the length of time it takes to recover the money you paid for these assets.

That, after all, is what depreciation is all about—writing off a certain amount each year until you've recovered the amount you paid for your property. In this way the government compensates you for the wear and tear your business assets receive over the years.

Recovery periods range from three to twenty years.

- The *three-year class* includes small tools.
- In the *five-year class* are light trucks, automobiles, computer equipment, typewriters, calculators, and copiers. Also included: assets used in research and development, oil and gas drilling, construction, and the manufacture of certain products, such as chemicals and electronic components.
- Assets in the *seven-year class* include office furniture and fixtures and most other machinery and equipment.
- There are also *ten-, fifteen-,* and *twenty-year classes*, but only a small number of assets—including land improvements, such as drainage pipes—fall into these categories.

Should you have any doubt into which class a particular asset falls, contact your local IRS office or ask your tax adviser.

LONGER CLASSES   You might have noticed that some depreciation periods are longer than they used to be. And that's bad news, since you get to write off a smaller amount each year.

Also, some property has been reclassified from a shorter to a longer category. Automobiles and light trucks, for instance, were in the three-year class before tax reform. Now they are five-year assets. You should check carefully for such changes before you assign a depreciation period to personal property you acquired after the 1986 Tax Reform Act.

ACCELERATED DEPRECIATION   The new depreciation rules aren't all bad, however.

To compensate for the longer lives now assigned to many business assets, the tax code prescribes a faster depreciation rate for most of this property.

You may now depreciate your assets—except those in the fifteen- and twenty-year classes—using the 200-percent-declining-balance method. If Congress adopts legislation now before it, you may also opt for the 150-percent-declining-balance method for all classes. Both methods are types of accelerated depreciation, which means you get to write off greater amounts in the first years of ownership.

In fact, in the first year of an asset's life, the 200-percent-declining-balance method yields deductions that are twice the amounts you'd get using straight-line depreciation. (The straight-line method produces the same write-offs from year to year.)

In each subsequent year, however, the 200-percent-declining-balance method lets you deduct progressively smaller amounts until, at some point, the write-offs you calculate under that method become the same or smaller than your annual deductions figured under the straight-line method. At that point you switch to straight line to finish depreciating your property.

The 150-percent-declining-balance method, which is used for assets in the fifteen- and twenty-year classes is, as you would expect, 1.5 times the straight-line depreciation in the first year of an asset's life.

You have a choice when the time comes to calculate write-offs on your business assets. You may use IRS-approved formulas (later in this chapter, under "By the Numbers," we'll tell you how), or you may use depreciation tables recently published by the IRS.

You may obtain a copy of these tables from your tax adviser or local IRS office. But even if you use the tables, you should understand the conventions, or rules, incorporated in them that apply to depreciation. Let's run through them.

IMPORTANT CONVENTIONS   The first important rule: A "half-year convention" applies when it comes to depreciating personal property. This convention assumes that property is depreciable for just half the taxable year in which you place it in service—IRS jargon for put to use.

Moreover, the half-year convention applies regardless of the date that you actually began using your asset. So the deduction you may take this first year is one half the amount that you'd take for a full year of depreciation.

The only exception to the rule: You get no depreciation deductions at all if you buy and sell an asset in the same year.

Caution: Uncle Sam doesn't want taxpayers who place a large number of assets in service during the last quarter of the year to claim a full six months' depreciation. So he imposes a 40 percent rule. This rule says that you may not use the half-year convention if you place more than 40 percent of your personal property into service in the last quarter of the year.

Instead, you must use a mid-quarter convention for all personal property you place in service during the year—even those assets you place in service *before* the last three months. The mid-quarter convention assumes that you placed your assets in service halfway through the quarter in which you actually put them into use.

When you have to use the mid-quarter convention, you may

end up with fewer total depreciation deductions than you could claim under the half-year convention.

BY THE NUMBERS   Let's run through an example of how the 200-percent-declining-balance method of depreciation and the half-year convention actually work.

Say you buy a new car on January 1, 1987. You use the car only for business. The car, which falls into the five-year class, costs $10,000.

And you depreciate it using the 200-percent-declining-balance method. To figure the first year's write-off, you divide $10,000 by five years and get $2,000. So you divide $2,000 in half to get $1,000.

Your depreciation deductions equal two times the amount you'd write off using the straight-line method, which, as we've seen, allows you to deduct the same amount each year. In this case you multiply $1,000 times 2 and get $2,000—the amount you may write off in the first year.

In the second year you depreciate your car by $3,200. How do we get this figure? Divide the remaining undepreciated value of the car—$8,000—by the depreciation period, five years. You get $1,600.

Now, since we're using the 200-percent-declining-balance method multiply this amount by 2. The result: $3,200.

Follow the same formula to calculate how much you may depreciate the third year under the 200-percent-declining-balance method: $10,000 minus $2,000 minus $3,200 equals $4,800; $4,800 divided by 5 equals $960; now you multiply by 2 to get $1,920 depreciation in the third year.

Let's run through the formula one more time, for the fourth year: $10,000 minus $2,000 minus $3,200 equals $4,800; $4,800 minus $1,920 equals $2,880, divided by 5 totals $576. And $576 times 2 equals $1,152.

But as we pointed out earlier, at some point during your car's depreciation life, straight-line depreciation begins to yield the same or a greater write-off than the 200-percent-declining-balance method. In our example, that point is in the fourth year.

Here's how to figure straight-line depreciation.

Simply divide the remaining undepreciated cost of your car ($2,880) by the total number of years remaining in its five-year useful life (2.5, because of the half-year convention). The answer—$1,152—is the same as you would get using the 200-percent-declining-balance method.

And you'll see that in year five your straight-line depreciation of $1,152 tops the $691 you'd get using the double-declining-balance method.

So in the fourth and fifth years you'll switch to the straight-line method of depreciation until you've written off your entire $10,000 purchase price.

To save you the trouble of calculating when it's time to switch from the double-declining method to straight-line depreciation, we've put together a simple chart. (Note: This chart uses the half-year convention.)

WHEN TO SWITCH

Recovery Class	Year to Switch
3 Year	3
5 Year	4
7 Year	5
10 Year	7
15 Year	7
20 Year	9

EXPENSING VS. DEPRECIATING You may not know it, but Uncle Sam allows you to deduct up to $10,000 of the amount you spend each year to acquire depreciable personal property.

Here's an example to illustrate how this tax break works. Assume that you're in the truck farming business. And you buy a pickup truck to transport your vegetables to market. The price tag: $15,000.

The law allows you to depreciate the truck over five years. But the expensing rules give you another option. You may deduct $10,000 of the purchase price this year and then depreciate the remaining $5,000.

There's one catch, though. The $10,000 annual ceiling is reduced dollar for dollar for every $1 in personal property you place in service in any one year over the first $200,000. So if you place $201,000 worth of assets in service, you may only expense $9,000.

CHOICES, CHOICES Under some circumstances the law requires you to use an alternative method to depreciate your property—one that is usually less generous.

You must use the alternative method when you finance your

property with tax-exempt bonds or when the property is used outside the United States. And you must use the alternative method for certain "listed property," including luxury automobiles and computers used no more than 50 percent in your trade or business.

To figure depreciation under these circumstances, you use the property's useful life as specified in the Asset Depreciation Range (ADR) system, which was used prior to 1981. If your asset isn't listed in the ADR system, use twelve years.

Then you depreciate your property using the straight-line method. And you use the same half-year or mid-quarter conventions we explained earlier.

When it comes time to compute your alternative minimum tax (AMT), you must use a modified version of the alternative depreciation method. Instead of the straight-line method, you opt for the 150-percent-declining-balance method for all property other than real property.

Tip: As we've just seen, in some cases the law *requires* you to use an alternative depreciation method. You may also *choose* to use an alternative method.

You may, for instance, use the straight-line method over the regular recovery period for any or all classes of property. You may also elect to use the alternative depreciation method for any class of property.

Remember, though, that the alternative method periods are usually longer than the regular recovery periods. If you choose either of these methods, then you do not use the 150-percent-declining-balance method when computing your alternative minimum tax.

Or, if Congress adopts legislation now before it, you may use the 150-percent-declining-balance method for regular tax purposes and switch to straight line at some point.

As you recall, you must use the 150-percent-declining-balance method for AMT purposes when depreciating personal property, unless you use the straight-line method for regular tax purposes.

Why would you want to use one of these alternative depreciation methods?

Many taxpayers find the straight-line method easier to administer. Other taxpayers may want to use the 150-percent-declining-balance method to compute depreciation for their regular tax *and* for AMT. That way they don't have to make two calculations. And, if they're subject to the AMT, they may end up saving money. That's because they wouldn't have to add to their AMT income the excess of depreciation allowed for regular tax purposes over depreciation allowed for AMT purposes. Both deductions would be equal. (See Chapter 20 for more on the AMT.)

LUXURY AUTOMOBILE LIMITATIONS   The law caps the depreciation you may claim for luxury automobiles used for business.

You may deduct no more than $2,560 in the first year, $4,100 in the second year, $2,450 in the third year, and $1,475 in each succeeding year, including years following the applicable five-year recovery period. This means that your depreciation deductions are limited during the normal five-year recovery period on business automobiles costing more than $12,800.

Here's an example. Say you buy a new car in 1988 and you use it exclusively for business. The automobile's price tag is a hefty $20,000.

The law caps your depreciation write-offs at $2,560 in year one, $4,100 in year two, $2,450 in year three, and $1,475 in each succeeding year. Under this schedule you'd have to hold on to your car for eleven full years before you would claim depreciation write-offs equal to the $20,000 you paid for your car.

And the law is even more strict if you use your automobile less than 100 percent of the time for business. Say your business use adds up to 75 percent. Your depreciation deductions are capped at $1,920 in year one (75 percent times the $2,560 ceiling), $3,075 in year two, $1,838 in year three, and so on.

TRANSITION   In general these new depreciation rules apply to all assets you place in service after 1986. Some personal property may, however, still fall within one of the transition rules that ease the change from the old law to the new.

You may, for example, use the old depreciation rules for property constructed, rehabilitated, or acquired under a contract that was binding on March 1, 1986, or earlier.

You may also use the old rules if you spent or committed to spend at least the lesser of $1 million or 5 percent of the cost of your property by March 1, 1986—as long as construction or rehabilitation of the property actually began by that same date.

But for any of this property to qualify under the transition rules, you must place it in service by:

• January 1, 1989, if it has an ADR life of more than seven years and less than twenty years
• January 1, 1991, if the ADR life is greater than twenty years

And only property with an ADR life greater than seven years qualifies for the transition rules.

QUESTIONS AND ANSWERS

QUESTION: My partner and I opened a flower shop on July 1, 1988. That same day we purchased a small van to make deliveries. We paid $10,000 for the van. Our partnership's tax year ends on December 31. May we claim the half-year convention?

You were in business only six months in 1988, so you must depreciate the van over half of the actual months in your first year—in your case, three months.

Your depreciation deduction for the van adds up to $1,000—that is, the $10,000 purchase price divided by five years equals $2,000; $2,000 multiplied by 2 (for the 200-percent-double-declining-balance method) equals $4,000; $4,000 divided by 2 (for the half-year convention) equals $2,000; $2,000 multiplied by six-twelfths (because you were in business only half the months of the year) equals $1,000.

Caution: If you use your personal automobile in your trade or business, you may be subject to the limitations on luxury automobiles (''listed property'') discussed earlier in this chapter.

Q: I want to use the $10,000 expensing allowance. How do I go about it?

You opt for the expensing allowance simply by taking it. You take your deduction for these expenditures—up to $10,000, of course—on Form 4562, the same form that you use to calculate and claim depreciation deductions.

Q: My partner and I own a trucking company. This year, we bought several open-road trucks. The total cost was $204,000. We decided to use the expensing allowance. I also own and operate a locksmith business, and I bought a van this year for $15,000. May I claim the full $10,000 expensing allowance on the van in addition to the $10,000 our partnership claimed?

The answer, in a word, is no. The rules say that a taxpayer may not claim an expense allowance of more than $10,000 in any single year.

So here's how your situation adds up.

Your partnership may claim an expense allowance of only $6,000—not $10,000. The reason: It purchased property that added up to more than $200,000.

Your half of the $6,000 expense allowance comes to $3,000. So you may claim an expense allowance of only $7,000 on the purchase of the van—that is, the $10,000 expense allowance ceiling less the $3,000 expense allowance from your partnership. You may depreciate the remaining cost of $8,000.

Tip: The partnership reports your share of the expense allowance on Form K-1, the same form that lists your share of income, losses, and credits from the partnership. You note the amount of the expense allowance reported on the Form K-1 on Form 4562, which you attach to your personal return.

Q: I am a 50 percent partner in three separate partnerships. Each has elected to take the full $10,000 expensing allowance. My three K-1's show that I should report $15,000—$5,000 for each partnership. May I deduct this amount on my individual return?

No, you may deduct only $10,000. The $10,000 expensing limitation applies both to the partnerships and to you individually.

CHAPTER 19

News from
the Tax Shelter Front

Tax shelters not only aren't what they used to be, they're not even called tax shelters any more. In fact, the rules and vocabulary relating to almost all investment-related income and losses have changed since Congress adopted the 1986 Tax Reform Act.

Tax shelters used to be investment vehicles that in their early years generated losses. Investors could use the losses to reduce their taxable incomes. With enough tax shelter losses, some investors cut their tax bills almost to nothing.

Congress thought this practice was abusive. So lawmakers made it practically impossible to use tax shelter losses to offset other income. Since that was the only point of many tax shelters, they quickly lost most of their glamour.

The 1986 tax law also gave us a new set of terms to use. Instead of tax shelters we now have passive investments.

Passive investments can generate two kinds of income. One is passive income, meaning income from the trade or business. The other is portfolio income, which includes interest, dividends, royalties, and so on. And the law now says that income from personal services fees and retirement plans is nonpassive income.

If all this seems a bit confusing at first, it is nonetheless important to master. That's because, as a general rule, only likes may offset likes.

Passive investment losses, for instance, may only offset passive investment income. Or, put another way, your passive losses may not reduce taxable income from nonpassive sources—salary or portfolio income, for instance. Here's an example to show what we mean.

Say you're a doctor in private practice and you invest in a

159

real estate limited partnership. In 1988 the partnerships produces a $10,000 loss. Meanwhile your income from your medical practice adds up to $120,000, and your interest income from other investments is $5,000.

Under the old law your adjusted gross income would have totaled $115,000—that is, $120,000 plus $5,000 minus your $10,000 loss.

But because your real estate partnership is now a passive investment, the losses it generates can't offset your nonpassive or portfolio income.

Under the new law, your AGI is $125,000.

In this chapter we'll lay out the restrictive rules on limited partnerships and other tax shelters and the exceptions—yes, there are a few—to those rules. We'll also show you how to handle losses and gains from tax shelter investments you held when Congress reformed the law.

WHAT'S PASSIVE?   First, though, a key definition. In the eyes of the IRS, a passive activity—subject to the rules we're about to discuss—is a trade or business in which you invest but are not a material participant.

So, the first issue to decide is whether you are or are not a material participant. In one situation—rental activity—the answer is easy. The IRS considers all rental investments to be passive regardless of whether you materially participate. (See Chapter 16 for more information about rental real estate.)

Rental investments include any investment that generates income from payments for the use of tangible property, rather than for services. Included, then, are real estate rentals, equipment leasing, and rentals of airplanes or boats, as long as no significant services are provided in making the property available to the lessees.

Limited partnership investments are *almost* always passive, because limited partners virtually never materially participate in managing the trade or business of the investment.

So to find out where you fit in any business activity other than rental activities and limited partnerships in which you clearly are not active, you have to return to the IRS phrase—"materially participate."

In Uncle Sam's eyes you materially participate in a trade or business if you're involved in its operations on a "regular, substantial, and continuous basis."

But what does that phrase really mean?

To decide whether you're a material participant in a business, the IRS has devised seven tests. If your involvement satisfies just one of them, you're a material participant. If you don't satisfy any of them, Uncle Sam considers your investment passive.

And note: You may be a material participant one year and a passive investor the next. Your participation is subject to reevaluation annually.

Test 1—More than 500 hours of material participation

If you spend more than 500 hours on an activity during the year, you are a material participant for the year. When applying this test, count any work that you do in connection with the activity as long as it's the type of work normally done by owners.

Furthermore, if your spouse also performs the work of an owner, you may add his or her participation to your own for purposes of this rule—and the tests that follow.

Tip: It doesn't matter that your spouses isn't a part owner of the business or whether the two of you file a joint return for the year. If the total hours the two of you worked exceeds 500, then you meet the requirements of the first test, and your investment isn't subject to passive loss rules.

Let's say, for instance, that Paul and Betty, a married couple, together put in more than 500 hours of work managing a restaurant that Betty owns.

They meet the requirements of Test 1. But if Paul's work had consisted of dishwashing—a job that owners don't usually perform—and the purpose of this effort was to avoid the passive loss rules, his hours wouldn't count toward the 500-hour threshold.

Caution: For purposes of this test and the ones that follow, Uncle Sam won't allow you to count the number of hours you spend in your capacity as an investor, unless you're directly involved in the day-to-day management of the business.

The role of investor includes studying and reviewing financial statements, preparing or compiling summaries or analyses, or monitoring the finances or operations of the business.

Test 2—Substantially all participation

If your participation, or the participation of you and your spouse, represents substantially all of the participation by anyone in an activity for the year, then you're a material participant. And unless the activity is a rental activity, the investment isn't a passive one.

Test 3—More than 100 hours of participation and not less than anyone else

This test has two parts.

First, you must spend more than 100 hours during the year operating the business. Second, you must spend more time than anyone else, including nonowners, working in the business. Meet both conditions of this test in nonrental activities and the business is exempt from the passive loss rules.

Test 4—More than 500 hours worked in several activities with more than 100 hours in each

The test itself isn't tricky, but the consequences can surprise you. The test says that if you spend at least 100 hours on each of two or more activities and a total of more than 500 on all of them, then you're a material participant in each of those business ventures.

That could be bad news. Maybe you wanted one of them to give you passive income or losses. Why? Consider this example.

Assume that John, a full-time attorney, invested in several real estate limited partnerships. He expects these investments to lose money for several years.

John is also a general partner in two other, very profitable activities—an auto-parts store and a dry cleaning business.

He spends about 300 hours per year in the auto-parts store and about 250 hours per year in the dry cleaning business. Both businesses have several full-time employees.

John is hoping to write off the passive losses from his real estate investments against the income from the dry cleaning and auto-parts businesses.

After all, he figures, he's not involved in either of the businesses for more than 500 hours, and others spend more time than he does working at them.

But John has a problem. Since his participation in each of these businesses is more than 100 hours and his total participation exceeds 500 hours, he meets the requirements of the fourth test. As a result, he's a material participant in both the auto-parts store and the dry cleaning business.

Consequently, the income from these businesses is not passive. The result: John can't use the income from his two part-time businesses to offset his passive real estate losses.

Caution: What if you invested in two businesses and both are posting a profit? You participate 140 hours in one business and 160 hours in the other.

Under Test 4 you're not a material participant. Your profits aren't passive. They're treated as nonpassive income, and you may not use these earnings to offset any of your passive losses.

Now, let's change the scenario. Say the two businesses are operating in the red. You lose again. Uncle Sam treats the losses as passive losses.

Test 5—Material participation in any five of the last ten years

If you've been a material participant in a business for any five of the most recent ten years, the IRS will consider you a material participant in the business for the current year—no matter how small your actual involvement.

What's the point of this test? Uncle Sam wants to prevent people from shifting income from the passive to nonpassive category, or vice versa, just to reduce their tax liability. Here's an example to show how that tactic might work.

Assume that Joe is the sole owner of Joe's Tool and Die, a very profitable sole proprietorship. He is also an investor in several real estate limited partnerships.

These limited partnerships produce sizable losses, and Joe wants to offset these losses against his profits from the tool and die business.

Joe has worked full time in his tool and die business since he started it in 1980. But he's decided to reduce the amount of time he spends on this business beginning in 1988, so he can pursue other business opportunities.

By reducing his involvement, Joe thought his income from the business would be passive. Unfortunately for Joe, he's tripped up by the fifth test.

He has been a material participant in the business since 1980, or seven out of the last ten years. Consequently, even though he doesn't participate in the business currently, the IRS will treat him as a material participant for purposes of the passive loss rule.

Test 6—For personal service businesses, material participation in any three prior years

Say you've materially participated in a personal service business—law, engineering, accounting, architecture, health, consulting, performing arts, actuarial science, and so on—in any three preceding years. What are the tax consequences?

In the eyes of Uncle Sam, you're considered a material participant for the current year and into the future.

This test means that once you've been a material participant in, for instance, an architectural firm for any three years, any income you receive *from that firm* in the future is nonpassive income no matter how few hours you put into the firm.

Residual fees, for instance, that inactive partners might receive from a personal service firm, are deemed nonpassive income.

Test 7—Facts and circumstances

This test is easy to state, but difficult to apply.

It says simply that the facts and circumstances in any specific case will be the final determinant of whether you are or aren't a material participant.

Unfortunately, the IRS hasn't issued much guidance yet on how it will look at facts and circumstances. Still, there are a few guidelines.

First, you may not automatically add, as time spent in the business, the number of hours you devote to management. You may include your management hours only if no one else performs and gets paid for managing the business and no one else spends more time than you managing the business.

Second, you must devote at least 100 hours to the business during the year to qualify under the facts and circumstances test.

If your participation is less than 100 hours, you're not a material participant in the business under this test, regardless of any other facts and circumstances.

One more note: Although the law doesn't require it, anyone who anticipates that material participation may be an issue would be smart to keep a daily log of the hours he or she puts into a business. If the decision is a close one, the log could be helpful backup.

AT A LOSS   Losses you rack up in 1988 from passive activities are good for only one purpose right now: offsetting your profits from other passive investments.

But what if you don't have profits from passive investments? All is not lost. You may carry your passive losses forward and use them to offset passive income in future years. The passive losses that you carry forward are called suspended losses. And you must keep track of your losses from each of your passive activities from year to year.

Here's an example to illustrate how suspended losses work. Let's say that the year is 1988 and you've invested in three limited partnerships—A, B, and C.

All these partnerships are passive investments. Partnerships A and B each generate $10,000 in losses this year. But partnership C rewards you with a $5,000 profit. In total, you lost $15,000 on passive investments—that is, $10,000 plus $10,000 (or $20,000) minus the $5,000 profit.

The passive loss rules won't allow you to deduct your $15,000 loss on your current tax return. So you carry forward the suspended loss to future years.

The losses from partnerships A and B are used pro rata—meaning in proportion—against C's $5,000 passive income, resulting in $7,500 of suspended loss to be carried forward for each partnership, meaning A and B.

Here's how we do the calculation: Multiply the suspended loss of $15,000 by the ratio of each partnership's loss to total losses.

For example, partnership A's suspended loss is $7,500—that is, $10,000 (A's loss) divided by $20,000 (A's loss plus B's loss), or 0.5 times $15,000.

Now, say the year is 1989. Partnership A earns $20,000. Partnership B once again generates a $10,000 loss, and partnership C posts another $5,000 profit. You have a net $15,000 profit for the year ($20,000 from A plus $5,000 from C minus $10,000 from B).

Here's the good news. You carry forward your total $15,000 loss from partnerships A and B and apply it against 1989's $15,000 profit. The result: You've reduced your income from passive investments in 1989 to zero.

Remember, the law says you may carry forward these suspended passive investment losses indefinitely. But that's not all. When you sell a passive investment, the law allows you to use all your suspended losses right away. And you may use these losses to offset not only your passive income, but earned income, or wages, and portfolio income as well.

What if selling your passive investment results in a loss? In this case the loss on the sale is not treated as a passive loss, but it is subject to the capital loss rules (see Chapter 13 for more information).

The suspended losses reduce, in order, the following items:

• Any current year income or gain from the passive investment, including any gain you recognize on the sale
• Any current year income or gain from all other passive investments
• All other income or gains, including wages

To illustrate this ordering rule, go back to our previous example. Now, say the year is 1989 and you decide to unload Partnership A. On June 30 you sell your entire interest to your neighbor John.

For the first six months of 1989 partnership A produces income of $2,000. And, when you sell, you realize a gain of $1,500. Partnerships B and C don't produce any income or loss during 1989. Your only other source of income: your $120,000 salary.

You'd obviously like to use at least some of your suspended losses to reduce your hefty income. And you may. In fact, you may use all your suspended loss from partnership A in 1989. But you must use it in the following order:

• Amount you use against current year's passive income, including the gain on your sale: $3,500 ($2,000 of current income plus your $1,500 gain)

• Amount you use against other net passive income from other passive investments: none

• Amount you use to offset your salary: $4,000 (your total suspended loss from partnership A of $7,500 minus $3,500 from above)

What about the $7,500 suspended loss from partnership B? It is still suspended and will carry forward to 1900. The reason: You didn't dispose of your interest in B.

SLOW AND STEADY   The rules we've described so far apply to investments you make after October 22, 1986, that is, the date the Tax Reform Act was enacted. But the law provides a phase-in period for investments you made on or before that date. (These investments include a binding obligation to purchase that was in effect on October 22, 1986.)

To qualify for this special treatment you must have acquired your interest in the business, and it must have begun operations by October 22, 1986. Even if it hadn't, though, it will still qualify for phase-in treatment if the business had a binding contract in effect on August 16, 1986, to acquire assets to use in its operations—as long as at least 50 percent of the business's assets were acquired by that date.

For the phase-in years you may use tax shelter losses and credits that the law will eventually zap completely to offset earned or portfolio income according to the following percentages:

- 1988—40 percent
- 1989—20 percent
- 1990—10 percent
- 1991—zero percent

So if you own both preenactment and postenactment interests in passive activities, you're going to have to do a little calculating to figure out how much of your current year passive loss qualifies for the partial deduction or phase-in.

Why? The tax rules let you apply the phase-in only to the lesser of:

- Your total passive loss for the year, or
- Your passive loss taking into account only preenactment interests

Let's say your passive investments produce the following results for 1988:

Activity A	Acquired Preenactment	$6,800
Activity B	Acquired Preenactment	2,800
Activity C	Acquired Postenactment	1,000
Activity D	Acquired Postenactment	500

How much in passive losses may you take in 1988? The answer: $1,400. Let's take a look at how we arrived at that figure.

As we've seen, the first step is to add up your losses from passive activities. Then subtract this amount from your profits. You now have the amount of the year's passive loss that would be disallowed—if you didn't consider the phase-in provisions.

Now we get to the next step. The rules also require you to add up your losses from passive investments you bought before October 23, 1986.

Then, it mandates that you compare your total loss from these preenactment investments with your total loss from all passive activities and see which figure is lower. You multiply the phase-in percentage times this lower number to get the loss you're allowed to write off against your regular income.

Here's how the numbers add up.

Your total 1988 passive loss: $3,500. Your passive losses from investments made by October 22, 1986 (the sum of activity A and C): $4,000.

The phase-in allowance applies to the lesser of $3,500 or $4,000, that is, $3,500. So multiply the phase-in percentage (40 percent) times $3,500. The result—$1,400—is the loss you may take for 1988 against your regular income.

Although the new tax shelter rules are phased in for regular tax purposes, don't expect this generosity for the alternative minimum tax. When you compute the AMT, you must add back to your taxable income any loss that the phase-out regulations allow you for regular tax purposes. (See Chapter 20 for more on the AMT.)

BETTER TO RECEIVE THAN TO GIVE   When you give away an interest in a tax shelter to a friend or relative, you lose your right to claim suspended losses. In this case, the recipient of your generosity must add these suspended losses to his or her basis in the investment.

What if, later on, the recipient sells at a loss? Then his or her basis is limited to the fair market value of the interest on the date you made the gift.

Moreover, sales you make to related parties—relatives, your closely held corporation, and so on—will also not let you immediately use your suspended losses. In this instance you carry forward the losses until the related party disposes of the investment in a taxable transaction.

For example, say you sell your limited partnership interest to your dad in 1989. You won't be able to use 1988's suspended losses from the partnership when you make the sale. Instead, you continue to carry these losses forward as suspended losses until your dad sells the investment to an unrelated party.

INSIDE STORY   The new law says that if an investment is subject to the passive loss rules, interest expense from that investment is not subject to the interest limits. (See Chapter 4 for more information on writing off interest expenses.)

And it makes no difference whether the interest is "inside interest"—that is, incurred by the limited partnership itself—or "outside interest," that is, interest on money you borrow to invest in the limited partnership.

What does this rule mean?

When you borrow money to purchase an investment, the interest is added to your partnership loss to determine your overall passive loss from the activity.

The one exception to this rule: Passive investments that report portfolio income, such as a real estate partnership that earns interest income on its excess cash reserves. In these cases you must classify a portion of your interest expense as investment interest, and it is subject to the new interest limits.

Here's an example. You're a new limited partner in ABC Partnership in 1988. And, for 1988, you have a passive loss before interest expense of $10,000. In addition, the ABC Partnership itself racks up $2,000 in interest expense. ABC reports no portfolio income.

The partnership is not required to treat any of its interest as investment interest. The entire $2,000 is included in your passive loss for the year. You do not need to treat this amount separately as investment interest on your return.

What if ABC did have portfolio income? In this case the partnership must allocate some of the $2,000 of interest expense to the portfolio income. ABC would then report this amount separately to you. And you would have to treat it as investment interest on your return.

Usually, losses you take from your passive investments won't have an impact on your investment interest limitations. But there's one exception. Losses allowed under the phase-in provisions reduce net investment income for the investment interest limitation.

NO CREDIT The same rules that apply to losses apply to credits. You may use tax credits passed along to you by shelters only to offset the tax on the net income from these investments. This provision applies mostly to a tax shelter that passes along such tax credits as energy credits and research and development credits.

Consider this example. Let's say you'd owe Uncle Sam a tax of $50,000 if you disregarded your net passive income. But you'd have to shell out $80,000 if you took into account both your net passive income and your other taxable income.

So the amount of tax that you attribute to your passive income comes to $30,000. And you're allowed to take any credits from your passive investments that don't top $30,000.

Like losses, you may carry forward credits to a future tax year. However, unlike losses, you can't use credits to offset tax on earned income and portfolio income when you sell your shelter.

You may increase your basis by any "suspended" credits before the sale. This provision gives you a lower gain or higher loss when you sell your property. If you go this route, you may no longer carry forward the suspended credit to offset other passive income.

WHAT REMAINS   The good news: You still have a few tax shelter benefits left. For example, rental real estate, low-income housing, and rehabilitation projects made it through reform with some tax breaks in place. (We cover all these topics in Chapter 16.)

Another exception to the passive activity rules was carved out for working interests in oil and gas properties. This exception, however, does not apply to limited partnerships or other types of deals that limit a participant's liability. How does the law define a working interest? It's one that includes development and operation expenses for the partner.

Losses generated by these interests are not subject to the limitations on losses from passive investments. You may deduct them from your regular income. And you don't have to materially participate in operations to do so.

Tip: Some syndicators are structuring oil and gas investments as general partnerships. The reason: General partners, unlike limited partners, aren't subject to the passive activity rules. That means if you invest in an oil and gas operation as a general partner, you may deduct from your ordinary income all expenses, including intangible drilling costs.

But know the risks before you invest. As a general partner you are fully liable for the debts and other obligations of the business. As a limited partner you are liable only up to the amount you invest.

LEFTOVERS   In earlier years you probably decided whether to invest in tax shelters based on the rate of return. But the rate of return included substantial tax write-offs.

These days you should continue to look to limited partnerships for solid economic returns. But you should exclude or minimize tax benefits when you evaluate the investment. Now, only high cash returns make these investments worthwhile.

Remember, you add together income and losses from all passive investments. So if you find yourself locked into some older investments that you expect will generate passive losses, follow the obvious strategy: Invest in vehicles that generate passive income. You may then use this income to offset your losses.

QUESTIONS AND ANSWERS

QUESTION: I invested in an oil and gas limited partnership and sold it at a loss. If this loss is a capital loss, how is it treated for tax purposes?

The capital loss rules take precedence over the passive loss rules in determining what losses you may take on your return when you sell your passive investment. (See Chapter 13 for a discussion of capital gains and losses.)

Let's say that you sell your entire interest in your oil and gas limited partnership in 1988. As a result you have a $10,000 long-term capital loss. Your investment also produced $5,000 of suspended passive losses in 1987. And in 1988 your investment brings you $3,000 in passive income. You have no other capital gains or losses.

The law allows you to claim only $3,000 in capital losses in one year. You must carry forward any remaining losses. So the long-term capital loss you deduct in 1988 is $3,000, and the loss you carry forward adds up to $7,000.

But you may also claim in 1988 your $5,000 in suspended losses. And this $5,000 offsets the $3,000 in income you realize in 1988 from your partnership. Moreover, you may use the remaining $2,000 in losses to offset your wages or portfolio income. The reason: You've disposed of your passive investment.

Q: Last year I invested in a building. And this year I lost my only tenant. It is virtually impossible for me to sell the building or convert it for use by someone else. Is there some way I can dispose of it, so I don't have to treat my loss for the year as passive?

Yes. You can abandon the property. The law also considers so-called abandonments as dispositions that let you escape the passive loss limitations. So you may claim your entire loss in the current year. The law can be tricky, though, when it comes to abandoning property. If you plan to go this route, consult your tax adviser beforehand.

Also, if you abandon your building after 1987, the suspended loss rules let you take all the losses you've been carrying forward.

How do you abandon an investment?

Uncle Sam considers your building abandoned if you can prove that you originally had a profit motive for investing in the building, and the property suddenly became useless. You must also show that you have permanently deserted the building and discontinued trying to rent or sell it.

But note: Just not using the building—or a decline in its value—is not conclusive evidence that you have abandoned your property. You must show that you have actually forsaken it. For example, the IRS would consider cutting off utilities, boarding up windows, and cancelling insurance as proof of abandonment.

Q: Can a limited partner materially participate in a business?

Generally, no, because state laws normally prohibit limited partners from being active in a business.

Limited partners who do become active risk losing their limited liability. Consequently, the material participation tests discussed above don't apply.

Exceptions exist, though.

The first exception deals with the first test, the 500-hour test. Even limited partners are material participants if they put 500 hours or more into the business.

The second exception relates to Tests 5 and 6. If a limited partner meets either the five-of-ten year test or the three-year test, he or she is a material participant regardless of the limited partner designation.

A third exception applies to people who are both general and limited partners in the same activity. The IRS considers them, on balance, to be general partners who must go back through Tests 1 through 6 to determine whether they're material participants.

Q: A few years ago I invested in a tax shelter, which is now generating taxable income. What do I do with this investment today?

Tax shelters were structured so that investors could claim tax deductions—accelerated depreciation, for example—in the early years of ownership. But these deductions diminished over time. Then the shelter was left with only paper profits or phantom income.

A shelter that generates taxable income but doesn't generate cash is known in investment circles as a "burned-out" shelter. If you find yourself with a burned-out shelter, consider these two strategies.

• Phantom income, is, in fact, passive income. So you can invest in a new tax shelter that generates passive losses to offset this income.

• Sell the investment. But be warned. You'll usually have to sell at a deep discount. And besides losing money on the sale, your disposing of the investment may create taxable income. But selling the shelter does enable you to avoid reporting phantom income on your tax return.

And you should find a ready buyer. In the past years, a new secondary market for tax shelter investments has emerged. Syndicators purchase these partnership units, then pool them and sell interests in the pools to taxpayers as "passive income generators" or PIG's.

Q: I have lots of passive losses, and I need passive income to absorb them. How can I generate this income?

One idea: Invest in limited partnerships that operate ongoing businesses that run in the black—a ski resort, golf course, or conference center, for example.

You should have no trouble finding this type of partnership. Your investment adviser or broker will know about some of these partnerships. You may also run across information on them in financial publications.

Here's a useful strategy if you own a profitable corporation that is not a personal service corporation or an S corporation. Transfer ownership of the investments that are generating passive losses to your corporation. The reason: The law allows a corporation to use passive losses to offset its regular business income.

Another alternative—if you're the owner of a corporation but don't materially participate in business operations—is to elect S corporation status. Since you don't materially participate, your income from the S corporation is considered passive. And you can use your passive losses to offset profits from your S corporation.

Q: My accountant says I should look into "paired investments." What are these vehicles, and are they appropriate for me?

Only you can decide whether an investment is right for your circumstances. But paired investments do hold appeal for may investors.

What are they? As their name implies, they're limited partnerships with two distinct businesses. One business generates income and, hopefully, cash. The other business generates losses—at least for tax purposes—to offset that income.

Paired investments are just another variation on the tax shelter theme. Our advice: Invest in one of these vehicles only if it makes economic sense.

Q: I've heard a lot about publicly-traded partnerships. For tax purposes, how do I treat income and losses from these partnerships?

You may not know it, but the rules governing publicly-traded partnerships—or master limited partnerships, as they are sometimes called—changed in 1987. Uncle Sam now treats net income form publicly-traded partnerships as portfolio income. That means you may not use this income to offset passive losses from other investments. What's worse, losses from publicly-traded partnerships are treated as suspended losses. And you may subtract these losses only from net business income from the same partnerships. But you may claim any unused suspended losses when you dispose of your partnership interest.

Q: I owned a limited partnership interest in a piece of rental real estate. We sold out in 1985 on an installment-sale basis, so I'm still receiving income. Is this income passive?

Yes, Uncle Sam treats the income as passive, even though the passive loss rules weren't in place when you sold your partnership.

CHAPTER 20

An Alternative Minimum Tax with Bite

You've got it made.

Your income this year is hefty, but your tax bill is almost embarrassingly low. How nice, you think—until you remember the dreaded alternative minimum tax (AMT).

The AMT was designed for people who—through the judicious use of deductions, credits, and deferrals—pay Uncle Sam little or no tax. With the AMT, which is really a totally separate tax system, the federal government is guaranteed to get its cut.

Here's how the AMT works. First, you figure your regular tax. Then you calculate your alternative minimum tax. If your AMT is greater than your regular tax, you owe the government the AMT amount.

Unfortunately, this exercise isn't as simple as it sounds. In fact, understanding the AMT rules—and doing the required calculations—is a challenge for even the savviest taxpayers. Nonetheless, the AMT is worth understanding, if only because understanding it may save you considerable money.

WHO'S SUBJECT TO THE AMT? If you claimed lots of deductions—particularly in the following categories—look out. There's a good chance you'll pay the AMT. The categories:

• Deductions from so-called passive activities, such as real estate and oil and gas limited partnerships
• Miscellaneous deductions
• Deductions for state and local income taxes, real estate taxes, and personal property taxes

175

- Deductions for investment interest, especially if it topped your investment income
  - Personal interest deductions
  - Deductions for interest on refinanced mortgages if the amount refinanced tops your old mortgage
  - Deductions for donations of appreciated property to charity

There's also a chance you'll pay the AMT if you exercised incentive stock options (ISO's) or invested in private-activity bonds. (These are bonds issued by state and local governments to raise money for private enterprise—for example, industrial bonds used by small businesses to build factories.)

What if you're not certain the AMT applies to you? The only way to know for sure is to "run the numbers."

This chapter shows you how in four stages. First, we help you figure out how much of your income is subject to the AMT. Second, we explain the exemption that may allow you to offset some of this taxable income. Third, we help you calculate what the IRS calls your tentative minimum tax. Finally, we show you how to keep your AMT to—well, to a minimum.

And if you're still confused, there's an outline in the Appendix that will help you quickly visualize the AMT system.

FIRST THINGS FIRST   Your starting point: Figuring out how much of your income is subject to the AMT. We call this amount your AMT income, or AMTI. Begin with your regular taxable income and make the following adjustments.

Itemized Deductions

Most itemized deductions that are allowable for regular tax purposes are not deductible for AMT purposes. So you must add them back to your regular taxable income when you figure your AMTI.

Specifically, you must add back state and local income taxes, real estate and personal property taxes, and medical expenses that are less than 10 percent of your AGI (even though the law allows you to deduct for regular tax purposes medical expense that top 7½ percent of your AGI).

You must also add back miscellaneous deductions—tax preparation fees and professional dues, for instance—that you wrote off for regular tax purposes.

Exceptions to the general rule on itemized deductions: home mortgage interest, investment interest that does not top invest ment income, and charitable contributions of other than appreciated property. All these items are deductible for AMT purposes.

Two more points: The phase-in rules for investment and personal interest for regular tax purposes don't count when it comes to the AMT. You may not deduct personal interest from your AMT income. But you may carry forward indefinitely—until you use it up—any investment interest expense that you can't use for AMT purposes in the current tax year.

Second, let's say you refinance your home mortgage. For AMT purposes, you may write off interest only on the amount of the refinanced mortgage that doesn't top your outstanding mortgage before you refinance.

So, if you refinance your mortgage to skirt the rules on deducting personal interest, the AMT rules ensure that you can't capture an increased interest deduction. (See Chapter 4 for the rules on deducting interest.)

But here's an exception: You may still deduct for AMT purposes interest on a mortgage you refinance, as long as you use the money you receive for home improvements, a trade or business, or investments. (In the case of investments, however, you may deduct interest only from investment income.)

And should you buy a luxury boat that qualifies as a second home, keep this rule in mind: The interest on the loan you take out to buy the boat may be deductible for regular tax purposes. But it is entirely nondeductible for the AMT. The reason: A boat doesn't qualify as a dwelling unit under the AMT system.

Passive Activities

If you think a passive investment is a stake in a limited partnership, you're absolutely right. But these investments—otherwise known as tax shelters—come in many other forms, such as rental property.

The definition of a passive investment: A trade or business in which you do not materially participate in management. Moreover, all rental activity is considered a passive investment—whether you materially participate or not.

During the Tax Reform Act's four-year phase-in period, which began in 1987, you may use a certain percentage of your passive investment losses to offset your earned income and portfolio income for regular tax purposes. But you're entitled to this break only if your investment was made before the new tax law was enacted. (See Chapter 19 for more information on the passive loss rules.)

You may not, however, use these phase-in losses to reduce this income when you compute your AMTI. In fact, passive investment losses are good for only two purposes in figuring AMT income.

You may carry these losses forward and deduct them against any passive investment income you may have in future years. Moreover, if you dispose of your entire interest in a passive investment, you may use these losses to compute your AMT income.

One word of caution: You must dispose of your tax shelter in a way that results in a taxable transaction. So if you give your shelter share away, you're out of luck. Your gift isn't a taxable transaction and you're not allowed to use any of the losses you've carried forward.

Tip: If you think you may be subject to the AMT, consider investing in vehicles that will generate enough passive income to soak up your passive losses. Otherwise, you may have to wait years before the losses produce any tax benefits for AMT purposes.

Stock Options

When you exercise an incentive stock option (ISO), you usually pay an amount that is less—sometimes considerably less—than the fair market value of the stock. The difference between the price you pay and the stock's value on the open market is known in tax lingo as the "bargain element."

And it's part of what makes ISO's so valuable as executive recruiting and retention tools for corporations. (See Chapter 24 for a full discussion of stock options.)

Alas, for AMT purposes this difference is a so-called preference item—that is, an item that receives favorable tax treatment under the regular tax rules. So you must add the bargain element to your AMT income in the year you exercise your options.

The news isn't all bad, though. The difference becomes part of the stock's cost basis. When you sell your shares, your gain—for AMT purposes—is less than for regular tax purposes.

Here's an example. In 1988 you exercise 1,000 ISO's that your company granted you in 1985. The option price is $11 a share and the fair market value of the stock when you bought it was $61 a share.

You now have a tax preference of $50,000—the difference between the option price you paid for your shares ($11,000) and the fair market value ($61,000). In 1989 you sell your 1,000 shares for $71 each. For regular tax purposes your gain comes to $60,000, that is, $71,000 less your option price of $11,000.

But for AMT purposes your gain totals a mere $10,000—$71,000 less your AMT basis for the shares, or $61,000 (the $11,000 option price plus the $50,000 bargain element you had to add to your AMT income in 1988).

Now, in 1989, when you calculate your AMT income, you subtract the $50,000 difference in the gain.

Tip: Before tax reform, AMT considerations often played a key role in determining when and how many stock options an executive would exercise in a single year. But changes in the rules governing the AMT and incentive stock options reduce the role the AMT plays in this decision.

Our advice: When it comes time to exercise your ISO's, don't put AMT considerations front and center. If it makes economic sense to exercise your options now, do so.

Depreciation

The law says that you must add back or subtract from your regular taxable income the difference between the depreciation you claimed for regular tax purposes and depreciation figured using the alternative depreciation lives.

Here's an example. Say in December 1987 you purchased the land and building where you maintain your office. The price tag—a reasonable $125,000. Of this amount, $100,000 is allocated to the cost of the building and $25,000 goes toward the cost of the land.

When you file your 1988 return, you claim a depreciation deduction for the structure. And you calculate this deduction using the straight-line method over 31½ years. So, in 1988, you may write off $3,175 in depreciation.

Now it comes time to calculate your AMT liability. Under the alternative method, your depreciation deduction would add up to $2,500. So the difference between the two methods—and the amount you must add back to your income for AMT purposes—comes to $675.

Now let's imagine that 32 years have passed. You still own the building, which by now is fully depreciated for regular tax purposes.

But here's where you finally get a break. The law says that, for AMT purposes, you are still entitled to a $2,500 annual deduction in years 33 through 40. So, rather than having to add back dollars, you get an additional write-off from your AMT income.

The law does make one exception to this rule for real property and leased personal property "placed in service" (IRS jargon for put in use) before 1987. In these cases, the law says, you must add back to your regular taxable income the excess of the depreciation you claimed using the accelerated method over the old straight-line depreciation. But later on you don't get to subtract the difference between the straight-line method and accelerated depreciation. (See Chapter 18 for a full explanation of these depreciation methods.)

Other Preference and Adjustment Items

There are a number of other preferences and adjustment items that are relevant to the AMT. Let's run through them.

• *Interest on tax-exempt "private-activity" bonds issued after August 7, 1986.* Income from these tax-exempt bonds isn't subject to tax under the regular system, but it is taxed under the AMT. Under regular tax rules, you may not write off interest on money you borrow to invest in private-activity bonds. But you may deduct this interest expense when you compute your AMT income—though, only to the extent that you have investment income.

• *The excess of percentage depletion over the tax basis of property generating the mineral deposit.* And what does this confusing phrase mean?

Here's an example. Say the year is 1988 and you own a 10 percent partnership interest in an oil and gas operation. You receive a share of the percentage depletion—that is, a deduction that reflects a decrease in the value of the operation.

Your share of the percentage depletion on the gross income of the oil and gas operation comes to $20,000. And your share of the adjusted basis of the land producing the oil and gas is $15,000. So the tax preference is the $5,000 difference. And you must add this amount back to AMT income.

• *Excess intangible drilling costs that come to more than 65 percent of the net income from productive oil and gas wells.* Obviously the adjustments you must make when you own shares in oil and as partnerships are complicated. So see your tax adviser if you count these among your investments.

• *The difference between the fair market value of property you contribute to a charitable organization and write off—as an itemized deduction—for regular tax purposes, and the cost of the property.* For example, say as a loyal alumnae, you give fifty shares of stock to your alma mater. The stock, for which you paid $2,000 two years ago, now has a fair market value of $5,000. For regular tax purposes you write off the $5,000 as an itemized deduction. But for AMT purposes you may deduct only the cost of the stock. So when you compute your AMT income, you must add back to your regular taxable income the $3,000 difference.

One last preference item you should know about: Research and development costs. You may deduct these expenses in the year you incure them for regular tax purposes. But for AMT purposes you must capitalize them—that is, write them off over several years, in this case, over a ten-year period.

So you may deduct 10 percent of these costs every year of the ten-year period, even though you already deducted them in full for regular tax purposes.

Tip: Here's a way to prevent research and development costs and intangible drilling costs from being treated as a preference item. Simply amortize all or a portion of these expenses for regular tax purposes and deduct them over ten years.

Of course, this strategy has its downside—namely, for regular tax purposes, you take a much smaller deduction in a single year. The bottom line: Do some calculations, and treat these costs in the way that saves you the most income tax.

MAKING ADJUSTMENTS When you've made all the required adjustments to your regular taxable income and accounted for all tax preference items, the result is your AMT income.

Now, the law says, you may reduce your AMTI by the following exemption amounts: $40,000 for taxpayers filing a joint return, $20,000 for married taxpayers filing separate returns, and $30,000 for single taxpayers. However, if your AMT income is high—an least by Uncle Sam's definition—you must reduce your exemption. Cut it by 25 percent of the amount by which your AMT income exceeds:

- $150,000 for married taxpayers filing jointly
- $75,000 for married taxpayers filing separately
- $112,500 for single filers

Therefore, you're entitled to no exemption at all if you and your spouse file jointly and your AMT income tops $310,000. Your ceiling as a single taxpayer is $232,500.

For example, if you and your spouse file a joint return with AMTI of $213,725, your AMT exemption is reduced from $40,000 to $24,069.

Here's how we arrive at that figure. We take AMTI of $213,725 less $150,000, or $63,725, and multiply by 25 percent. The result equals $15,931. We then subtract $15,931 from the $40,000 AMT exemption to get $24,069.

One more point: When you compute your AMTI, the rules allow you to deduct the personal exemptions you take for regular tax purposes. However, a pending technical correction to the tax code may change this rule. So check with your tax adviser before filing.

COMPUTING THE TENTATIVE MINIMUM TAX   So far, you've calculated your AMT income, then adjusted it by the appropriate exemption amount. At last you're almost ready to compute your alternative minimum tax. Take your adjusted AMT income and multiply it by 21 percent. The result, after you subtract any allowable foreign tax credits, is your tentative minimum tax (TMT).

Compare this TMT to your regular income tax (again, after you take any allowable foreign tax credits). If the TMT is larger than your regular tax, you must fork over the difference—the alternative minimum tax—to Uncle Sam, in addition to your regular tax.

Not so fast, though. You may not be done yet. You still have to figure out your minimum tax credit (MTC). Doing so is easier if you understand a few of the underlying concepts.

PREFERENCE ITEMS   The adjustments that you have made so far to your regular taxable income in computing your AMT income fall into one of two categories. Either they are "deferral preferences" or "exclusion preferences."

Deferral preferences don't permanently reduce your tax liability. As you might expect, they only defer that liability until some later time.

On the other hand, the government never recaptures the tax revenue it loses when you reduce your liability by using an exclusion preference item.

Which is which, and why do you care?

There are only four exclusion preference items: the percentage-depletion preference, all itemized deduction adjustments, the appreciated-property charitable-contribution preference item, and the tax-exempt bond preference item. Everything else is a deferral preference item.

How does knowing the difference help you reduce your taxes

in future years? After you've computed your AMT as we described above, compute it again using only the exclusion preferences. The difference between this adjusted AMT and the AMT you originally calculated is your minimum tax credit.

You may carry this tax credit forward indefinitely (although you may not carry it back) to offset your regular tax liabilities in future years. You may reduce your regular tax, however, only to an amount equal to the TMT in the year you carry forward this amount.

Still confused? An example may help.

Say in 1988 you pay $17,000 of AMT, all of it resulting from your exercise of incentive stock options—a deferral tax preference item. This amount then becomes your MTC carryover.

In 1989 you have a regular tax liability of $63,000 and a TMT of $61,000. So you may use $2,000 of that $17,000 MTC carryover from 1988 to reduce your tax payment to Uncle Sam.

However, if you're unfortunate enough to have to pay the AMT year after year, the minimum tax credit won't do you much good.

PLANNING TO MINIMIZE THE AMT   When it comes to planning for the AMT, you must consider both short-term and long-term strategies. Your short-term strategies: Accelerate or defer income and deductions. For long-range planning, you should focus on the types of investments you make.

Say you've invested most of your money over the past few years in real estate or oil and gas limited partnerships. If you think you'll be subject to the AMT either this year or in the future, you may want to shift your investments into vehicles without AMT implications—stocks or mutual funds, for example, or corporate bonds.

When you map out your long-term strategies, you should also focus on the tax treatment you elect for depreciable assets such as rental property.

For example, you may want to opt for the longer alternative method of depreciation for regular tax purposes. That way, you don't have to add to your AMT income the difference between accelerated depreciation and alternative depreciation.

WHY MORE TAXPAYERS WILL PAY THE AMT   Starting in 1988 more people will pay the AMT than ever before. Here's why. When Congress adopted the 1986 Tax Reform Act, it voted to not only expand the AMT, but toughen it up as well.

For starters, Congress boosted the AMT rate from 20 percent to 21 percent. This new AMT rate is 75 percent of the top regular tax rate of 28 percent.

In the past the ratio was only 40 percent (a 20 percent AMT and a 50 percent top regular rate). As the ratio goes higher, it is more likely the AMT rate will apply to more taxpayers. Also, as we've seen, more income is subject to the AMT than in previous years. And the phase-out of the exemption amount as income goes higher will cause more taxpayers to fall into the AMT trap.

Our advice: Don't assume you're not subject to the AMT. Run the numbers this year and every year. And project your tax situation for two years at a time, since what you do this year will affect your AMT situation next year. Remember, forewarned is forearmed.

If you don't want to go through the trouble of calculating your AMT income, use the table printed at the end of this chapter. It shows you the total amount of preferences and adjustments you may have, based on a given level of regular taxable income, before you're subject to the AMT.

If you think you have to worry about the AMT only when you prepare your tax return, think again. The law requires you to pay 90 percent of your final tax bill through withholding and estimated tax payments. So if you're subject to the AMT, you may find you need to increase your estimated tax payments. (See Chapter 27 for more on estimated tax payments.)

QUESTIONS AND ANSWERS

QUESTION: Let's say I sell property that I placed in service after 1986. Will I have the same gain or loss for regular tax purposes and for the AMT?

No. And here's the reason: You're depreciating your property by a different method for the AMT. So you end up with a different AMT basis—that is, your adjusted cost or your cost less depreciation—which, in turn, affects your gain or loss. Consider this example.

Say you purchase a building on May 1, 1987 for $200,000. You sell it on June 1, 1988, for $210,000. For regular tax purposes your depreciation deductions for 1987 and 1988 amount to $6,878. For the AMT, however, your depreciation deductions total $5,417.

So your basis for the regular tax system is equal to $200,000 minus $6,878 of depreciation deductions, or $193,122. And your gain comes to $16,878.

But your basis for AMT purposes total $200,000 minus $5,417, or $194,583. So your gain comes to $15,417. And your AMT income is reduced by $1,461—the difference between $16,878 and $15,417—in 1988.

Q: I overpaid my state income taxes in 1987 and received a refund in 1988. I know I have to report my refund as income for regular tax purposes in 1988 since I took the deduction in 1987. But how do I treat it for AMT purposes?

As we've seen, Uncle Sam won't allow you to deduct state and local income tax payments for AMT purposes. The good news: You don't have to report any state and local tax refunds as income when you calculate your AMTI.

Q: If I don't itemize on my tax return, I claim a standard deduction for regular tax purposes. What about for the AMT?

Sorry, but the standard deduction is for regular taxes only. You get no such deduction for the AMT.

Q: I've run the numbers for 1988 and 1989. It looks like I'm subject to the AMT in 1988 but not in 1989. What's the best course of action for me?

As we've seen, deferral preferences don't permanently reduce your tax liability. They only defer that liability until some later time.

On the other hand, the government never recaptures the tax revenue it loses when you reduce your liability by using exclusion preferences.

Our advice: Ask your tax adviser to help you divide your deductions into two categories—deferral preference items and exclusion preference items. The idea is to postpone until 1989 paying expenses that you may claim as deductions for both regular and AMT tax purposes.

If you pay in 1988, you'll get a smaller tax benefit if your item was deductible for AMT purposes (for example, charitable contributions). Or you could waste potential deductions if the items were not deductible for AMT purposes (for example, state and local taxes).

You might postpone exercising an ISO until 1989—if it makes economic sense. Doing so lets you sidestep the 21 percent AMT on the bargain element in 1988.

Q: I'm subject to the AMT in 1989 but not in 1988. What should I do?

Clearly, your situation is the direct opposite of the one we've just described. And the course of action you should take is the direct opposite, as well. So you should:

• Defer income. You want more of your income taxed in 1989 when you'll pay tax at a lower rate.

• Accelerate deductions, especially those that aren't allowed for AMT purposes. By accelerating these write-offs to 1988, you'll realize some benefit from them. An example: prepay 1988 state and local income taxes.

• Consider accelerating the exercise of an ISO. But make sure exercising these options won't subject you to the AMT in 1988.

Q: Do I always end up with a preference item when I exercise ISOs?

In most cases your preference item is the difference between your option price and the market price of the stock at the time of exercise.

But under legislation now before Congress, Uncle Sam gives corporate insiders—officers or directors of public companies—another option. You're allowed to postpone reporting your gain from option shares for six months. So your preference item is the difference between your option price and the market price of the stock at the end of the six-month holding period.

Something else you should know: If you sell your stock in the same year you exercise your option, you record no preference item. And this rule applies to everyone, not just corporate insiders.

Say you sell your stock before you meet the ISO holding requirements—that is, one year from the date of exercise and two years from the date of grant. You report a preference item unless you sell the stock in the year of exercise.

ARE YOU SUBJECT TO THE AMT?   The chart that follows lists the maximum amount of preferences and adjustments you may chalk up in 1988 before you're subject to the AMT.

Regular Taxable Income	Preferences/ Adjustments	AMT	Regular Tax
$ 40,000	$ 34,900	$ 7,330	$ 7,330
60,000	41,570	12,930	12,930
80,000	50,190	18,940	18,940
100,000	59,300	25,540	25,540
120,000	64,440	32,140	32,140
140,000	69,580	38,740	38,740
160,000	74,720	45,340	45,430
180,000	79,870	51,940	51,940
200,000	83,640	58,180	58,180
220,000	84,940	63,780	63,780
240,000	90,380	69,380	69,380
280,000	103,710	80,580	80,580
320,000	117,050	91,780	91,780
360,000	130,380	102,980	102,980
400,000	143,710	114,180	114,180

Note: Assumes the taxpayer is married, files a joint return, and claims four personal exemptions in 1988

CHAPTER 21

What You Need to Know about Retirement Plans

A retirement plan is one of the few ways left to reward yourself or your employees for a job well done—without realizing current taxable income. But figuring out the impact of taxes on your retirement planning can get confusing.

There are so many different retirement plans. And the type of plan you may use depends on whether you're an employee or self-employed—or both.

Moreover, the complex rules about when you can and can't withdraw your money and how you're taxed when you do can be mind-boggling. So, let's simplify matters.

First we sort all the plans into just a few categories—you'll find the similarities among plans are much more striking than the differences. Then we devote most of the chapter to covering the tax considerations involved in taking money out of each kind of plan.

TYPES OF PLANS　There are really only three types of retirement plans: those you create and contribute to yourself, those your company runs and contributes to, and those to which both you and the company may contribute. Most people may participate in more than one type of plan.

Let's look briefly at each type.

Individual Retirement Accounts

Individual Retirement Accounts (IRA's) are retirement plans that you contribute to and create. IRA's, unfortunately, lost much of their appeal as a result of changes made by the 1986 Tax Reform Act. They're no longer as useful to individuals who are covered by employer-sponsored retirement plans. Still, they aren't totally without value.

The law allows you to contribute to an IRA the lesser of $2,000 or 100 percent of your compensation each year—$2,250 if you and your nonworking spouse file jointly.

But you may deduct this contribution only if neither you nor your spouse is covered by a tax-deferred retirement plan or your AGI falls below a certain level.

Whether your annual contribution to an IRA is deductible or not, the account's earnings still accumulate tax free until you withdraw your money at retirement. (See Chapter 22 for more on IRA's.)

Keogh

If you work for yourself, you should have a Keogh for saving and sheltering part of your self-employment income. Keoghs are bona fide wealth-building tools.

To have a Keogh plan, you must be self-employed. That is, you must have income from your own business—whether or not you also work for someone else. And if you have employees, you must include them in your Keogh plan.

Having a Keogh doesn't preclude you from having an IRA. But you should know that a Keogh is a qualified plan under the tax law. So if you set one up, you're in the same deductibility boat as someone who is an employee. That is, your income must fall within certain levels or your IRA contributions aren't deductible.

You pay no tax on your Keogh contributions or on any earnings that accumulate until you begin to collect benefits, usually at retirement.

Keoghs come in two varieties: defined-contribution plans and defined-benefit plans.

A defined-contribution plan allows you to contribute some fixed percentage of your earnings to the plan each year. To make matters more complicated, these plans themselves come in two varieties: profit-sharing plans and money-purchase plans.

You may contribute up to 15 percent of your self-employment income with a profit-sharing plan or up to 25 percent with a money-purchase plan. But in either case your contribution must not total more than $30,000.

You should know, too, that you have to subtract your contribution to figure your net self-employment income. So, in practice, you're contributing only 13.043 percent of your self-employment income to your profit-sharing plan or 20 percent to a money-purchase plan.

With a defined-benefit plan you contribute annually whatever amount is required to fund a specified retirement payout. The payout is fixed, and the contribution is based on actuarial tables for your life expectancy.

The only limit: The annual benefit after retirement may not top the lesser of $94,023 (adjusted annually for increases in the cost of living) or 100 percent of your average earnings for your three consecutive years of highest earnings. Note, though, that your contribution can't top your current annual income.

Many people steer clear of setting up a defined-benefit Keogh. The reason: The paperwork and the cost of maintaining the plan are greater than with a defined-contribution plan. But for many people the benefits outweigh the hassles involved—especially if you're over age forty-five.

Here's why. Let's say you're fifty-five years old and currently earn $100,000 in self-employment income. The most you could put away with a defined-contribution money-purchase plan is $20,000 (20 percent times $100,000).

But say you want to fund a benefit of $59,000 after you retire at age sixty-five. Based on actuarial computations, you could sock away as much as $41,000 this year in a defined-benefit plan—nearly $21,000 more.

Caution: If you have employees, you must provide them with comparable benefits. And you must weigh the cost of doing so with the benefits you'll realize from the plan.

Tip: To take advantage of a Keogh, you must create your plan no later than the last day of your taxable year, which for most people is December 31. But you don't have to make your actual contribution until the due date of your tax return, including extensions.

Caution: You may not know it, but starting in 1989, Uncle Sam requires you to make contributions to defined-benefit plans quarterly.

Tip: If you do business as a sole proprietor, you set up your Keogh plan. But if you're a partner in a partnership, the partnership must establish the Keogh plan.

Tip: Although you may contribute the least amount to a profit-sharing plan, this type of arrangement does have one advantage. You're free to skip a contribution any year you like. If you have a money-purchase or defined-benefit plan, you must make an annual contribution or pay a penalty.

Tip: You may also "pair" or combine a money-purchase plan with a profit-sharing plan. The advantages: You may, if you want, contribute and deduct a full 20 percent of your self-employment income, just as if you chose to fully fund a money-purchase plan. But you have more flexibility in the amount you *must* contribute each year.

Here's how pairing works.

You set up a money-purchase plan to shelter 6.957 percent of your income. Now you may contribute up to an additional 13.043 percent (for a total of 20 percent) to a profit-sharing plan.

And the amount you put into the profit-sharing plan is entirely up to you. So you may still protect from Uncle Sam's long reach as much as $30,000, or 20 percent of your income, whichever is less.

We recommend this paired strategy for people who want to set aside more than 13.043 percent of their earnings in a retirement plan but don't want to tie themselves to contributing a hefty percentage of their income year after year.

Employer-Sponsored Retirement Plans

These are plans created, and for the most part funded, by the company that employs you. As with Keoghs, employer-sponsored plans come in two flavors: defined-contribution plans and defined-benefit plans.

And, as with all retirement plans, any earnings that accumulate in employer-sponsored plans remain untaxed until you begin withdrawing funds at retirement.

Hybrid Plans

There are several retirement plans that combine some features of employer-sponsored plans with the IRA concept. For instance, 401(k) plans are a hybrid.

Your employer will create and administer a 401(k) plan and may contribute to it. Employees use 401(k) plans much as they do IRA's—as a place to stash a tax-deferred portion of their salary or wage income until they need to withdraw it, usually at retirement. (See Chapter 23 for more information on 401(k) plans.)

Another hybrid, the Simplified Employee Pension (SEP) plan, is quite similar to an IRA. An employer—rather than maintaining his own pension fund—makes contributions to the IRA's of his employees.

And the employer may deduct his contributions. Moreover,

you don't have to count your employer's contributions to your SEP as part of your income.

You may also make contributions to your own SEP—up to a cap of the lesser of $7,313 or 15 percent of your compensation.

Individuals who participate in union pension plans, called Section 501(c)(18) plans, may also make deductible contributions to these union plans—subject, however, to the same limitations that apply to 401(k)s. That is, no more than $7,313—or 25 percent of compensation—may be contributed by any one person during any one year to any single plan or combination of plans.

TIME TO WITHDRAW It's when you want to take money out of your retirement plan—no matter which type of plan you have—that the tax consequences become acute. How and when you withdraw the funds can make a big difference in how much tax you'll pay.

Whenever you begin to withdraw your funds, you really have just a few options. You may pull money out of your plan at retirement or before retirement. And you may pull it out in one lump sum or spread your withdrawals over time. Let's see how the tax law views each of these options.

First we'll consider withdrawal at retirement—both in lump-sum and in periodic payments. Then we'll look at the early withdrawal option.

One point some people may need to keep in mind regardless of how they decide to withdraw their funds is the potential penalty they may incur for excessive distribution.

Here's the general rule: If the total distribution you receive tops $150,000 in one year, you owe a 15 percent penalty. Special rules apply if the totally vested benefit in your retirement plan on August 1, 1986, was more than $562,500. If you fit into this category, see your tax adviser about the election which can be made in your 1988 return.

Also, the penalty is assessed separately if you get a lump-sum distribution. The penalty is imposed only on the amount that exceeds $750,000.

Tip: If you think your yearly retirement benefits will exceed the limit, you may want to take some distributions earlier. The best way to know: Run the numbers and consult your tax adviser.

Caution: This penalty applies whether you're over or under 59½. But the IRS will not assess the 10 percent early withdrawal penalty (see below) on the excess distribution.

LUMP-SUM WITHDRAWAL The obvious disadvantage to taking your accumulated savings out of a retirement plan in a single lump sum is that you incur a big tax liability in the year you do so. But the tax law allows you to mitigate that liability somewhat—except in the case of IRA's—by using a device called five-year averaging.

Five-year averaging can reduce the tax rate levied on lump-sum withdrawals. Here's why. Even though you pay your full tax in the year you receive your lump sum, you calculate the tax as if you received the money evenly over five years.

To figure your taxes on five-year averaging, first compute the tax on one fifth of the lump-sum distribution in the year that you're taking it. (You use the rates for single taxpayers—even if you're married—and don't take into account any other income.) Multiply that number by five. This figure is the total tax you'll owe. And the amount would be smaller than the tax you'd pay if you included the whole amount in your income in one year.

Be aware, though, that you may use five-year averaging just once, and not until you've reached age 59½.

Because the five-year averaging rules were enacted by Congress in 1986, the law still includes some special deals for individuals who were born on or before December 31, 1935. These folks have an additional option open to them in dealing with lump-sum distributions.

They may use five-year averaging. Or they may use ten-year averaging rules. If they take this latter course, however, they must apply the tax rates that were in effect in 1986.

If you fall into this age category, the only way to know which option is the better tax choice is to do both calculations and compare the results.

Anyone eligible to use ten-year averaging under this transition rule, however, must also be aware that if you use it on a lump-sum distribution you receive before you reach age 59½, you may not use the averaging device—either ten- or five-year averaging—ever again.

One last point: Uncle Sam may consider part of your distribution as a capital gain. If that's the case and you elect ten-year averaging, you may pay less tax. That's because the maximum 1986 capital gains rate of 20 percent was less than the highest 1986 ordinary rate of 50 percent. Our advice: If you find yourself in this situation, see your tax adviser *before* you withdraw your money.

PAYMENTS OVER TIME   Suppose you don't take your retirement plan benefits in a single lump. Your alternative is to withdraw the money in the form of an annuity—annual payments, the size of which depends upon your life expectancy or, in some cases, the life expectancy of you and your spouse. (The IRS uses its Standard Annuity Tables to determine life expectancy.)

The payments are taxable—unless, that is, you have made nondeductible contributions to the plan. If so—and this is true for many individuals—some part of each payment will be nontaxable. That part is based on the "exclusion ratio," and it reflects the proportion of nondeductible contributions you've made to the total value of your retirement plan.

You may only continue to exclude that portion of your regular benefit payments from taxable income, however, until you reach your actuarial life expectancy. At that point, as far as the law is concerned, you've pulled all your nondeductible contributions out of the plan. The payments that follow this statistical milestone will be fully taxable.

EARLY WITHDRAWALS   You may tap your retirement fund early, but you must comply with quite a number of restrictions to avoid paying expensive penalties on early withdrawals.

If, for instance, you leave a job before age 59½ and your employer requires you to take your pension benefits with you, you'll incur a 10 percent early withdrawal penalty unless you roll the account over into an IRA or other qualified retirement plan within 60 days.

You may also avoid the penalty if:

• You use the distribution to pay for deductible medical expenses.
• You receive the benefits (after separation from service) in the form of an annuity spread over your life or the joint lives of you and your beneficiary. (Payments must be substantially equal and made at least annually.)
• You retire after reaching age fifty-five but before age 59½. (No penalty applies if you meet your plan's requirements for early retirement.)
• You receive distributions from an Employee Stock Ownership Plan (ESOP) before January 1, 1990.

QUESTIONS AND ANSWERS

QUESTION: May I take out a loan from my retirement fund?

You may borrow from your retirement fund, if the plan so allows. But the loans may constitute a taxable distribution—and the early withdrawal penalty may apply if specific requirements are not met. For a rundown of the rules governing loans from retirement plans, see Chapter 23.

Q: Is there any point at which I must begin withdrawing funds from my retirement account?

No matter what kind of retirement plan you have and how you decide to take the money out, the law requires you to begin withdrawing your benefits not later than April 1 of the year following the year you reach the age of 70½.

One exception: Employees who reached age 70½ by January 1, 1988, may defer the distributions until they actually retire.

Failure to begin taking your benefits in time will subject you to a 50 percent penalty on the amount that's required to be distributed each year.

CHAPTER 22

Your Guide to IRA's

Individual Retirement Accounts (IRA's) were among the best retirement saving plans around. They were, that is, until Congress clipped some of their more generous features.

And now? Well, don't dismiss IRA's. They are still a useful part of many retirement portfolios. Just know their new limitations.

The greatest appeal of an IRA used to be that as long as you weren't more than age 70½, the contributions you made—up to the $2,000 annual limit—were fully tax deductible.

Today that's true for only two types of people: those who aren't eligible for an employer-sponsored retirement plan, and those whose incomes fall below specified levels.

If both you and your spouse aren't eligible for a company retirement plan, the rules governing your ability to make tax deductible contributions to an IRA weren't affected by the 1986 Tax Reform Act. Both of you are still free to write off IRA contributions equal to the lesser of your earned income or $2,000 a year—$2,250 if you have a spouse who doesn't work outside the home.

But if your company has a retirement plan and you're an active participant in it, you may lose some or all of the deductibility of your annual IRA contribution.

How? Let's take a look.

For people with company retirement plans the first test of IRA deductibility is income. If you're married and file jointly, you may still make a fully deductible IRA contribution as long as your joint adjusted gross income (AGI) is no greater than $40,000.

In this case AGI is your adjusted gross income before you claim a deduction for your IRA but *after* you've deducted any losses from investments. Also, your AGI includes any taxable Social Security benefits you receive.

If your joint AGI falls between $40,000 and $50,000, part of your contribution is still deductible. Couples with AGI's of $50,000 or more may not deduct IRA contributions at all.

Figuring the partial deduction is easy. Just subtract your joint AGI from the $50,000 cap. Then divide the result by $10,000. That answer is the fraction of the maximum IRA contribution that you may deduct. Confused? Here's an example.

Say your joint AGI is $42,000. Subtract that amount from $50,000 to get $8,000. Divide $8,000 by $10,000 to get 80 percent. This is the percentage of the IRA base—$2,000—that you may contribute to an IRA and deduct. So you may deduct $1,600. (See appendix 5.)

Of course, you're free to *contribute* the full $2,000. But don't count on pocketing a deduction for the extra $400.

The rules and the calculations for single people are just the same—except that the income limits are different. With an AGI below $25,000, a single person may deduct the entire IRA contribution. Over $35,000, none of it is deductible.

Between the two, there's a partial deduction.

A single person with a $30,000 AGI, for instance, may deduct half of his or her maximum IRA contribution (the $35,000 cap minus $30,000 of AGI equals $5,000, which, when divided by $10,000, comes to 50 percent).

Tip: If your income falls within the phase-out ranges, Uncle Sam allows you to deduct at least $200—even if your calculation indicates that your deductible contribution should be limited to $10.

WHAT HAPPENS WHEN YOU FILE SEPARATELY It doesn't matter that only one spouse participates in another retirement plan. If you file jointly, you're treated as if both of you do.

If you file separately, though, it's another story. In that case the spouse who is not covered by a qualified plan may contribute up to $2,000 to an IRA and deduct the contribution. (However, should Congress adopt legislation now before it, this loophole will be gone for 1988 and beyond. The rule will apply only if you live apart for the entire year.)

The other spouse who's covered by a qualified retirement plan, however, is subject to another strict set of requirements. His or her IRA deduction is phased out beginning with the first one dollar of AGI he or she reports. And when that spouse's AGI reaches $10,000, no deduction is allowed.

Say, for example, that you and your spouse file separate

returns. And you, but not your spouse, is covered by a retirement plan.

Your separate AGI adds up to $5,000, so you subtract $5,000 from $10,000 to get $5,000. Then you divide $5,000 by $10,000 to get 50 percent. Finally, you multiply 50 percent times the maximum IRA contribution of $2,000 to get the amount you may deduct—$1,000.

Whatever limit the rules place on the size of your or your spouse's annual deductible IRA contribution, you'll pay a penalty if you contribute too much—meaning more than $2,000 in any one year.

If you exceed your contribution limit, the IRS will demand that you pay an excise tax equal to 6 percent of the excess contribution. And, as we will see later, you also face a 10 percent penalty when you withdraw the money. You can avoid both these penalties if you withdraw your excess contribution before you file your tax return for the year.

HOW ACTIVE IS ACTIVE?   There's room for confusion about what the IRS means by being an active participant in a company-sponsored retirement plan. So let's clear the matter up.

As a general rule, the IRS considers you an active participant in a pension plan if the plan's rules say that you're covered—even if you decline to participate. So just being eligible for one of the following employer-provided retirement plans makes you an active participant:

* Qualified pension, profit-sharing, or stock bonus plans, including Keogh plans
* Qualified annuity plans
* Simplified employee pension plans (SEP's)
* Retirement plans for federal, state, or local government employees
* Certain union plans (so-called Section 501(c) (18) plans)
* Tax-sheltered annuities for public school teachers and other employees of charitable organizations

Say you meet the eligibility conditions under your employer's defined-benefit pension plan. But under the plan's rules you won't be credited with any contributions your employer makes on your behalf unless you contribute to the plan. Even if you don't make a contribution—and therefore aren't credited with benefits—you are considered an active participant.

Vesting—that is, becoming eligible to receive benefits—also has nothing to do with determining whether you're an active participant.

Say, for example, that your company offers a profit-sharing plan. You're an active participant once your employer contributes something to your account for the year. It makes no difference that you're not vested for, say, five years.

Uncle Sam also considers you an active participant if you participate in a retirement plan for just part of the year.

Suppose you change jobs in November 1988. You move from Old Company Inc. to New Corp. Tough luck, says New Corp. You're not eligible for our pension plan in 1989, your first year on the job. So, you say to yourself, "I'll just make a tax deductible IRA contribution that year."

Oh, no you won't. Old Company's pension plan doesn't end its tax year until January 31. You are eligible and therefore "active" in that plan for part of 1989. So the deductibility of your IRA contribution is limited for the whole year.

The point to take away from this example is simply that timing is an issue when it comes to determining the deductibility of your IRA contribution.

Tip: You calculate your AGI *after* you make your Keogh contributions. Say, for example, that you are self-employed and you and your spouse file a joint return. Your earnings from your business add up to $40,000, and the two of you report interest and dividend income of $5,000.

You contribute $8,000 to a Keogh account. Under the rules, you may make a fully deductible $2,000 IRA contribution because your joint AGI—$37,000 before you subtract your IRA contribution—is less than the $40,000 threshold amount.

FOR BETTER OR WORSE   You don't have to hold a job to have an IRA. Your nonworking spouse may start a so-called spousal IRA—as long as you file jointly and your nonworking spouse's earned income totals less than $250.

If you meet these two requirements, each of you may open and make contributions to an IRA. The limits? Together, collectively, you may contribute as much as $2,250 in any single year. No more than $2,000 of that amount, however, may go to either account.

How much you write off on your tax return depends on your circumstances. You're subject to the same rules on deductibility as other taxpayers.

So, how do you split up your contribution? The answer depends on your long-term objectives. If you want to keep your savings in an IRA as long as possible, make the greater contribution to the IRA of the younger spouse. If you want to get at your savings sooner, put it in the older spouse's account.

Of course, if neither of you is active in a company-sponsored plan and your spouse's income exceeds $250, you don't lose out. Your spouse just opens his or her own IRA and contributes as much as 100 percent of his or her income (up to $2,000) to it.

Tip: If you own your own business and your spouse helps out from time to time, consider paying him or her for services rendered.

Here's why. Your spouse may sock away all or part of his or her earnings in an IRA and claim a tax deduction for the contribution.

Let's say the year is 1988 and you pay your spouse $2,000 a year for bookkeeping services. She reports income from no other source.

The two of you file a joint return listing AGI of $30,000. The result: Each of you may make a tax deductible contribution to an IRA of up to $2,000.

Caution: Make sure you pay your spouse with a payroll check—the IRS may not consider a deposit in a joint bank account as an actual payment of wages. And be prepared to show that your spouse's employment is genuine.

You should also know that the 1987 tax law boosted the cost of this strategy. Now, wages paid to a spouse are subject to Social Security taxes of 15.02 percent for 1988—that is, 7.51 percent paid by the employee and 7.51 percent paid by the employer.

HOW MANY IRA'S?   If you're eligible, it doesn't matter how many IRA's you have—one or a dozen. Set up as many as you like. But you should know that many institutions charge an annual maintenance fee for each IRA. The fees can run as high as $50, which can get expensive if you open lots of accounts.

The effect of these fees is to reduce the net return on your investments. The fees are deductible, but only if you pay them from non-IRA funds and only to the extent that they and all your other miscellaneous itemized deductions top 2 percent of your AGI.

The rules also allow you to borrow money to make an IRA contribution. The only question: May you deduct the interest on the loan?

The answer depends on whether the interest is classified as personal interest or investment interest. And the rules aren't clear on this point.

Under the 1986 law you may deduct only 40 percent of your personal interest expenses in 1988 and 20 percent in 1989. You may deduct investment interest only from your investment income. (For more on the rules governing interest deductions, see Chapter 4.)

CHOOSING THE RIGHT ACCOUNT AND MANAGER

Who should manage your IRA, and what sort of investments should be in it? You may choose as the manager of your IRA the institution where you have an account—a bank, for instance, or a savings and loan or brokerage house. Or you may manage it yourself.

As to what investments belong in an IRA, almost any investment vehicle makes sense—with just a few exceptions.

What you obviously don't want in an IRA are tax-free investments—municipal bonds, for instance. The beauty of an IRA is that it allows you to defer taxes on an investment's earnings. If the earnings are already tax free, you lose. Here's how.

The income from tax-exempt bonds, say, is tax free—that is, it is not subject to federal taxation. The income from an IRA is tax deferred—that is, you pay tax on it when you withdraw it. If you use IRA dollars to invest in tax-exempt bonds, income from those bonds is paid to your IRA. And when the income is withdrawn, it is taxed. In effect, you've turned tax-free income into taxable income.

Among the IRA investments you should consider:

• Bank certificates of deposit (CD's) that pay market rates of interest. Deposits are insured up to $100,000 at most institutions.

• Money market mutual funds offered by brokerage houses and other financial institutions.

• Mutual funds of all types (except municipal bond funds).

• Stocks, including individual issues. You may, for example, open a self-directed IRA at a brokerage firm. You select the stocks you like and reinvest any dividends—thereby preserving the year-to-year tax-free feature of your IRA.

• Flexible-premium annuities offered by insurance companies (these are known as Individual Retirement Annuities).

About the only investments the law says you may not make with IRA dollars are those in art objects, antiques, stamps, and other collectibles. You also may not invest IRA dollars in gold or silver coins (except gold and silver Eagle coins minted by the U.S. Treasury).

Also, you may not use your IRA dollars for "self-dealing"— that is, you may not use IRA funds to purchase assets from yourself or from a company you own. For example, you couldn't use IRA dollars to purchase stock in a corporation you own.

What's more, you may not borrow from your IRA. Nor may you use your IRA as collateral for a loan. If you do use IRA dollars in any of these forbidden ways, the IRS treats the amount you invested as if you had withdrawn it from your account.

What happens then? You pay tax at your normal rate on that amount of income, and if you're younger than 59½, you pay a 10 percent early withdrawal penalty too.

Whichever investments you choose for your IRA, you're no more stuck with them than you are with non-IRA investment choices. As far as the IRS is concerned, you may buy and sell stocks and mutual funds, switch to CD's, or move into the money market as often as you see fit.

The institutions with which you place your IRA, however, may put the brakes on some of this activity. For instance, a bank may penalize you by an amount equal to three months of interest if you withdraw funds early from a certificate of deposit.

You may roll over your IRA from one institution to another without penalty just once each 365 days. So if you roll over only part of the balance in your IRA, you are not allowed to roll over the remainder until 365 days later. But this limitation need not inhibit you if you have your IRA at an institution that offers a variety of investment vehicles. You may switch among these vehicles as often as you choose.

Say you maintain your IRA at a brokerage firm. You may, for instance, switch from stocks to mutual funds to bonds and back again without penalty. You do, of course, pile up commission fees and other transaction costs.

Tip: Here's a way around the once-every-365-days limit on rollovers. Switch your funds via a "trustee-to-trustee" transfer.

You authorize the trustee of the institution that now holds your IRA dollars to transfer these funds directly to the trustee of another institution. Since you never touch the money—it goes from one institution to another—it isn't technically a rollover. And it isn't subject to the once-every-365-days limit.

Tip: Uncle Sam says that your IRA may not loan you money. But here's a way to borrow from your IRA using the rollover rules.

As we've seen, the law says that you may roll over IRA money once every 365 days. And the money isn't taxable to you unless you hold the funds for more than 60 days. The result: You may withdraw your IRA dollars, use the money for up to 60 days, then roll it over into another IRA—all without any tax consequences.

Note: In the eyes of Uncle Sam, IRA's you maintain at several institutions are considered separate accounts. What does it matter?

Say you maintain two IRA accounts, one at a bank, the other at a brokerage firm. On October 1, 1988, you roll over the money from the bank to a mutual fund company.

Delighted with the mutual fund's performance, you decide— four months later—to roll over the money from the brokerage firm to the mutual fund company.

Breathe easy. You can do it without penalty. The reason: The 365-day rule applies separately to each account.

SHOULD YOU MAKE A NONDEDUCTIBLE CONTRIBUTION?
If you're not eligible, for whatever reason, to make deductible contributions to an IRA, should you make any at all? It's not an easy question to answer—even though the pros and cons of this decision are relatively straightforward.

The pros?

The most obvious is that even though you may not deduct your annual IRA contribution, the earnings from your IRA investments accumulate and compound tax free. That means they build up faster than if you were paying tax on them every year.

And the cons?

Once you put money into an IRA, it's locked in until you reach age 59½—unless you're willing to pay a 10 percent penalty for early withdrawal.

Of course, if you're almost that age already, early withdrawal probably won't be a problem. Go ahead and contribute to your IRA.

Some people feel that investing in tax-free bonds is a reasonable alternative to making a nondeductible IRA contribution. And they have a point.

The earnings from these bonds are tax free. And you don't have to pay a penalty if you want to get at your money. Moreover, you're not limited to investing $2,000—or $2,250 for you and your nonworking spouse. But the bonds come with two potential drawbacks.

You can get locked into the bonds. If interest rates rise and the value of your bonds falls, you'd have to take a loss to sell. So you're stuck with the bonds until rates fall again.

The other potential problem with tax-free bonds is that, depending on the market, their yields are sometimes low compared to the after-tax yields of other securities. So they can be a poor investment.

Should you or shouldn't you make a nondeductible IRA contribution? It depends on your age and the financial markets.

But remember this: The option is time-limited.

After the deadline passes for making this year's contribution—deductible or not—there's no changing your mind. Once missed, the opportunity is gone forever.

TAKING IT OUT   You may take your money out of an IRA at any time.

But if you don't want to pay a penalty equal to 10 percent of the amount withdrawn that is taxable, you must wait until you reach the legal age of 59½. (Disabled individuals may make penalty-free withdrawals at any age.)

We talk about early withdrawals shortly, but first let's cover the normal route. Say you're older than 59½ and you want some or all of your IRA money.

How do you get at it? And does it matter?

Yes, it certainly does.

In general, there are two ways to withdraw money from any retirement fund. You may take it out bit by bit, as you need it, over a period of years. Or you may withdraw it in one lump sum. There are perfectly good reasons why you might choose either option.

Maybe you just need a little money every year to augment your Social Security and company-paid retirement income. So gradual withdrawal makes sense for you. Or maybe you need a large sum of cash to pay off the mortgage on your house. You want your IRA money all at once.

Hold on, though, because the lump-sum alternative triggers an unfortunate tax consequence.

IRA's are different from all other tax-deferred retirement plans in one important respect. As a general rule, with other plans, you may, for tax purposes, spread a lump-sum withdrawal after age 59½ over five years. You get the money all at once. But, even though you pay the tax all in one year, you're taxed as if you had spread the withdrawal over a five-year period.

Not so with IRA's. Your lump-sum withdrawal is taxed at ordinary income rates in the year you make the withdrawal. This rule isn't a bar to lump-sum withdrawals, of course. But it is a consideration you ought to keep in mind before deciding to empty your IRA in a single shot.

However you decide to withdraw IRA funds, you're going to owe some tax. Remember, at least some of the money you contributed to the IRA over the years was untaxed income, and all the earnings from your IRA investments have been accumulating tax free.

Now it's time to pay the piper. The principle that governs your tax liability at this point is simple enough: If the money you're withdrawing was taxed once, it isn't taxed again. The way you apply this principle in figuring your taxes is pretty simple too.

Let's say that you've had an IRA for ten years. Now you want to begin withdrawing from it. For the first eight years you made tax-deductible contributions, $2,000 each year. Your total deductible contributions: $16,000.

During the last two years you also contributed $2,000 annually, but those were nondeductible contributions. Your total nondeductible contributions: $4,000. And, you are pleased to learn, your savvy investment decisions have resulted in accumulated IRA earnings of $10,000.

So, all together you've got $30,000 in your account.

What if you make a lump-sum withdrawal? Easy. You owe tax on the $16,000 in deductible contributions and on the $10,000 in accumulated earnings, but not on the $4,000 in nondeductible contributions. You're taxed on $26,000 of your $30,000 withdrawal.

But what if you want to withdraw just part of it—say, $4,000 in the first year? May you withdraw just the $4,000 that represents the nondeductible contributions you made and thereby escape paying income tax? No, you may not. Any withdrawal you make is taxable in the same proportion as the tax-deferred portion of your IRA bears to the total.

In this case, $26,000 of the $30,000 in your IRA—or 87 percent—has been contributed or has accumulated tax free. So 87 percent of any withdrawal you make that first year will be subject to tax. (Of course, this proportion will change slightly from year to year as earnings continue to accumulate tax free in your IRA while you make periodic withdrawals.)

The same rule of proportion applies even if you have several separate IRA's—some with mostly deductible contributions and others with nondeductible contributions. For purposes of computing the taxable proportion of any withdrawal you make, the IRS considers them all one.

Tip: Remember, once you reach age 59½—but before you reach age 70½—you may withdraw your IRA dollars any time you choose and in any amount without penalty. Plan accordingly.

Another point: If you take an extremely large distribution from your IRA, you may be subject to a 15 percent excise tax on excess distributions. (See Chapter 21 for more on this topic.)

As we've seen, if you want your IRA money before you reach age 59½ and you're not disabled, you will pay a penalty—10 percent of the untaxed funds you withdraw. The same rule of proportion applies here as applied in the example above.

If, say, 80 percent of the money in your IRA consists of deductible contributions and accumulated earnings, you pay a 10 percent penalty as well as regular income tax on 80 percent of any early withdrawal you make. But you can avoid the penalty. Just take your distribution in the form of lifetime annual payments.

The law demands that these payments be of approximately equal amounts. Also, the payments must be based on your life expectancy or joint lives or life expectancies of you and your beneficiaries—as determined by IRS tables.

Say, for instance, that you're fifty with a life expectancy of thirty-three years, according to the IRS tables. Your IRA contains $50,000. You may take annual distributions of $4,340 (assuming an 8 percent interest rate) from the account without incurring a penalty.

Just as it discourages early withdrawals, the law also takes a dim view of late IRA withdrawals. The law requires you to begin pulling your accumulated IRA funds out before April 1 of the year following the year you reach age 70½.

Exactly how much you must withdraw depends on your life expectancy or, if you choose, the joint life expectancies of you and your beneficiaries.

If you don't withdraw the required amount, the law says, you start paying a hefty penalty. It equals 50 percent of the difference between the amount you withdrew and the amount you were required to withdraw. Here's an example.

Say you're age 71½. Based on your life expectancy, you must withdraw a minimum of $6,000 a year from your IRA. But in 1988 you make a mistake. You withdraw only $3,000.

What are the tax consequences?

You pay a penalty that equals 50 percent of the difference between the amount you withdrew—$3,000—and the amount you were required to withdraw—$6,000. In this case you fork over $1,500—that is, 50 percent times $3,000.

To get the maximum deferral from your IRA, consider naming your child or another younger person as beneficiary. That way your joint life expectancy will be quite long. And the amount you'll have to take out of your IRA account will be much less than it would be otherwise.

As should be clear by now, the rules on IRA's are more stringent. But these plans still offer a good opportunity for many people to squirrel away funds for retirement.

If you're young—in your twenties, for example—you shouldn't underestimate the long-term value of tax-deferred earnings on an annual contribution of $2,000. So consider making nondeductible contributions to an IRA. (However, if your employer offers a 401(k) plan, contributions to it are a much better deal. See Chapter 23 for information on these plans.)

Whether an IRA—even a nondeductible one—still makes sense for you, depends, of course, on your own circumstances.

The key point: Take your personal situation into account. Lay out all the pros and cons each and every year before making your decision.

QUESTIONS AND ANSWERS

QUESTION: What's the deadline for making a contribution to an IRA?

For 1988 you may contribute to an IRA any time after January 1, 1988, but no later than April 15, 1989—the due date of your annual tax return.

Q: I've heard that there's a new form people who make nondeductible IRA contributions must fill out. Is my information correct?

If you do make nondeductible IRA contributions, you must report the amount on Form 8606. Uncle Sam will use this form to keep track of the nontaxable part of an IRA.

Q: I think individual tax rates are going up. So should I withdraw some or all of my IRA dollars now?

The answer depends on two factors—how high you think income tax rates will go and your personal tax situation.

Say, for example, that you're under age 59½. You're in the top 33 percent tax bracket, and you withdraw $10,000 from your IRA.

On that amount, you pay ordinary income taxes of $3,300—33 percent times $10,000—plus a 10 percent penalty of $1,000 (10 percent times $10,000). Your total tax bill adds up to a hefty $4,300, or 43 percent of the amount you withdrew from your IRA.

If you think tax rates will rise above 43 percent, you may want to withdraw your money now. If not, you'll probably want to wait to take your dollars out.

But there's another reason not to withdraw your money from an IRA before you reach age 59½. Interest and earnings on money deposited in an IRA accumulate tax deferred. That's not true of dollars invested outside of tax-favored vehicles.

Tip: It's always a good idea to consult your tax adviser *before* you withdraw money from an IRA—or, for that matter, any other tax-favored retirement plan.

CHAPTER 23

Why a 401(k) Plan May Be Right for You

It's true that the name 401(k) doesn't tell you much. It refers to the part of the tax code that describes these attractive retirement plans. But don't let a name put you off. Taking advantage of an employer-sponsored 401(k) is easy—and the benefits are substantial.

Substantial benefits? Yes, two of them, actually.

First, the money contributed to a 401(k) and the earnings that accumulate in it are tax deferred. That means your savings grow more rapidly than they would otherwise.

How much faster?

Well, compare two investment plans, one tax deferred and one not. With both plans, you invest in the same mutual fund each year for twenty years. The fund earns 10 percent a year, and you reinvest these earnings, less any taxes due, in the account. Your marginal tax rate is 28 percent.

In order to compare apples to apples, let's say that in the taxable fund you invest $7,313 (the maximum the law allows in 1988 for tax deferred plans) from your salary—less the $2,048 you owe Uncle Sam in taxes—or $5,265 each year. At the end of twenty years this taxable fund has grown to more than $236,000. Not bad, you say, and you're right.

But the tax deferred fund is larger still—more than $460,000— for two reasons. You have been able to invest a full $7,313, since money earmarked for a 401(k) isn't taxed currently, and you haven't had to pay federal income tax on the earnings as they accumulated.

Tax deferred, of course, doesn't mean tax free.

It only means that you don't pay taxes on the money contributed to a 401(k) or the earnings that pile up until you withdraw the funds.

Let's go back to our example. The true value of the tax deferred fund isn't $460,000 but $331,000—that is, $460,000 minus the $129,000 in income taxes you pay when you withdraw the money. Still, you come out nearly $95,000 ahead in your tax deferred 401(k) fund.

But we said there were two substantial benefits to a 401(k). The second: The law allows your employer to help you build your 401(k) retirement fund. Many employers, in fact, contribute to employee's 401(k)s—up to a certain limit. It's almost like giving yourself a raise.

No doubt about it. A 401(k) retirement plan is an attractive arrangement. But, as you might expect, Congress has established limits to keep it from becoming too attractive.

So, to get the most out of your 401(k), you need to know the rules. There aren't many—at least when it comes to joining a plan.

If your company sponsors a 401(k) plan, signing up is simple. You authorize your employer to create an account for you and regularly deduct an amount from your pay.

Let's say your salary adds up to $50,000 in 1989. You instruct your employer to subtract $400 a month from your pay and deposit it in a 401(k) plan.

When you get your W-2 form for the year, it won't show your entire $50,000 salary. Instead, it will report that you were paid $45,200—$50,000 less the $4,800 deducted for your 401(k). The $4,800 is treated as "deferred compensation" and isn't reported as current income to you.

Caution: Although you don't currently have to pay federal income tax on the money that you contribute to your company-sponsored 401(k), this amount is still subject to federal Social Security (FICA) tax in the year that you earn it.

WITHIN LIMITS   Not surprisingly, there are limits to the amount of money you and your employer may contribute annually to a 401(k) plan. But these limits seem rather generous when compared, for instance, to the $2,000 cap on IRA contributions.

The government sets two limits on 401(k)s.

One caps the amount that you may contribute to your own retirement plan. The other restricts the amount that you and your employer together may contribute. The federal government adjusts both of these figures annually for inflation.

If you play your cards right, you can ensure that your plan receives the maximum total contribution while minimizing your personal 401(k) expense.

In 1988 the maximum amount an employee may salt away annually—tax deferred—in a 401(k) is $7,313—$9,500 in the case of a tax-sheltered annuity.

What, you ask, is a tax-sheltered annuity?

It is a kind of tax deferred account for teachers, church workers, and employees of other nonprofit groups or institutions. It is usually sold by life insurance companies in the form of a contract that guarantees a payment to you at some future date, usually at retirement.

The second ceiling limits the amount that you and your employer together may contribute to a 401(k) and all other defined-contribution plans (see Chapter 21). In 1988 the ceiling is $30,000 or 25 percent of your after-contribution salary, whichever is less.

Say, for instance, that your salary comes to $100,000 in 1988 and you contribute $7,313 to a 401(k). How much may your employer contribute?

Calculate 25 percent of your after-contribution salary. That amount adds up to $23,172 ($100,000 minus $7,313, then the result—$92,687—times 25 percent).

Since $23,172 is less than $30,000, that is the most that you and your employer together may contribute to all your defined-contribution retirement plans.

You've already put away $7,313, so your employer's maximum contribution is not $22,687—that is, the $30,000 ceiling minus your $7,313 contribution—but just $15,859 ($23,172 minus $7,313).

So maybe you would be better off reducing your own contribution? First, let's assume that your employer does not use a matching formula to tie his contribution to the amount you pay in. Instead, he contributes a certain percent of your compensation.

Now, in the above example, if you were to reduce your contribution from $7,313 to $5,000, your after-contribution salary would total $95,000 ($100,000 minus $5,000).

And 25 percent of that amount comes to $23,750.

By reducing your contribution, you have raised the maximum ceiling on the total retirement contribution for the year by $578 (the difference between $23,750 and $23,172). And you have also allowed your employer to increase his contribution.

The company may now chip in as much as $18,750 ($23,750 minus your $5,000 contribution). Less sometimes can be more.

TAKING IT OUT   Two sets of rules govern withdrawals from 401(k)s. One set is imposed by the federal government, the other by your employer. And you must abide by both when you make a withdrawal.

You should know that the rules imposed by your employer may never be more generous than those outlined by Uncle Sam—but your employer's rules may be *less* generous. So familiarize yourself with the provisions of your employer's 401(k).

The IRS rules governing access to funds in a 401(k) plan are similar to the restrictions that apply to other retirement plans.

You may receive your money, without penalty, when:

- You reach age 59½, regardless of whether you're working or not
- You reach age fifty-five or older and retire early
- You die or become disabled

If, at any of these times, you choose to make your withdrawal in a lump sum, you can reduce your taxes if the withdrawal is eligible for five-year averaging. (We explained the tax consequences of lump-sum withdrawals in Chapter 21.)

Remember, too, that you may take your money out with no penalty to pay medical expenses that would ordinarily be deductible. (See Chapter 6 for more information on writing off medical expenses.) And, after you leave your job, you may receive your money in the form of an annuity—that is, periodic payments over your lifetime.

As for financial hardship, you may withdraw your money from your 401(k) if your employer's plan allows—but you still pay taxes and a 10 percent penalty.

And your company may distribute the cash in the plan to you when your employment ends—even if you haven't yet reached age 59½.

In this case, Uncle Sam gives you just 60 days to roll the 401(k) funds over into an IRA or another approved retirement plan. Any amount that you don't roll over is taxed as ordinary income—and you pay a 10 percent penalty to boot if you're younger than age 59½.

If your employer's plan allows, you may withdraw your money from a 401(k) in the form of a loan. (That's generally not the case with other retirement plans, such as IRA's.)

But borrowing from your 401(k) plan, while possible, has restrictions attached to it. The law limits loans to the lesser of:

$50,000, or the greater of $10,000, or one half of your vested 401(k) account balance. And the $50,000 limit is reduced by the excess, if any, of:

• The highest outstanding loan balance during the one-year period before the date of the new or extended loan, over
• The outstanding loan balance on the date the loan is made

Confused? Here's an example. On January 1, 1988, your outstanding loans from your 401(k) plan total $40,000. Seven months pass, and on August 1 you want to borrow more money. Since you paid back $15,000, your loan balance for outstanding loans is now $25,000.

How much more may you borrow? You may take out $10,000 —that is, $50,000 minus the outstanding current balance of your existing loan ($25,000), minus the difference between the highest outstanding loan balance during the previous year ($40,000) and the outstanding balance of your existing loan ($25,000), or $15,000. And it makes no difference if you pay off the $40,000 balance by August 1.

Stated more simply, you may take out $10,000—that is, $50,000 minus the highest amount outstanding during the prior year ($40,000).

Also, you must repay the loan within five years, unless you use the money to buy a principal residence. In that case, you may take as long as your plan allows—usually 15, 20, 25, or 30 years, the terms of typical mortgages.

Moreover, the law requires that you repay your loan in equal payments, which you make at least quarterly over the term of the loan. The interest you pay on the loan must be "reasonable"— which is to say that it may not be too low or too high.

But whatever it is, you may not deduct it, even if the deduction would otherwise be allowed—as mortgage interest, for instance. The reason for this rule: The legislators figured you shouldn't be able to deduct interest that you are, in effect, paying to yourself.

You do get a break, though, if you took out a loan from your 401(k) plan before 1987. In this case, Uncle Sam allows you to deduct your interest under the interest rules. For example, interest on a loan used to buy stock is classified as investment interest (see Chapter 4).

But if you took out a loan after 1986, you're out of luck. The interest isn't deductible—no matter how you used the money.

And here's more bad news: When it comes time to cash out of your 401(k), you're taxed on the amount of interest that you paid in. It's treated in the same way as any other interest or dividends that accumulate on the amounts you've contributed.

Caution: If you leave your current job with a 401(k) loan outstanding, you usually have to repay it immediately or the IRS will treat the loan as a distribution.

In which case you'll pay taxes.

You'll also pay the early-distribution penalty, unless you're one of the exceptions to the rule—if you're age 59½, for example.

HAPPILY EVER AFTER It may seem that 401(k)s are hemmed in by a lot of rules and restrictions. But, as we've seen, they actually carry fewer restrictions than many other retirement plans.

In fact, a 401(k) is one government-created retirement plan that has few drawbacks. So if your company offers one, accept with pleasure.

QUESTIONS AND ANSWERS

QUESTION: Where should I invest my 401(k) funds?

You really don't have much choice about where to invest your 401(k) plan dollars. Unlike an IRA—where you have control of how your funds are invested—you must choose from among the options your employer offers for your 401(k) plan.

Some 401(k) plans limit you to a single investment option. Others let you split your account among two or more choices.

Q: Does my participation in a 401(k) plan affect the level of other benefits I might receive?

You'll want to check with your employer to find out.

Why? The value of some benefits—life insurance, for instance, and contributions to profit-sharing plans—is often tied to your total earnings. And what you get in these other benefits may vary depending on how the company tallies up your compensation.

The key point is this: Does the company reduce your compensation by the amount you've contributed to your 401(k)? Or does it add that amount back to your pay before calculating the value of your other benefits? Employers aren't required to do the latter.

Ask your company about what procedure it follows.

CHAPTER 24

Stock Options as Employee Incentives

It would be hard to imagine better aids to employee recruitment and retention than stock options and stock appreciation rights.

Both let employees share in the success of their employer. And, from the company's perspective, both boost employees' incentive to work for that success.

Some companies restrict options to top executives. Others spread this benefit down the line. Often, options are a negotiable part of a total compensation package.

You can use stock options and stock appreciation rights to your best advantage if you understand the tax rules that govern them. These rules aren't difficult, and they do provide lots of flexibility, which means you have choices to make. This chapter helps you make those choices.

HOW OPTIONS WORK When your employer grants you a stock option, you're gaining the right to buy a specific number of shares of your company's stock at a specific price within a specific period of time. You don't have to buy, but you may—at your option, so to speak.

Of course, like any other investor, you are free to buy your company's stock through a broker. The beauty of option stock, which you purchase through your company, lies in the price you pay.

Say, for instance, that for your outstanding performance last year the boss gave you a bonus—an option on 2,000 shares of company stock. The "option price"—the price you pay for the stock if you exercise the option—is $12 a share, the fair market value of the stock when your option is granted.

Now, a year later, the market price of the stock has soared to

$20 a share. You decide to exercise the options. When you do, you pay $24,000—that is, $12 times 2,000 shares—for stock that's currently worth $40,000. Not a bad deal.

But it's an even better deal if your options are incentive stock options (ISO's). As it happens, options come in two varieties— ISO's and nonqualified stock options (NQO's). The difference lies mainly in the tax benefits that ISO's enjoy.

There's no tax due on an incentive stock option until you eventually sell or exchange the stock, and then only if you sell or exchange it at a profit.

With NQO's, on the other hand, there's an intermediate tax bite when you exercise the option, as well as the tax you pay when you sell the stock at a profit.

Let's return to our example.

If your boss had granted you nonqualified options instead of ISO's, you would have incurred a tax liability when you exercised them. The IRS taxes you on the difference between the option price, $12, and the market price, $20, at the time you exercise the option.

If you're able to sell the stock, say, a year later for $30 a share, you're taxed again—this time as capital gains on the difference between $20 and $30.

With an ISO you're taxed just once—when you finally sell the stock for $30 a share. But with an ISO the entire amount of your gain—that is, the difference between the $30 a share you receive at the sale and the $12 a share option price that you originally paid—is taxed as a capital gain. (For more information on capital gains, see Chapter 13.)

You can see the advantage of the ISO. You pay no tax until you actually realize a gain when you sell or exchange your stock.

With the NQO, on the other hand, you pay tax on your paper profit when you exercise the option. That means that you not only must have cash to buy the stock when you exercise an NQO, you also need money to pay Uncle Sam. There is one plus, though. You increase your basis in the stock—that is, the stock's cost to you—by the amount of your reported gain.

Beware, though: The bargain element—the difference between the price at which you buy your stock and the fair market value—on the exercise of ISO's is a preference item when you compute your alternative minimum tax (AMT).

So, timing is an issue. You may not want to exercise an ISO if it will throw you into an AMT situation. (See Chapter 20 for the details about the AMT.)

Which is the better deal? ISO's? NQO's?

It depends, of course. You may be better off from a tax perspective with ISO's. But ISO's do come with a set of rules that can make them less desirable for other reasons.

These rules are what define an ISO. If a stock option doesn't conform, it is, by definition, an NQO. Even if an option qualifies as an ISO, you may be able to treat it as an NQO if its terms give you that option. So, let's take a look at these rules and the restrictions they impose.

Employee Status

From the day you receive the ISO until three months before you exercise it, you must be employed by the company (or a related company) granting it.

So, if your employer's plan allows it, you may actually leave your company, exercise the option within three months after your departure, and still obtain the favorable tax benefits.

If, however, you leave a company due to permanent and total disability, you have up to one year to exercise your ISO's. Sick leave or any other company-approved leave doesn't count, however.

If you die, your options go to your beneficiaries, who may, in turn, exercise them.

Option Period

You must exercise your ISO within ten years of the date it is granted—unless you own more than 10 percent of your company's stock. In that case, the option period may not top five years.

Another rule: The company must grant ISO's within ten years of the date the shareholders formally approve the stock option plan or the plan is adopted, whichever is earlier.

Fair Market Price

The rules say that the option price must not be less than the fair market price of the stock on the date the option is granted.

But a special rule applies to individuals who own more than 10 percent of a corporation's stock. In their case only, the option price must be equal to at least 110 percent of the fair market value of the stock on the date the ISO is granted.

$100,000 Ceiling

Of all the ISO's you are granted after 1986, no more than $100,000 worth (valued at the time they're granted) may become exercisable for the first time in any single year.

If you violate this rule, the first $100,000 of options still qualifies as ISO's. But the remainder falls into the category of NQO's.

You calculate the first $100,000 of options that qualifies for ISO treatment by adding together your options in the order you receive them. Here's an example.

Say your company grants you two options that are first exercisable in 1988. You receive the first—to purchase 6,000 shares at $10 a share, or $60,000—on January 15. You receive the second—to purchase 7,000 shares at $10 a share, or $70,000—on July 15.

The first option—of $60,000—qualifies as an ISO. So does $40,000 of the second option. The remainder of the second option ($70,000 minus $40,000, or $30,000) falls into the category of an NQO.

Understand, however, that this limit is not on the value of stock options your employer may grant you. If the company thinks you're that valuable, it may grant you any amount in options. Rather, the limit is on the value of the stock options that are first exercisable by you in any year. (You determine the value of the option by multiplying the number of shares in the option by the fair market value of the stock at the time the option is granted, which in most cases is the option price.)

Say, for instance, that your employer grants you $300,000 worth of options in 1988. The entire amount would qualify as ISO's—as long as the terms of the grant stated that you couldn't exercise more than $100,000 in 1988, and the second and third $100,000 in 1989 and 1990, respectively.

You don't have to exercise them, or you could wait and exercise all three in 1990. But you couldn't be allowed to first exercise more than $100,000 in any one year.

If, however, your employer grants you $150,000 worth of options in 1988, all of which can be exercised in the same year, the corporation should be instructed at the exercise date to issue you a separate stock certificate and identify the certificates as an ISO exercise in the stock transfer records for $100,000 of the stock.

Otherwise, each share of stock will be treated as two thirds acquired by ISO and one third acquired by the exercise of an NQO. The separate designation will provide you with greater flexibility in recognizing income in future years.

Order of Exercise

You must exercise ISO's granted to you in 1986 and earlier in the order in which they were granted. But you may exercise ISO's granted in 1987 and later in any order you choose.

Let's say you hold an option to purchase 2,000 shares of stock at $15 a share, another to buy 1,000 at $10 a share, and still another to purchase 5,000 at $5 each. You received the $15-per-share option in 1985, the $10-per-share option in 1986, and the $5-per-share option in 1987.

You may exercise the post-1986 option—the $5-per-share option issued in 1987—before the other two.

But you must exercise options issued before 1987 in the order in which they were granted. So you must exercise the option you were granted in 1985 before you exercise the 1986 option.

Capital Gains

This rule is less important since the 1986 Tax Reform Act eliminated preferential tax rates on long-term gains. But the law says you must still keep track of long-term and short-term gains and losses.

You may claim long-term tax treatment of gains from the sale of stock bought with ISO's only if you hold the shares for the later of:

- More than two years from the date the option was granted, or
- More than one year from the date you exercised it

Otherwise, your gain—the difference between the option price and the amount you collected when you sold your stock—is taxed as ordinary income.

Say you receive an option on July 3, 1988. You exercise the shares six months later—on January 3, 1989. Under the law, in order to have your gain considered long-term, you must hold the shares until after July 3, 1990—that is, two years after the option was granted to you.

Transferability

Only you and your heirs may exercise ISO's, which means that you may not contribute your options to an IRA or other retirement plan. (The IRS doesn't want you deferring gains on options even longer than the options themselves permit.)

No one else—not even your spouse—may exercise your ISO's during your lifetime, and you may not assign options in a divorce settlement. It's not surprising, therefore, that options are often an issue during separation or divorce negotiations.

Both sides must devise a formula to compensate for the fact that much of your wealth may consist of nontransferable stock options.

This rule also means that you may not sell your right to exercise an option or use the right as collateral for a loan.

With all the restrictions that apply to them, why might you still prefer ISO's to NQO's? Tax deferral is perhaps the best reason.

As we pointed out earlier, you report no gain for regular tax purposes until you sell or exchange your ISO stock. This fact and another feature available in many plans—that you may use company stock you already own to pay for the exercise of an ISO—allow you to use a powerful tax strategy.

Say that you join a young company whose shares are selling for $2. At the time you join, you buy 1,000 shares of stock and receive ISO's for 5,000 shares at $2 a share. In five years the stock price hits $10, and you decide to exercise your option.

You do so by paying with the 1,000 shares you bought earlier. Now you own 5,000 shares worth $50,000 at the current market price, but your investment cost was just the $2,000 you paid for that initial stock. And this transaction is tax free until you sell the option shares.

Now, let's say that you use this same strategy, but instead of paying with shares you bought, you pay with shares acquired under an ISO. The same rules apply—but only if you've held the stock for the longer of two years after you were granted your ISO's or one year after exercise.

Otherwise, the shares you exchange no longer qualify as ISO's. You have made a so-called disqualifying disposition—that is, you've disposed of ISO stock before meeting the holding period requirement. So you must pay tax on your profit—that is, the appreciation—at ordinary income rates when they're exchanged.

Another benefit of ISO's: The capital gains income they yield is sometimes useful. For instance, you may need capital gains to offset capital losses. Without the capital gain from an ISO sale, you could claim only a maximum of $3,000 in losses against ordinary income.

NQO's, however, have their place. With NQO's you don't have to worry about the alternative minimum tax. Nor do you have to worry about limits on when you can exercise your options or sell the stock you've acquired.

STOCK APPRECIATION RIGHTS   At the beginning of the chapter we mentioned stock appreciation rights—SAR's for short.

With SAR's you never actually buy your company's stock. But you still profit from the stock's appreciation.

Let's say your company gives you a one-year SAR on 5,000 shares of stock when the market price is $2 a share. A year later the stock price has risen to $3.

You could get a check for $5,000 (less any withholding tax, of course). Or your company could give you $2,000 (again, less any income tax withholding) plus 1,000 shares of stock valued at $3 a share. At any rate, your total compensation comes to $5,000.

The gain is taxed at ordinary rates—just like the gain on a nonqualified stock option. But unlike the option, you never have to put up any cash of your own with an SAR.

ASK FIRST Options and SAR's can be remarkably profitable for employees. So be sure to check out their availability when you take on a new position.

QUESTIONS AND ANSWERS

Question: I'm a corporate insider. Any tips for me?

If you're a corporate "insider"—an officer or a director of a public company—take heed. You must conform to special requirements regarding ISO's and NQO's. Among these requirements is the so-called six-month rule. Here's an example to illustrate how this rule works.

Say you're the president of a company. You sell company stock at a gain within either six months before or after exercising your option. Under the six-month rule, you may have to forfeit to your company your entire profit on that sale.

Insider regulations are quite strict and complicated. You need to choose carefully when you exercise and when you sell your options.

As we've seen, the rules restrict when you may sell your stock. And because they do, you may postpone recognizing your paper gain from the exercise of an NQO until the end of the six-month period. (In this case, your holding period begins when you recognize the ordinary income.) However, if you prefer to report the income at the time of exercise, you may elect to do so.

Our advice: If you're an insider, ask your tax adviser or attorney to help you evaluate your personal situation. Enlist his or her help as soon as you get an option. That way, you won't unknowingly violate these rules and jeopardize your gain.

CHAPTER 25

What You Need to Know about Your Children's Taxes

Children may once have brought joy and tax shelter to your happy home. Now, by and large, you have to settle for the joy. Since tax reform, more children than ever before will file tax returns. And the youngest of these youngsters will probably pay taxes at a higher rate too.

In this chapter we cover when and how children file. We also show you how the new rules on children's taxes may change your own tax strategies as a parent. And we tell you how the rules governing trusts have changed.

Let's begin with who has to file. Keep in mind that the key point here is not how old your children are but how much they make.

FILING REQUIREMENTS AREN'T AS EASY AS ABC

The limits on filing are far from straightforward. They say that dependent children with unearned incomes greater than $500, or with gross incomes greater than the standard deduction, must file returns.

The standard deduction? That's the tricky part. It is the greater of $500 or the amount of a child's earned income—up to a limit of $3,000 in 1988. In subsequent years the limit will be adjusted for inflation.

As a consequence, a child with modest unearned income and less than $3,000 in gross income may still have to file a tax return.

Consider this example. Assume that Molly reports unearned income—from interest and dividends—of only $400 in 1988. That's less than the $500 filing limit.

But she also earns $1,000 working at a summer job. Her standard deduction, then, is limited to the amount of her earned income—$1,000. But her gross income is $1,400—higher than her standard deduction. Molly has to file. And she must also pay tax on $400 of her income.

When you—or your tax adviser—calculate Molly's tax liability, you subtract the standard deduction, which in her case equals her earned income of $1,000. The remainder is the amount subject to tax.

In past years Molly would have claimed a personal exemption for herself and reduced her taxable income. But not since 1987.

The rules changed then, and now Molly, a dependent of her parents, may not use the personal exemption, $1,950 in 1988, to reduce her taxable income. Only Molly's parents may claim her and take the personal exemption.

Since Molly's parents are entitled to claim her as a dependent, Molly may not claim herself. There's no option here. If the parent may claim the child's personal exemption, the child may not. (For more information on the personal exemption, see Chapter 2.)

One additional point. Congress is considering a proposal that would allow parents to report the unearned income of a child under age 14 on their return. If parents go this route, the child wouldn't have to file a return. The provision would apply only to a child with income of less than $5,000 which consists entirely of specified types of unearned income (interest, dividends, and Alaska Permanent Fund dividends). The election should not be made if estimated tax payments for the taxable year are made in the child's name and Social Security number. However, this change in the rules would not apply to 1988 returns. So check with your tax adviser about the status of this proposal.

IT TAKES TWO   At this point it makes sense for us to separate children into two groups: those who have reached the age of fourteen and those who have not.

Why? Because the tax law does. The distinction is a result of Congress' effort to put an end to a common tax-saving strategy known as income-shifting. Parents, using this popular tactic, would shift income to their children, so it would be taxed at the child's lower marginal rate.

Parents may still use this strategy with children who are fourteen years of age or older, but not for their younger offspring.

It doesn't matter when during the year your child turns fourteen. In other words, your child is taxed as a fourteen-year-old all year—even if his or her birthday isn't until December 31.

FIGURING YOUR CHILD'S TAXES   The rules enacted under the 1986 Tax Reform Act say that the net unearned income of children under fourteen—that is, the income that comes their way from investments, not from wages—is taxed at the higher of the parents' rate or the child's rate. (The parents' rate is almost always higher.)

This rule makes the calculation of the younger kids' taxes a bit difficult. The trick is to determine "net" unearned income.

First, you add together all your child's unearned income from interest, dividends, capital gains, and so forth. Then you subtract $500, because the first $500 of unearned income is taxed at the child's rate no matter what the child's age.

Finally, you reduce the balance by the greater of: $500 of the standard deduction or, if the child itemizes deductions for the year, $500 of itemized deductions; or any amount of deductions that are directly connected with the production of the unearned income, such as investment-adviser fees, as long as this amount is greater than $500 *after* you apply the 2 percent floor for most miscellaneous itemized deductions. (See Chapter 8 for more information on the 2 percent rule.)

Now what you have is "net" unearned income. Let's run through an example to see how your youngsters might fare.

Assume that the year is 1988 and you're in the 28 percent tax bracket. Your hard-working thirteen-year-old, Rachel, earned $800 babysitting and raking leaves this year, and she received $2,000 in unearned income—interest and dividends from stocks and bonds that you've given to her over the years.

Let's compute her net unearned income. Beginning with the $2,000 in interest and dividends, subtract $500—because the first $500 of Rachel's unearned income, no matter what her age, is taxed at Rachel's rate, not yours.

Now we reduce the remaining $1,500 in unearned income by the greater of: any deductible expenses—in excess, of course, of 2 percent of Rachel's adjusted gross income (AGI)—related to producing that income (in Rachel's case, there were none); $500 from the standard deduction or up to $500 in itemized deductions (again, none in Rachel's case).

So you take $500 from the standard deduction and subtract it from her remaining $1,500 of unearned income. The result?

Only $1,000 of Rachel's unearned income ($2,000 minus the

$500 taxable at her marginal rate minus $500 from the standard deduction) is taxed at your marginal rate. The $1,000 is her net unearned income.

What about her wages? Any earned income—in this case, the $800 Rachel was paid for babysitting and raking leaves—is taxed at her rate. But Rachel pays tax on just $500 of her earned income.

Here's why: The law allows her to claim a standard deduction equal to the greater of $500 or her earned income (up to the $3,000 limit in 1988). So she's entitled to a standard deduction of $800—the amount she received for her work.

We know that she's already applied $500 of her standard deduction against her unearned income. That leaves $300 that she can use to reduce her earned income. Subtracting this $300 from $800 leaves $500, the amount of Rachel's earned income subject to tax.

Her tax liability on earned income comes to $75 (15 percent times $500). On her unearned income, however, she owes Uncle Sam a total of $355—$75 from the $500 taxable at her 15 percent marginal rate plus $280 from the $1,000 taxable at her parents' 28 percent marginal rate. Her total tax: $430.

Here's a simple way of figuring the tax on your child's net unearned income—that is, the unearned income that will be taxed at your rate. First, calculate the net unearned income. Add it to your taxable income. Then calculate your tax. Next calculate your tax bill without adding in your child's income. The difference between these two figures is the amount of tax due on your child's net unearned income.

Caution: If you're the parent of more than one child under the age of fourteen, the rules say you must add all their net unearned incomes to your taxable income. Then you calculate your tax again. If the result is an increase in your tax bill, you then must allocate a pro rata portion of this increase to each of your children.

CHILDREN'S AMT   Children under the age of fourteen may be subject to alternative minimum tax (AMT) rules, but only if their parents are. So, if you have to pay AMT, here's how to figure your child's tax.

First, calculate the child's net unearned *minimum* taxable income. Basically, this calculation involves adding back certain preferences, such as miscellaneous deductions, and making certain AMT adjustments. (See Chapter 20 for detailed help in making these adjustments.)

Then, just as you did in figuring the child's normal tax, add his or her unearned minimum taxable income to your AMT income. If this increases your AMT liability, the amount of the increase is the amount your child owes in AMT. Don't forget, the child's AMT bill is in addition to his or her regular tax liability.

Children fourteen and older will rarely be subject to AMT, but if you suspect that this might happen, consult your tax adviser to see how the child might avoid future AMT liabilities.

FURTHER CONSIDERATIONS   It bears repeating: any dependent child with $500 or more in unearned income must file a return—even if he or she owes no tax.

Furthermore, the source of the unearned income makes no difference. It might come, for instance, from dividends paid by stocks given by grandparents or purchased with the child's own money. And the stocks may have been given or purchased long before Congress adopted the 1986 tax law. Nonetheless, the same tax rules apply. The net unearned income generated by the stock is taxed at your rate or your child's rate, whichever is greater.

What if Rachel's parents are divorced? Then her net unearned income is taxed at the rate of the parent who has custody. If her parents have joint custody, her rate is the same as the parent with the higher rate—just as it would be if her parents were married but filed separate returns.

If both parents are deceased, a child pays taxes at his or her own rate.

A child who is fourteen, or who turns fourteen during the tax year, pays tax almost like an adult. By that we mean that a fourteen-year-old's marginal tax rate on unearned income depends strictly on his or her income level—not on the income of his or her parents.

But older children are entitled to claim a standard deduction of only $500—or their earned income if this amount is greater, up to $3,000—and they may not reduce their taxable income by their own personal exemption. As we've seen, as long as they are dependents, their parents—not they—may claim that exemption.

WHY THE IRS WANTS YOUR KIDS' SOCIAL SECURITY NUMBERS   The law now requires you to list on your return the Social Security numbers of all your children who are five years of age or older (two or older if Congress adopts legislation now before it). It also requires that each of your children must note your Social Security number on their returns.

Why? The IRS plans to use these numbers to make sure that you don't claim deductions to which you're not entitled. For example, if you claim a personal exemption for your child, the IRS will check to see if your child is claiming one for himself or herself as well.

Getting a Social Security number for your child is a simple process. Start by asking your local Social Security office for a copy of Form SS-5. Then fill out the document and send it in.

When you mail the application, include proof of your child's age and citizenship. A public birth certificate is the best evidence. But a hospital record of birth or a religious record showing age or date of birth is also acceptable.

Since you are applying on behalf of your child, you must prove your identity. Acceptable evidence includes a driver's license, church membership or confirmation record, U.S. passport, voter's registration card, or military record.

Caution: The law also gives children under the age of fourteen access to your tax return. Not a big deal, you say. But it might be for divorced parents.

If you and your ex-spouse have joint custody of a child under fourteen, then, as we mentioned earlier, the child pays the same rate on his or her net unearned income as the parent with the higher rate pays—just as he or she would if you were still married and filing separate returns. So, the only way the child will know which parent has the higher rate is if he or she, and your ex-spouse, have access to your return. As a practical matter, there's not much you can do to avoid disclosure.

INCOME-SHIFTING The new treatment of younger kids resulting from the 1986 tax law revisions means that the opportunities for income-shifting—moving income from a family member with a higher marginal rate to one with a lower marginal rate—are more limited than in the past.

In fact, because the tax law now draws a clear distinction between children who have reached the age of fourteen and those who have not, we can separate income-shifting strategies that apply to children into two categories. Some are appropriate for the older group, some for the younger, and some for both.

Now we'll take you through a number of income-shifting devices. With just a little calculation, you can decide which will pay off for you.

FAREWELL TO CLIFFORD TRUSTS   Before we begin, a reminder that one of the most popular devices for shifting income, the Clifford trust, is now defunct—thanks to the 1986 tax law.

A Clifford trust allowed the person establishing the trust—the grantor—to get back the assets or cash he or she contributed at the end of the trust term—usually after a minimum of ten years.

While the trust was in effect, however, its income was taxed either to the beneficiary or to the trust. In both cases, the rates were a good deal lower than the grantor's.

Today the game has changed. The new rules require that the grantor—not the beneficiary—report and pay taxes on the trust income. So if you give assets to your child, you must make an outright and irrevocable gift if you want to have the income treated as your child's.

But there is one exception to this rule. If you established a Clifford trust before March 1, 1986, it remains valid. Income from the trust, however, is taxed according to the new rules. So if your child is under fourteen, the money will be taxed at your presumably higher rate. For children over fourteen, of course, the income remains taxable at their rate.

What if you, the grantor, make a new contribution to a Clifford trust that was established before March 1, 1986? Earnings generated by this contribution are reported as income to you, the grantor.

MAKING GIFTS TO CHILDREN FOURTEEN OR OLDER
Because the unearned income of children fourteen years of age and older is taxed at the child's rate—which is usually lower than the parents'—shifting income to these senior offspring can produce tax savings. How large?

Say you invest $20,000 at 10 percent compounded annually for five years, and you're in the 28 percent bracket. You'd have just $8,314 in after-tax earnings at the end of five years.

But let's say you and your spouse gave your fourteen-year-old son Max the $20,000 and allowed him to make the same investment.

His earnings probably would be taxed at only 15 percent. So

at the end of five years Max would have after-tax earnings of $10,073—$1,759 more than your own.

Put another way, Max's after-tax rate of return on the investment would be 8.5 percent compared to the 7.2 percent net rate of return that you were able to earn.

The bottom line: Giving the $20,000 to Max increased the *family's* net income by $1,759 over five years.

What's the best way to shift income to your children?

Probably the most sensible and simplest method is through the Uniform Gifts to Minors Act (UGMA) or the newer Uniform Transfers to Minors Act (UTMA).

Under these acts parents—or any person, for that matter—may give money to a child and keep those assets under a custodian's control.

You may select a member of your family, a legal guardian—or any adult you trust—as the custodian. One word of warning, though: It usually is not a good idea for the donor—the person who gives the money—to serve as custodian.

Here's the reason. Say a favorite relative, Aunt Virginia, is the donor, and she also acts as custodian. And say she dies before your child reaches the age of majority. Under these circumstances the money she's given your child is subject to estate tax.

The situation isn't so bad, though, if her estate is small—less than $600,000. Nor does it matter as much if Aunt Virginia is married. In this case her entire estate passes—free of estate tax—to her husband, thanks to the so-called unlimited marital deduction.

You don't have to worry about legal fees in setting up an UGMA or UTMA account. Just go to a financial institution, such as a bank, and ask for the appropriate forms.

One last point about these accounts: The UTMA may make more sense if you want to make sure your child uses the account's assets for college.

With an UTMA account, the custodian does not have to distribute assets until your child reaches twenty-one, or even twenty-five in some states.

With an UGMA account, however, the custodian must distribute the money when your child reaches majority, which is eighteen in many states. Moreover, the UTMA account lets you invest in real estate. With an UGMA account, real estate or other personal property transfers are prohibited by law. You may transfer only money, securities, annuities, and insurance contracts.

It's easy to see that shifting capital to your older children is an effective way of reducing the family tax burden. There are just two caveats, though.

First, you and your spouse may not give a child more than $10,000 each (other than money you give for support) in any year without facing a possible gift tax problem.

What's the difference between a gift and support? The distinction is not always clear-cut. In Uncle Sam's eyes, support items include food, clothing, lodging, medical expenses, babysitting costs, educational expenses, and so forth.

But what if you're an exceptionally generous soul and buy your sixteen-year-old daughter a $35,000 sports car? Does the IRS consider the car a gift or part of your child's support?

Chances are Uncle Sam will decide that the car is a gift. While the courts have ruled that a child's transportation expenses count as support, the IRS would probably consider a $35,000 automobile excessive.

Second, as we've seen, once you've turned over your hard-earned cash to your child, it legally belongs to him or her—not to you. Legally, you can't dictate how the money is spent.

If Max decides to withdraw the $20,000 you gave him toward college expenses and buy a used Porsche instead, legally he's free to do so. Sorry, Mom and Dad.

But giving gifts to children fourteen years and older is still an attractive income-shifting device. As we'll see, it's less effective for younger siblings.

You do, however, have alternatives when it comes to shifting income to younger children.

INCOME-SHIFTING TO THE YOUNGER SET   As long as a child is younger than fourteen, the government will tax most of the child's unearned income as if it were received by the parents.

But don't despair. This unfortunate rule doesn't mean that gift giving has lost all its value as an income-shifting device to lower the family's overall tax burden.

As we've already discussed, the first $500 of the younger child's annual unearned income is not taxed at all, and the second $500 is still taxed at the child's lower rate.

Take advantage of these rules. It still makes sense to shift some income-producing assets to younger children, even if the tax savings aren't dramatic.

Say you give your four-year-old son $3,000 and invest the

money in a mutual fund that yields a 10 percent annual return. Your marginal tax bracket is 28 percent.

Since his annual interest is less than $1,000, he pays no tax on his first $500 of annual earnings and only 15 percent on the second $500. And, at the end of ten years, the $3,000 would have grown to $7,700.

What if you kept the $3,000, invested it in the same mutual fund, then gave the account to your child when he turned fourteen?

You'd pay tax on your annual earnings at 28 percent, so the account would have grown to only $6,000. By taking advantage of this $1,000 break, your family accumulated $1,700 more than it otherwise would.

But you should try to keep your child's unearned income to less than $1,000 until he or she reaches age fourteen. So what should you do instead?

Take a look at these other devices.

Savings Bonds

Ironically, one of the best income-shifting devices for younger children comes from the government itself. Series EE Savings Bonds make a terrific tax shelter for children age two and older. Here's how.

Current EE bonds mature in twelve years. (Bonds you bought between November 1982 and October 1986 mature in ten years. These maturity dates are based on interest rates—the higher the interest, the shorter the maturity period.)

The interest on these bonds—unless you elect to report it annually—isn't taxed until the bonds mature and you cash them in. (If you cash them in before they mature, any interest you've accumulated to date is taxed at the time you redeem them.) And note that interest from Series EE bonds is not subject to state or local income taxes.

So, you can give your child cash and allow him or her to buy EE bonds. Or you may buy the bonds in your child's name. The only requirement: Your child needs a Social Security number when you buy the bond or when you cash it in. If you put your number on the bond, Uncle Sam taxes the interest to you—unless you specify that the bond is a gift at the time you buy it.

You or your child may purchase EE bonds for as little as $25 or as much as $5,000. (The face value equals twice the amount of the purchase price.) The only catch: Uncle Sam imposes a cap on savings bonds purchases of $15,000—a face value of $30,000—per person per year.

It does make more sense, however, to buy the smaller denominations. That way you can cash your bonds in gradually.

You can buy EE bonds through banks and savings and loans, payroll deduction plans, the Federal Reserve, or the Bureau of the Public Debt (Parkersburg, WVA 26106-1328). You can also buy Series EE's by calling, toll free, 1-800-US BONDS and charging the purchase to your Mastercard or Visa.

As long as your child is age two or older, Series EE bonds won't mature until after he or she has turned fourteen. And at that point, when they are redeemed, the interest will be taxed at the child's lower rate.

There are no sales charges when you buy an EE bond. And if your child keeps the bond until it matures, he or she will receive—at the very least—its full face value.

But your child might actually receive more than the face value. Here's why. The interest rates on these bonds vary—but only upward. The government guarantees that at maturity you'll get at least twice what you paid for them, even if interest rates have dropped precipitously. But if interest rates go up, your child will collect more than the face value. So these bonds make an excellent hedge against inflation.

Can you hold the bonds past the maturity date? We don't know yet. In the past Congress has extended the maturity date for savings bonds. But it hasn't yet done so for Series EE bonds issued during the 1980s. If it does, though, the interest on these bonds continues to pile up—tax deferred.

Caution: Don't list yourself as co-owner of your child's savings bonds. Here's why. If you die, the bonds are included in your estate.

Tip: If the Series EE bond you purchased for your child matures before he or she turns fourteen—and Congress hasn't extended the maturity period—roll over the EE bonds into Series HH bonds, another type of savings bond. That way your child defers taxes on the interest that's accumulated on the EE bonds, until he or she redeems the HH bonds or they mature.

Series HH bonds, which mature in ten years and pay, semiannually, a flat annual interest rate of 6 percent, are available only if you exchange Series EE bonds. So the HH bonds' interest would be currently taxable at your rates if your child is under fourteen. But the EE interest that's accumulated remains tax deferred.

Growth Stocks

The same principle applies to buying growth stocks.

These are shares issued by fast-growing companies that probably aren't paying current dividends. And if there are low dividends (less than $500) or no dividends, there's no tax to pay until your child sells the—one hopes—appreciated stock after he or she turns age fourteen.

Then the gain is taxed at the child's lower rate.

Single Premium Annuities

An annuity is defined as a contract sold by an insurance company that guarantees a payment to the beneficiary at some future date.

With a single premium annuity, you pay an insurance company a lump sum up front. At the end of a fixed term, the annuity starts to pay benefits. The advantage: The funds accumulate, tax deferred, until your child—the beneficiary—starts receiving payments.

So buy your child a policy that begins payments after the child turns fourteen or when he or she enters college. Again, your child won't be taxed on that income until that time, and presumably at his or her rate, rather than at your own.

Caution: There's a movement afoot in Congress to curtail some of the advantages of single premium annuities. You should ask your tax adviser about the status of this legislation before you invest in one of these policies.

Appreciating Property

You may make a gift of any appreciating property to your child—land, collectibles, gold, coins, stamps, or art. He or she can then sell the property after turning fourteen—and the gain is taxed at his or her lower rate.

Tax-Exempt Municipal Bonds

These bonds are issued by cities or states for local projects. They're free of federal income taxes. And if you buy municipal bonds issued in your own state, you usually don't pay state taxes either.

So purchasing one of these bonds for your child—or buying shares in a municipal bond fund—lets him or her avoid taxation altogether. (However, income on tax-exempt, so-called "private activity" bonds issued after August 7, 1986 are taxable for purposes of the alternative minimum tax.)

Remember, buying municipal bonds or shares in a bond fund is not a way to shift income from one family member to another. But it is a way to avoid taxation.

So you may want to give your child money to purchase these bonds. (Remember, you and your spouse each may give a child up to $10,000 a year with no gift-tax consequences.)

Tip: Buy zero-coupon municipal bonds or bond funds in your child's name. Zero-coupon bonds are quite similar to U.S. Savings Bonds. They're sold at a deep discount from their face value and pay no current interest. When they mature, you receive the full face amount.

On ordinary zero-coupon bonds, the IRS "imputes" annual interest to the buyer. And you must pay taxes on this amount. And when you buy zero-coupon municipal bonds, you're home free.

THE FAMILY BUSINESS   Say you own a business and it's a sole proprietorship—that is, you report your business income on Schedule C of your Form 1040.

You have an opportunity to shift income right in your own backyard. Just put your child to work in your business and you'll reap a double tax benefit.

First, your child's wages are considered earned income, which is always taxed at the child's lower rate, regardless of his or her age.

Second, the wages that you pay your kids are legitimate business expenses. So they're tax deductible.

And that's not all. Here are two other benefits.

Under a special provision in the tax law, you don't have to pay Social Security taxes on your child's wages as long as he or she is under eighteen.

What's more, your child may open an Individual Retirement Account (IRA) and shelter some or all of his or her earnings. Under the rules, a child may sock away the lesser of $2,000 or 100 percent of his or her earnings in an IRA.

Contributions and earnings to an IRA are tax deferred—that is, your child pays no taxes on the contribution or earnings that accumulate until the money is withdrawn, usually at retirement. (But keep in mind: An IRA is a long-range investment. If your child withdraws money before age 59½, he or she will have to pay income taxes and a 10 percent early withdrawal penalty to boot. We cover IRA's in Chapter 22.)

Say in 1988 your child contributes $2,000 to an IRA and

deducts the full amount. Next he subtracts $3,000 for the 1988 standard deduction.

His deductions, then, add up to $5,000. So that means he could earn as much as $5,000 in wages in 1988 without paying federal income tax.

One word of warning: You have to be sure that the job is a legitimate one and that you can justify the salary that you pay. Blatant abuse—paying twelve-year-old Sally $10 an hour to sweep up—may attract Uncle Sam's attention and ire.

The business doesn't have to be a sole proprietorship, but if the family firm is a corporation or partnership (other than a family partnership), you'll have to pay Social Security and unemployment compensation taxes on wages you pay your children. And your children will have to pay Social Security taxes on their wages. Obviously, doing so will eat up some of your income tax savings.

The exemption applies to partnerships only if the parent-and-child relationship exists between the child and each of the partners—for instance, a family partnership where the mother and father are the only partners.

CHILD CARE CREDIT   The child or dependent care credit was designed primarily to help parents defray the cost of child care. For the most part, the credit may be taken by single parents who work outside the home or by married couples if both spouses are employed outside the home.

To qualify for the credit, you must meet a host of requirements. For one, the expenses you incur must be necessary in order for you to be employed or actively seek employment away from home.

Also, you must bear financial responsibility for maintaining your household, and you must spend money for the care of any of the following dependents while you're on the job:

• Youngsters under age fifteen who are dependents
• Dependents who are physically or mentally incapable of caring for themselves—a person with Down's syndrome, for example

The child care credit ranges from a low of 20 percent to a high of 30 percent of expenses paid during the year. The percentage is based on your AGI. If your AGI comes to $10,000 or less, the 30 percent credit applies; if it tops $28,000, the 20 percent credit applies.

What if your income falls between $10,000 and $28,000? The

30 percent credit is reduced by 1 percent for each $2,000 of AGI in excess of $10,000. For instance, a person with AGI of $14,000 would qualify for a 28 percent credit.

The credit applies only to "employment-related" expenses of up to $2,400 for one dependent and $4,800 for two or more dependents—so the maximum credit is $1,440 (30 percent times $4,800). The IRS defines employment-related expenses as the cost of people to care for your dependent or provide household services—cleaning, cooking, and so on.

Caution: If your child care expenses exceed your earnings, watch out. Uncle Sam says the credit may be applied only to expenses that are equal to or less than your earned income. (If you're married, you must use the earned income of the spouse who makes the least.)

Say you earn $2,000 working part-time, and your spouse earns $25,000 working full-time. Also, you and your spouse collect $3,000 interest from your money market fund. So your joint AGI is $30,000. You pay someone $2,400 to care for your child while you're on the job.

Under the law, you may claim only $2,000 of child care expenses. And your credit totals $400 (20 percent times $2,000), not $480 (20 percent times $2,400).

Tip: Say you're married and file a joint return. You work outside the home and your spouse is a full-time student. Uncle Sam gives you a break.

You're entitled to claim a child care credit, even though your spouse is a student and not employed outside the home.

When it comes time to calculate your child care credit, the rules assume that your "student spouse" earned $200 a month for each month he or she attended school full-time. If you claim a credit for more than one child, the amount jumps to $400 a month.

QUESTIONS AND ANSWERS

QUESTION: Last year my three-year-old daughter received a number of small-denomination U.S. Savings Bonds as gifts. The interest from the bonds was minimal, and she has no other investment income. Should she report the interest annually or let it accumulate until the bonds mature?

Children under age fourteen may receive up to $500 of investment income each year and pay no taxes—thanks to the standard deduction.

So if the annual interest on your daughter's bonds is $500 or less, report the interest income annually, rather than allowing it to build up until the bonds mature.

One drawback to this strategy: Once your daughter elects to report the interest annually, that decision is irrevocable. If her investment income tops $500 one year, she is not allowed to postpone reporting the income until the bond matures.

What's more, her decision to report interest annually applies to all U.S. Savings Bonds that she owns at the time—plus any bonds that she acquires in the future.

Q: I own my own business and I report my earnings on Schedule C of my Form 1040. My net profit for 1988 should add up to $45,000. Should I hire my kids—aged twelve and thirteen—to help with the filing and cleaning? Will this strategy save me taxes? And, if so, how much?

Let's say you pay each of your kids $250 a month, or $3,000 a year, for their efforts. And you deduct this amount, $6,000 in total, on your Schedule C.

This write-off reduces your business profits of $45,000 by $6,000. So you save $1,680 in federal income taxes—that is, your federal income tax rate of 28 percent times your tax deduction of $6,000.

You also save $781 in Social Security taxes—the Social Security self-employment rate of 13.02 percent times $6,000. (In 1988, only the first $45,000 in income is subject to self-employment taxes.)

Your total tax savings add up to $2,461. Meanwhile your kids pay no federal taxes on the amount they receive, since it's equal to their 1988 standard deduction (assuming, of course, that they report no unearned income). And neither you nor your children pay Social Security taxes on their wages. So by paying your kids to help you—rather than just giving them money—you slash your family tax bill by $2,461.

Not a bad deal, you say. But what if your earnings—after you deduct what you've paid your child—top the $45,000 Social Security cap? You save income taxes—but no Social Security self-employment taxes when you employ your children.

Still not a bad deal, you say, and you're right. One drawback: The Social Security benefits you receive at retirement are based on the amount you pay in. So, potentially, you could receive less in Social Security when you retire.

CHAPTER 26

Tax-Wise Ways to Finance Your Child's Education

As astronomical as college costs are today, they're going to climb even higher in years to come. In fact, they're expected to nearly triple by the year 2000.

This kind of price escalation isn't a worry if you've won the state lottery. The rest of us, however, have to plan ahead, which includes tax planning.

So, that's what we'll do in this chapter.

In the first section we'll suggest tax-efficient ways to put money aside for college expenses ahead of time. Then we'll show you how to get the most out of the cash you set aside for college costs—including minimizing the share that has to go to Uncle Sam.

PLANNING AHEAD What's the best way, taxwise, to finance your child's education? The answer, as you might expect if you've read Chapter 25, depends on whether the child you're saving for has reached fourteen years of age yet. That's because your opportunities to minimize the tax bite are far fewer until your child does reach age fourteen.

So first let's look at the techniques that apply in the case of a younger child. Even with the harsher rules, you do have some options when it comes to cutting the tax bite on college savings.

PRE-FOURTEEN STRATEGIES Say you've set aside a few dollars for your child's education. And you want to put them in an investment that pays current income—dividends or interest, for example.

Should you make the investment in your name? Or should you

make it in your child's name? If your child is under age fourteen, it doesn't much matter.

Here's why. As we've seen, a child under age fourteen pays taxes on his or her unearned income at the higher of the parents' rate or the child's rate. And the parents' rate is almost always higher.

The only significant difference is that younger children aren't taxed on the first $500 of unearned income, and the next $500 is taxed at their lower 15 percent rate. Given a maximum 1988 tax rate of 28 percent, this small break could yield a tax saving of up to $205 each year.

But keep in mind: Because of a 5 percent surtax on income falling between certain levels, some higher-income taxpayers will find themselves paying tax at a 33 percent marginal rate. And for these people the tax savings could jump to $255 each year.

These savings help a little, of course, but not much.

So about the best tax strategy you can use when putting aside education money for younger children is one that involves tax deferral—delaying the tax until the child reaches fourteen. After that point more tax saving is possible.

How can you defer taxes? Look again in the preceding chapter at the strategies we suggest for the under-fourteen-year-old. As you recall they include buying:

• Series EE U.S. Savings Bonds
• Nondividend-paying growth stocks
• Single premium annuities
• Appreciating property
• Tax-exempt municipal bonds

Another option you might consider for your pre-fourteen child isn't exactly a tax-deferral device. The effect is much the same, however.

Minor's trusts allow you to make one or more gifts to a child—subject to the usual $10,000 per person per year limit, or, in tax lingo, the annual gift-tax exclusion. This rule means that you and your spouse can add up to $20,000 a year to each of your children's trusts without worrying about a gift tax.

The principal and earnings that accumulate remain in the trust until the trustee—who may be anyone you'd like—distributes them.

The trust document, which creates the trust, must specify that the trustee has the discretionary power to distribute the property and income for the child's benefit until the child reaches age twenty-one. Of course, you're free to specify how and when you want the assets distributed, but unless the trust document grants the trustee the authority to carry out your wishes, the gift-tax exclusion does not apply.

Note: It's a good idea not to name yourself as trustee. If you do and if you die, the assets of the trust would be included in your taxable estate.

The income earned by the property in the trust is taxed each year, but at a partially reduced rate so long as you allow earnings to accumulate within the trust.

The reason is that Uncle Sam taxes the trust, not the recipient. The first $5,000 of income in a minor's trust is taxed at only 15 percent in 1988, the rest at 28 percent. The result is an annual tax savings of $650. Income distributed from the trust, on the other hand, is taxed under the so-called kiddie tax rules (see Chapter 25).

Another tax advantage of a minor's trust is that the rules allow you to specify when a child is to receive the dollars in trust. If you want to ensure that a child spends his or her money on college, pick eighteen or twenty-one as the age for distribution of the funds.

Another important point: When income and principal are eventually distributed to a child at age eighteen, say, there is no need to recalculate the tax on that income to account for the period of accumulation. With other types of trust you might have to perform this complicated recalculation.

The minor's trust you establish does have to comply with two major conditions.

All the assets in the trust must be distributed to the beneficiary by the time he or she reaches age twenty-one. And, should the child die before reaching age twenty-one, the trust document must provide for the assets and accumulated income to be paid to his or her estate or be subject to the child's general power of appointment—legal talk that means the child must have the right to name the recipient of the balance in the trust in the event of his or her death.

Is a minor's trust worth the trouble—and the expense? Remember, you're going to have to pay administrative fees to a bank or other institution that acts as trustee. (These fees range from 0.5 to 2 percent of the trust's principal.) The answer is:

Probably, if you have a lot of money—$10,000 a year or more, for instance—to put into it.

Say, for instance, that you and your spouse together give your child $20,000 each year for three years, beginning with the child's first birthday.

Assume that the trust funds earn income at a 10 percent annual rate and that taxes on the first $5,000 of annual income are paid at the 15 percent rate.

By the time the child reaches eighteen and the tuition bills come due, the trust will have grown to $215,572. Had you simply saved the money and paid taxes at your normal 28 percent rate, the fund would have grown to only $195,958. You're $19,615 ahead by having set up the trust fund.

Don't forget, though, to offset this amount by the administrative costs of the trust. These charges vary from institution to institution (they're deductible if they exceed 2 percent of the trust's adjusted gross income). Ask your bank or trust company about the charges it imposes.

A word of caution: If the income from the trust is used to support your child, it is taxable to you. The laws defining legal support vary from state to state.

There's another type of trust that can also be useful. Called a Crummey Trust after the court decision that recognized it, this trust basically allows the distribution of principal and income at the trustee's discretion but does not require the mandatory termination of the trust when the child reaches twenty-one. Instead, the trust document may allow distribution of the principal in stages.

The catch, however, is that the trustee must notify the beneficiary child annually of his or her right to withdraw over a reasonable period—usually 30 to 60 days—any gifts made to the trust each year.

Whether the child actually withdraws anything from the trust or not, he or she will be taxed each year on the amount of the trust that *could* have been withdrawn. Another drawback: Income that accumulates above this amount is subject to recalculation of income tax under the complex throwback rules.

Because Crummey Trusts are complicated, and because under some circumstances they may actually increase the overall tax liability of a child older than fourteen, you should probably consult your tax adviser before creating one.

Keep in mind, as well, one other idea—which we also covered in the previous chapter—for your under-fourteen-year-old child.

Parents who are business owners can shift some of their income to their younger tykes by putting the youngsters to work. (See Chapter 25 for more information on employing your child.)

POST-FOURTEEN STRATEGIES   Just because your child has reached age fourteen doesn't mean that it's too late to start saving for college expenses.

It's true that you don't have as much time to accumulate assets when your child is this old. On the other hand, it's only when the child reaches fourteen that Uncle Sam truly becomes your partner in the savings effort. From this point on the child's unearned income will be taxed at his or her rate, not yours.

So at this point you can begin to do some income-shifting—transferring income on which you would pay a high tax rate to your, now, less-taxed youngster.

How do you shift income? Usually by gifts.

Just give a child $10,000 or $20,000 with no strings attached? Not exactly. To make sure the kids don't blow their college money on something you'd consider foolish, you'll probably want to use the Uniform Gifts to Minors Act (UGMA) or the Uniform Transfers to Minors Act (UTMA). (See Chapter 25 for more on UGMA or UTMA accounts.)

WHAT TO DO WHEN SAVING TIME IS OVER   Your child is a high-school senior and ready to choose a college. The time for long-range planning is over. Either you've earmarked money for covering college expenses or you haven't. In either case, now you have to come up with the cash. So, what do you do?

You've got three options, which you'll probably want to use in some combination. You can tap your capital, including whatever assets, if any, you or your child have been accumulating against this day. You or the prospective freshman can borrow money. And you can always apply for financial aid from the government or from the school.

Let's run through the options to see what possibilities they offer and how you can coordinate them.

TAPPING CAPITAL   If you've specifically put aside some savings or assets as college money, you'll have no reluctance to liquidate them when the bills come in.

But even if you haven't had such foresight, you can nevertheless tap some of your assets and still get a bit of tax help from Uncle Sam.

Let's say that you own stocks or bonds that have appreciated in value. Naturally, you might think of selling some of them to raise college cash. But if you sell in 1988, you're going to be taxed on the gain that you realize at a 28 percent tax rate.

Why not, instead, give the stocks or bonds to your college-bound daughter?

She'll have to pay the taxes on the appreciated value of the securities. But she'll pay taxes only at her 15 percent rate—as long as her gain plus her other taxable income doesn't top $17,850, which is the limit for single people paying at the 15 percent rate. By giving her the assets to sell, there's more after-tax money left to pay the college bills.

How much more?

Assume that a stock you bought many years ago has appreciated in value by $15,000. If you sell it, you get the $15,000 appreciation minus $4,200 ($15,000 times 28 percent) in taxes. In other words, out of the $15,000 gain, you get to keep $10,800.

If you give the stock to your daughter and she sells it, her tax bill will add up to just $2,250 ($15,000 times 15 percent). She gets to keep $12,750 of the $15,000 gain. So by giving the stock to her, she winds up with $1,950 more than you would to put toward tuition bills.

Just bear in mind, though, that she doesn't have to sell the stock. Once you give it to her, you've lost legal control over what she does with it.

BORROWING POWER If you have to borrow to finance a youngster's education, probably the best way is through a home-equity loan. Why? The interest is deductible.

As a result of tax reform, you can't fully write off the interest you pay on a student loan unless the loan is secured by your home. On any other sort of loan, interest is only 40 percent deductible in 1988 and less so in subsequent years. (See Chapter 4 for details on interest deductibility.)

On the other hand, you may deduct interest on a home-equity loan of up to $100,000 no matter how you use the money. That fact makes home-equity loans very attractive for financing education costs.

Caution: Your kids can always borrow some or all of the cash they need for college from you—provided you've got it to loan.

But beware. You must be careful to treat the transaction in a businesslike manner or Uncle Sam might consider the loan a gift. So make sure to write up a promissory note that states the amount your child borrowed, the interest rate, and the repayment schedule.

And note too: Zero-interest loans to offspring don't impress Uncle Sam. He will impute, meaning attribute, interest income to you and interest expense to the borrower.

Furthermore, whether it's a zero-interest loan or one made at fair market rates, you actually incur a tax disadvantage when you loan money to your children. These loans result in greater income to you, the higher-bracket taxpayer. And they produce a limited deduction to your child, the lower-bracket taxpayer, because the interest is personal interest and subject to the phase-out rules. (For more information on interest deductions, see Chapter 4.)

So taxwise, it's not a smart move.

SCHOLARSHIPS AND FELLOWSHIPS There have been recent changes in the tax rules applying to scholarships and fellowships. Despite the changes, however, degree-seeking candidates awarded scholarships or fellowships may still exclude from their income much of the money they receive. And it makes no difference whether they're in graduate or undergraduate school.

If your son, for instance, is in a degree-granting program, he may exclude from income amounts he uses for tuition and books, equipment, supplies, and other course fees. But amounts that are earmarked for room, board, or other living expenses are fully taxable.

Moreover, he must pay tax on wages he receives for research, teaching, or other services that the school may require as a condition of receiving the scholarship or fellowship.

QUESTIONS AND ANSWERS

QUESTION: I've heard a lot about prepaid tuition plans. What are these plans? Are they a good idea?

Prepaid tuition plans actually come in two varieties.

With the first type, you pay all four years of tuition when your child becomes a freshman. Because you pay at the first-year price, you're protected against future increases.

These plans may be a good idea under two conditions: You can afford the hefty up-front cost, and you're fairly certain your child won't want to transfer. In any case, it makes sense to check whether your money is refundable if your son or daughter does switch schools.

The second, and newer, type of prepaid plan is a much dicier proposition. These plans, which have been established by some colleges and at least one state, let you pay four years' tuition—at a steep discount—when your son or daughter is a mere tot. When your child is old enough to enter college, his or her tuition is already paid for—presumably at a price far below current levels.

One drawback is immediately obvious. Should your child decide against the college you've paid for, or should that institution close its doors, you may lose your money entirely. Or the college or state may refund only the amount you've paid in—with no allowance for many years' interest on your cash.

Granted, some schools are forming umbrella plans that allow your scholar a choice of institutions. But there's no guarantee any of these colleges will appeal to your youngster.

And the plans may have tax-related drawbacks. So far the IRS has ruled on just one program. It found that the plan created by the Michigan legislature triggered three tax liabilities.

First, it triggered a gift tax to the parent when he or she purchased the contract. Furthermore, the IRS said, the $10,000 annual gift-tax exclusion did not apply in the case of prepaid education programs.

Second, the plan created a tax liability on the earnings of the trust in which the funds were deposited.

Third, the prepaid plan also triggered a tax liability for the child when he or she began school. The amount taxed is the difference between the annual tuition cost and one quarter of the cost of the tuition contract (assuming that the contract covered four years of tuition). This means that the income earned by the original purchase price of the contract is actually taxed twice— once when it's earned by the trust and then again when the child receives the education.

The IRS ruling on the Michigan plan means that its only real savings (if any) to the individual who buys it is the difference between the future value of the current price paid and actual tuition charge when the child enters school. You'll also want to determine whether the income earned by a prepayment trust in your state is subject to state as well as federal taxes. If it is, that's another reduction of savings overall.

Q: My parents have offered to pick up the tab for my daughter's schooling. Are there any tax angles I should know about?

You're in luck.

Generous grandparents may pay your child's educational expenses and still make tax-free annual gifts of up to $10,000 each ($20,000 as a couple) per recipient.

The only qualification: They must pay the college or university directly. So make sure they write their check to the school—not to you or your daughter.

Q. My son was planning to live in a dorm. But friends tell me that it may pay off to buy a small condominium for him to live in instead. Do you agree?

There certainly can be tax advantages to seeking alternative housing for your son.

Say you buy an off-campus apartment. You may, under the tax law, treat this unit as your second home and deduct mortgage interest and property taxes. (Uncle Sam allows you to deduct these expenses on your principal residence and one other house.) Meanwhile, your son has a free place to live.

Or you could rent the apartment to your son and deduct—subject to the passive loss rules—mortgage interest, property taxes, maintenance, utilities, depreciation, and other expenses associated with maintaining rental property. If you end up with a loss, you may be able to use it to offset your regular income.

But the laws in this area are complex.

First, Uncle Sam requires that the house be your son's principal residence. Also, you must charge him and any of his friends a fair-market rent. And you must actively manage the property yourself—that is, you must participate in collecting rents, authorizing repair work and maintenance, and so on.

If your adjusted gross income is $100,000 or less, you may deduct from your income up to $25,000 in losses from rental real estate in which you actively participate each year. But this cap is gradually phased out if your AGI falls between $100,000 and $150,000. So when your AGI reaches $150,000, you're entitled to use the losses you incur, but only against other passive income.

When your child graduates, you can sell your property. You may now deduct any losses you were unable to take while you owned the property. And, with luck, your property will have appreciated in value. (See chapter 16 for more information on the tax rules governing real estate.)

There's also a tax bonus to setting your son up with a place he can share: You may hire him to manage the property.

Your son can earn up to $3,000 tax free, provided he has no other income, and you can write that off against the rent his friends pay you. Just be sure that the amount you pay Junior for his job is reasonable, or the IRS may challenge the arrangement.

CHAPTER 27

The Lowdown on Estimated Taxes

Almost all of us make estimated tax payments to the IRS, and most of us do it the easy way—through payroll withholding. That way we never see the cash. Our employers simply pass it along to Uncle Sam before we get our hands on it.

But most people who are self-employed or who report unearned income, such as dividends, interest, and alimony, face the responsibility of making their own estimates of income taxes due. And they have to make quarterly tax payments.

What if your employer withholds too little from your paycheck? You, too, must pay estimated tax to the federal government.

Failing to pay or underpaying estimated taxes is serious business. It results in penalties—and penalties aren't deductible on your federal or state tax return.

In this chapter we cover the estimated tax rules. We show you how to figure your payments, avoid underpayments, and minimize the penalties if you do underpay.

The IRS expects to get your estimated tax payments once a quarter. For calendar-year taxpayers, the due dates are *April 15, June 15, September 15, and January 15*.

If the due date falls on a Saturday, Sunday, or legal holiday, your payment is considered on time if you make it on the next business day.

You should know that the IRS considers the postmark on the envelope the date of payment—as long as the envelope is postmarked by the U.S. Post Office and not a private postage meter. If you're uneasy about the reliability of the U.S. mails, you might want to send your payment by registered or certified mail.

That way you'll have proof positive—via your receipt—that you mailed your estimated tax on time.

How much, exactly, must you pay by the due dates? The tax law requires that your four quarterly payments total either:

- 100 percent of the tax you paid during the previous year—that is, the amount of tax shown on your previous return, assuming you had a 12-month taxable year, or
- 90 percent of the tax that you will owe in the current year—that is, the amount listed on the tax return you file for the current year

So the IRS gives you an option—which you may use to your advantage. How? Consider this example. Assume that last year your tax liability came to $35,000.

This year, you estimate, it will total $40,000. The question is, how much should you fork over to the IRS in quarterly payments during the current year?

You may send Uncle Sam either $35,000—the amount of last year's tax—or $36,000—90 percent of the $40,000 you estimate you will owe this year.

Naturally, you choose the $35,000 option.

Tip: Uncle Sam says you may skip your January estimated tax payment if you file your return and pay your tax bill in full on or before January 31.

Tip: People who make their living farming or fishing get special treatment under the tax law. They need to make only a single estimated tax payment of two thirds of their estimated current year's liability. And that payment isn't due until January 15 of the following year.

What's more, they need to make no estimated payments at all if they file their tax returns and pay their full tax bills by March 1.

Also exempted from the quarterly payment requirement are individuals whose estimated current-year tax liability—after credit for taxes that are withheld by their employers—is less than $500. Teenagers often fall into this category.

Excluded, too, are people who owed no tax last year. (These individuals must be U.S. citizens or they must have been U.S. residents for the entire previous 12-month period.)

Tip: The law provides an alternative method—the so-called annualization method—that you may use for determining what you owe.

250 **The Price Waterhouse Personal Tax Adviser**

This method is used primarily by self-employed people with seasonal or fluctuating incomes. With this method you may pay installments that actually reflect the income you earn in the period immediately before the installment is due.

If your annualized tax installment is less than you'd pay under the minimums we just described, you may safely pay it without being accused of underpaying. But you must attach Form 2210, "Underpayment of Estimated Taxes by Individuals," to your Form 1040 to show that you are not subject to the penalty.

To help you annualize your income and figure your adjusted self-employement income for each quarter, the IRS provides worksheets in IRS Publication 505, *Tax Withholding and Estimated Tax*, and in the instructions to Form 2210.

THE TAB FOR UNDERPAYMENT If you come up short on your quarterly estimated tax payments, the IRS will impose a penalty on the amount of the shortfall.

The amount of the penalty varies—it rises or falls with current interest rates. Moreover, unlike in past years, if you borrow money to pay your estimated income taxes, the interest you pay on the loan is not fully deductible.

This interest is classified as personal interest, which, thanks to the 1986 Tax Reform Act, is only 40 percent deductible in 1988 and 20 percent deductible in 1989 (see Chapter 4). So should you borrow to avoid the penalty? The answer is probably yes in 1988—as long as you pay the interest by December 31.

Clearly, the tax law supplies some very sound reasons for making sure that you satisfy the IRS' quarterly payment requirements. But the specifics of those payments are a bit tricky sometimes, and the unwary taxpayer may find that he or she has quite unwittingly underpaid the taxes due.

So far, we've talked just about the total of your quarterly estimated payments for the year. What about each individual payment? The government requires that each of your quarterly payments equal or exceed 25 percent of either:

- 100 percent of last year's taxes, or
- 90 percent of the current year's estimated taxes

Then there's the alternative minimum tax (AMT) to consider. This year more taxpayers than ever before will pay the AMT. (See Chapter 20 for more on the AMT.)

And the amount of AMT you might owe counts when it comes

to determining the percentage of estimated tax you must pay in order to avoid a penalty. So does the amount of Social Security self-employment tax that you may owe on, say, fees you receive as a freelance consultant.

When any single quarterly payment falls short—even if you make up the shortfall in a subsequent payment—the IRS maintains you underpaid and will impose a penalty. And this rule holds true even if you eventually receive a tax refund when you file your 1988 return.

Say, for example, that your tax last year added up to $40,000 and that this year it will total $80,000. Your quarterly payments are either $10,000 (one quarter of $40,000) or $18,000 (one quarter of $72,000, which is 90 percent of $80,000).

No fool, you pay $10,000 for each of the four quarterly installments. If you make those payments, you won't be guilty of underpaying—even though your estimated payments amount to only half of your current year's tax liability. Of course, you will have to come up with the $40,000 unpaid balance when you file your tax return.

On the other hand, assume that money is tight and that you pay only $4,000 in each of the first three installments. Although you have underpaid each installment by $6,000 ($10,000 less $4,000), the IRS will first apply your estimated tax payment to any underpayment in the order in which such installments were required to be paid. The IRS starts the penalty clock on each underpayment on the date the installment was due.

But you can limit the penalty—or perhaps even eliminate it. Here's how. If on the fourth installment you hand over $28,000 to the IRS (the $10,000 due on the fourth installment plus the $18,000 you underpaid on the first three installments), the penalty clock stops running.

You still owe a penalty, the size of which depends on current interest rates, but you have put a cap on its accrual.

Or you could eliminate the penalty altogether—provided you are drawing a salary that is subject to tax withholding. You see, unlike the estimated payments, which are credited to your account when you make them, the IRS simply totals all your payroll withholding at the end of the year. Then it credits one fourth of the total to each of your four quarterly installments.

So you may ask your employer to increase the amount of your tax withholding at the end of the year by simply filing a new Form W-4, "Employee's Withholding Allowance Certificate," and claiming fewer withholding exemptions. That way, you can make up the shortfall from any earlier underpayment of estimated quarterly payments.

To see how this strategy works, just take the last example and assume that you made those three quarterly estimated tax payments on income that you earn from freelance consulting. You're also employed as an executive of a large oil company, and you usually receive a holiday bonus.

To eliminate the underpayment penalty you've incurred on your freelance income, you simply have your company withhold an extra $28,000 ($18,000 in underpayments plus the final $10,000 installment) from your year-end bonus check. As long as the extra payroll withholding is done before the end of the tax year, you're off the penalty hook.

But now, suppose the situation is different. Suppose you don't want the IRS to credit your withholding equally to all four quarterly installments. Instead, you want Uncle Sam to credit the amount withheld in the quarter in which the withholding actually happened.

Why? Well, it could be useful in minimizing the penalty. Let's say that you quit your job on April 1. For the first three months of the year, your income from salary and bonuses is subject to withholding that totals $24,000.

Based on your investment income, you calculate you'll owe the IRS $10,000 a quarter in estimated Taxes. Because cash is short, you don't make the quarterly payments.

Later you come into some money and you want to stop the underpayment penalty that's been accruing. So you make one estimated tax payment of $16,000 on January 15. If the IRS pro rates your withholding as it normally would, it would credit $6,000 ($24,000 divided by 4) to each quarterly installment.

But what if you could claim credit for the $24,000 withheld from your salary and bonus on the dates it was actually withheld?

In that case the IRS would consider your first two $10,000 installments paid in full. You would have underpaid the third installment by just $6,000—that is, the $10,000 due minus $4,000 remaining from your withholding. Since you made up for this underpayment with the $16,000 that you sent the IRS in the fourth installment, you've minimized your penalty.

To claim credit for the amounts you had withheld, all you have to do is retain proof—such as copies of paycheck stubs—of the dates of the actual withholding. Attach these copies to Form 2210 and include the form with your 1040.

MAKING AMENDS If your tax picture changes during the year—your income goes up, say, or your expenses decrease—you should consider amending your estimated tax payments.

Let's say your income increases. In this case you should total up your tax liability for the year, then subtract the tax payments you've already made. Now, divide the result by the number of quarters remaining in the year—three, say—and pay the extra tax in three equal installments.

Your first installment may still fall short if you pay only estimated taxes and don't have tax withheld from your wages. For example, assume your tax liability last year came to a whopping $70,000. This year you estimate that you'll owe a more modest $40,000.

So you base your estimated tax installments on 90 percent of $40,000, or $36,000. And each of your quarterly payments comes to $9,000.

On September 15, however, you revise your tax liability for the current year to $60,000. So you must change the estimated tax you owe to $53,000 ($60,000 times 90 percent).

Since you have already made $18,000 in estimated payments on April 15 and June 15, your remaining estimated tax comes to $36,000, which you'll pay in two installments on September 15 and January 15.

Because your first two payments fall short, Uncle Sam might penalize you, unless your withholding is enough to cover the shortfall, or you satisfy the IRS that you're entitled to a waiver—a subject we get to shortly.

To minimize the penalty, you should consider a September 15 payment of $22,500 and a January payment of $13,500. In this way the penalty for the first and second quarters would be cut off as of September 15.

And if your income decreases? Again, add up your tax liability and subtract the tax payments you've already made. You may find you've already paid the required amount. One drawback, though: If you are entitled to a refund, you must wait until you file your current return to receive it.

SOME DISCRETION While the underpayment penalty is mandatory in most cases, the IRS may—but is not required to—waive it in three situations where it would be unfair.

There is one condition, though: You must file Form 2210 with your return and attach an explanation of the circumstances entitling you to a waiver. The three situations:

- Your underpayment is due to a disaster or a casualty.
- It is the result of "unusual circumstances"—a phrase, alas, that the IRS to date has not defined.
- You retired after reaching age sixty-two or became disabled in the current or previous tax year, and your underpayment is due to reasonable cause, not willful neglect.

IT'S NEVER TOO LATE   Now, more on Form W-4.

If you found yourself overwithheld or underwithheld when you completed your 1987 return, you should file a new W-4 in 1988 to more accurately reflect the tax you expect to owe.

As in 1987, when you fill out the worksheet provided to figure the number of allowances you may take, you must take into account your spouse's income and your nonwage income, such as interest or dividends. Don't forget that the value of certain fringe benefits you receive from your employer is also subject to withholding. So the number of exemptions you claim may well be less than those you claimed previously.

The sooner you revise your W-4 to reflect these changes, the more your withholding will approximate your actual tax liability for 1988. And this fact is important.

Why? As we've seen, you must pay 90 percent of your current year's tax liability or 100 percent of last year's tax to escape underpayment penalties.

Let's say the number of withholding allowances you're entitled to decreases to fewer than the number you've claimed on your new W-4. In this case you must file a new W-4 within 10 days of the event that led to the decrease in allowances—you and your spouse divorce, for instance.

And here's another rule: If you claim more than ten withholding allowances, your employer must send copies of your W-4 to the IRS. And you may then be asked to verify your allowances.

The IRS wants to make sure you fill the form out correctly. So Uncle Sam may fine you $500 if he discovers you deliberately filed—with no reasonable basis—a Form W-4 that results in your having less tax withheld than you should.

But take heart. The IRS has repeatedly stated that taxpayers who make honest mistakes in calculating their withholding are not the targets of the $500 penalty.

The law also imposes criminal penalties—of $1,000 or a year in jail or both—if you willfully supply false or fraudulent information or fail to supply information that might require an increase in your withholding.

Tip: If both you and your spouse are employed, the IRS recommends that the spouse with the higher salary take all the withholding allowances. That way, your withholding will more closely approximate your actual tax liability.

If you have more than one job, or your spouse works, you may claim all your allowances on one job or you may claim some on each job. However, you may not claim the same allowances on both jobs.

Say, for example, that you spend your days working for XYZ Corp. and your nights for ABC Co. You claim your four with-holding allowances—for your four children—when you fill out your Form W-4 with XYZ. When you file a W-4 with ABC, you claim no withholding allowances for your children.

Caution: Your employer may not refund you any taxes that have been overwithheld. You must request a refund when you file your annual tax return.

APPLYING OVERPAYMENTS TO YOUR ESTIMATED TAX BILL   If you overpay your taxes in one year, should you apply the overpayment to your estimated tax bill?

It depends. If your overpayment is approximately the same as you'll owe on your first installment, it's usually a good idea. After all, your first installment is due April 15, and there's little sense in writing a check to cover an amount that the IRS already has in its hands.

But what if the overpayment substantially exceeds the amounts you owe in the first and second quarters? Pay your first and second quarter installments from the overpayment, then ask for a refund of the remainder. Of course, if you anticipate a significant drop in income for the year, and you expect to pay little or no estimated tax, request a refund for the overpayment when you file your return. Why? Once you request that an overpayment be applied to your estimated tax, you can't change your mind.

QUESTIONS AND ANSWERS

QUESTION: If I make a joint payment of estimated taxes with my spouse, must I file a joint return?

Making joint estimated tax payments with your spouse does not mean that the two of you must file a joint return. You may still file separately, and you and your spouse may divide up the estimated payments any way you want.

Q: If my spouse and I make separate estimated payments, can we file a joint return?

The answer is yes if you and your spouse are legally separated under a decree of divorce or separate maintenance, have different tax years, or if either of you is a nonresident alien.

CHAPTER 28

Your Guide to IRS Penalties

Penalties aren't levied just on those who cheat, or try to cheat, Uncle Sam. Being late, negligent, or plain careless can cost you extra money on top of taxes due.

In this chapter we'll show you how to avoid inadvertently subjecting yourself to IRS discipline. And if you do find yourself on the wrong side of an agency ruling, the information here will at least help you minimize the damage.

INTEREST OWED AND OWING Penalties aside, if you owe the government money, you must pay interest on the amount due—from the very day that it's due. Filing extensions doesn't change the fact that interest on any unpaid amount that you owe begins to accrue on April 15.

Likewise, you may collect interest from the IRS on overpayments. The rate will be lower than the one you'd pay if you owed the agency money.

The rules say the IRS must fork over your refund within 45 days from April 15 or the date you file your return—whichever is later.

What if the IRS fails to meet this deadline?

The agency must pay you interest on your refund. What's more, it must calculate the interest due you from April 15 or the date on which you file your return, again, whichever is later.

Both rates—what the IRS pays and what you pay—are compounded daily and adjusted quarterly based on the federal short-term rate. This amount is the average market yield of Treasury bills and other U.S. obligations with terms of three years or less.

When the IRS owes you, it pays the short-term rate plus 2 percent. If you owe the IRS, however, you pay the short-term rate plus 3 percent. Since 1987 these rates have averaged 9 percent and 10 percent, respectively.

Any interest the IRS pays you is taxable. But any interest you pay the IRS is considered personal interest, and it is only partially deductible through 1990. After 1990 you may not deduct any of it. (See Chapter 4 for more information on interest deductions.)

DON'T BE LATE   Late filers and late payers are both subject to their respective penalties. And if you're a late filer and a late payer, you're subject to both. The penalties are in addition to interest that's due on the unpaid amounts. Let's take late filing first.

If your return isn't filed by the date it's due (or by the next business day, if the deadline falls on a Saturday, Sunday, or holiday), the IRS imposes a stiff penalty: 5 percent of the total tax due for each month or fraction of a month that you're late.

There is a cap on this late-filing penalty, though. The penalty may not add up to more than 25 percent of the tax you owe.

What happens if you're just one day late filing your income tax return? You pay the full 5 percent for the first month. If you're more than 60 days late, you pay the full 5 percent, but, at minimum, you pay the lesser of $100 or 100 percent of the tax due.

Further, even if your return is mailed to Uncle Sam on time, the IRS may consider it late if it's either unsigned or lacks enough information to compute the tax.

What determines whether your return is late is the postmark on the envelope you mail it in. If you've addressed it correctly, affixed the right postage, and gotten an official postmark that beats the deadline—and if the return actually makes it to the IRS—it's not late.

If the return never arrives, however, the burden is on you to prove that you mailed it—a difficult task unless you have the receipt from a certified or registered mailing.

If you don't owe any tax—for instance, if your payroll withholding more than covered your tax liability for the year—you don't owe a penalty for late filing.

What happens if you file but just don't pay? More fines, of course, but late payers' penalties work a bit differently.

Initially the agency assesses you one half of one percent of the tax not paid for each month or fraction of a month that the tax remains due.

Say you file your tax return on April 15 and it shows you owe $1,000 to Uncle Sam. and you don't pay that amount until three months after you file. You owe a penalty of $15—that is, one half of one percent times $1,000 times three months.

And if you still don't pay up?

Usually the IRS then sends you four or five notices demanding payment. These letters are mailed to you over a period of six months or so. Then, 10 days before it does so, the agency lets you know through a levy notice that it intends to file a lien against your assets.

Beginning with the month after the levy notice expires, the penalty rate doubles. From then on it's one percent of the unpaid tax for each additional month the tax remains unpaid.

No matter how late you are in paying, though, the penalty may not exceed 25 percent of the taxes due—unless you're both a late filer and a late payer.

If the late filing and late payment penalties both apply for the first five months, the IRS reduces the late filing penalty by the amount of the late payment penalty.

In other words, you're not subject to more than a 5 percent combined penalty in any one month—a maximum of 25 percent during the first five months.

Caution: In the eyes of the IRS a postmark from an office postage meter isn't official. So think twice before you use your company's postage meter.

Tip: There's only one proven way to avoid the late filing penalty—that is, file your return on time. Even if you owe Uncle Sam money, go ahead and file your return by April 15. Then make arrangements with the IRS to pay the amount due.

The agency may waive the late payment penalty if you show reasonable cause for not paying on time—serious illness or financial hardship, for example.

REASONS FOR UNDERPAYMENT Now let's say that you've filed your return on time and paid all the taxes you claim to owe. So there are no late filing penalties due.

But what if it turns out you owe more tax than you claimed to owe? The IRS recognizes three reasons for underpayment: honest mistakes, negligence, and fraud.

What's the difference? An honest mistake is, well, just that. You added 5 and 3 on your return and got 4. If you make an honest mistake, the IRS will give you 10 days from the day it notifies you of the underpayment to pay up.

If you don't pay within 10 days, the penalty is one half of one percent per month of the amount you haven't paid. This penalty may not exceed 25 percent of the underpayment.

Negligence is a bit harder to define. It includes acts of omission and commission. The most common is keeping inaccurate or inadequate books or records. It's automatically negligence if you fail to include on your return an amount that was shown on Form W-2 or 1099.

Other examples include taking clearly improper deductions, making substantial errors in reporting income, continuing to deduct items that were held to be nondeductible in previous years, or failing to offer any explanation for understatements of income.

Whether something constitutes negligence always depends on a taxpayer's circumstances. For example, whether your books are adequate depends on the size and complexity of your business. The IRS generally holds a highly educated person to a stricter standard than one who is less educated.

If you rely on a tax professional for advice or preparation of your return, you probably won't be found negligent unless you negligently failed to supply your accountant with adequate records.

The agency's finding of negligence is presumed true. In other words, in the case of an error that results in an underpayment, the burden falls on you to prove that you weren't negligent.

Not so with fraud, though. Fraud is a deliberate attempt to evade the tax law. Here, the burden of proof lies with the IRS.

So, how are the penalties applied?

If, after an audit, the IRS decides that you underpaid as a consequence of negligence, it may assess a fine—5 percent of the total underpayment, plus an amount equal to one half of the interest that would accrue between the original due date of the return and the day the penalty is assessed.

But if the IRS can prove that the underpayment resulted from fraud, the penalty assessed is 75 percent of the underpayment attributable to fraud plus an amount equal to one half of the interest that would accrue between the original due date and the day the penalty is assessed.

What if the underpayment is only partially due to fraud? The other part was simple error.

It doesn't matter. If the IRS concludes that only part of an underpayment is due to fraud, it treats the entire underpayment as fraud. You must then prove that it wasn't all due to fraud. If you're successful, the fraud penalty applies only to that portion of the underpayment attributable to fraud. If Uncle Sam concludes you've been negligent as well, the negligence penalty applies to the amount that's not attributable to fraud.

Congress is considering a change in the way these penalties are calculated. That portion of the penalty currently calculated like interest will no longer apply.

But interest on the remaining 5 percent or 75 percent portion of the penalty will accrue from the date the return was filed, rather than from the time the penalty is assessed.

Here's an example of how the IRS levies negligence and fraud penalties. The agency audits your return and finds a $1,000 underpayment.

Part of it, $100, was due to a math error.

Another part, $200, was the result of negligence. You inadvertently mixed personal expenses with your business travel-and-entertainment deductions.

But $700 of the underpayment, the agency decides, was fraudulent. You deliberately omitted income from your return. You reluctantly agree.

How do the penalties apply? The 75 percent fraud penalty applies only to $700—that part of the underpayment attributable to fraud. And the negligence penalty applies to the remaining $300 underpayment, even though part of it stemmed from an honest mistake.

The interest portion of the fine—one half of the interest due—applies only to $900 of the underpayment (the $200 attributed to negligence and $700 to fraud).

And don't be confused by the inclusion of half the interest in the underpayment penalty fine. It's part of the fine. You still owe the full amount of the interest due on the underpayment as well as the penalty.

SUBSTANTIAL UNDERSTATEMENT
The tax law draws a distinction between underpayment, which we just covered, and something it calls "substantial understatement."

You're guilty of substantial understatement when the amount of tax shown on your return falls short of the tax you should have listed by $5,000 or by 10 percent, whichever is greater. The penalty for substantial understatement is 25 percent of the amount by which your tax was understated.

Here's how substantial understatement could happen.

Assume that you're a talent agent who spends lavishly on lunches and dinners in search of contracts for your clients. The

IRS, in an audit, disallows many of your entertainment expense claims.

Consequently, you owe Uncle Sam an additional $6,000 in taxes. On top of that, you owe a $1,500 substantial understatement penalty.

There's one exception to the understatement penalty.

Say you take a position in your return that's not clear under the tax law—you deduct points on your refinanced mortgage, say, instead of amortizing them.

As long as you disclose in the return all the facts and your authority for taking that position—for example, a revenue ruling, a court case, or your interpretation of the law—the IRS won't assess the substantial understatement penalty.

In other words, you don't have to be right. You only have to be honest and present your case fairly and squarely to Uncle Sam.

FRIVOLOUS RETURNS   The IRS is a collection agency, not a debating society. It doesn't want to read about your antiwar sentiments, for instance, on one of its 1040 forms.

People who deliberately use their tax returns to register a protest or make a point about public policy may find their social activism rewarded with a $500 penalty for filing a frivolous return. The IRS may impose the penalty if the person filing the return makes a claim that delays or impedes the processing of the return or the payment of tax that is plainly, and legally, due.

What's frivolous? A position isn't frivolous simply because it's novel. Rather, a frivolous claim is one that has been repeatedly rejected as utterly meritless.

Examples include claiming clearly unallowable deductions, such as a discount because the U.S. is no longer on the gold standard, or claiming a deduction for the proportion of taxes that would have gone to support the Defense Department.

The burden of proving your return is frivolous falls on the government, but he $500 fine is based on the irregular return, not on any tax underpayment. So the penalty may apply even if you actually paid the correct amount of tax.

Now, we're not suggesting that you shouldn't stand up and be counted. We're only pointing out that there may be a cost involved if you use your tax return as a soapbox.

TAX SHELTER PENALTIES   Promoters and investors who play loose with the laws that apply to tax shelters face substantial penalties, increased during the last round of tax reform.

For promoters, failure to register a tax shelter carries a minimum fine of $500. And the fine can go as high as one percent of the total amount invested. Failure to register a tax shelter partnership that raises $3 million, for instance, can cost the organizer $30,000.

Neglect to maintain a list of those who invest in the tax shelter you've promoted, and the IRS may find you $50 per name omitted—up to a maximum of $100,000.

And, as an investor, forgetting to report a tax shelter identification number on your return may net you a $250 wrist slap from the IRS, which takes its tax shelter rules very seriously. (For more information on tax shelters, see chapter 19.)

FILING FORMS   The agency is also serious about getting the information it needs to track taxpayers' taxable income. Employers who don't file information returns—forms 1099—with the IRS or who fail to supply a copy of the form to taxpayers face stiff fines.

For each form not filed with the IRS, the fine is $50, up to a maximum of $100,000. The same holds true for each form not supplied to a taxpayer, so that the total maximum fine may hit $200,000. Incorrect information on a 1099 submitted to the IRS, or to a taxpayer, results in a $5 fine up to an annual maximum of $20,000.

And as a business owner or taxpayer you'll be dealing with more form 1099's than ever before. Recent changes to the law now require 1099's to be filed for real estate transactions and for royalty payments amounting to more than $10 in any calendar year.

In the case of real estate transactions, the person responsible for closing the transaction—usually the settlement attorney or title company representative—must file the form. If those people aren't present, then the primary mortgage lender, the seller's broker, or the buyer's broker, in that order, must furnish copies of the 1099 to the buyer, seller, and the IRS.

In the case of royalty payments, the person or organization that pays the royalties must fill out the required 1099s.

As should be clear by now, Uncle Sam is serious when it comes to income taxes. And he backs up his beliefs with hefty penalties if you transgress.

The only way to ensure that you don't get slapped with penalties is to educate yourself about the workings of the tax law. Then check to be sure that you've filed a completely accurate return and paid the full amount of taxes due.

QUESTIONS AND ANSWERS

QUESTION: I was due a refund of $300. But the IRS send me $3,000 instead. I deposited the full amount in my checking account. Soon afterward I sent the IRS a check for $2,700 to cover the error. They say I owe interest for the time the money was in my account. Do I have to pay it?

A recent change in the tax law reduces your interest liability in the event of an IRS administrative error. If Uncle Sam should overpay you by $50,000 or less—send you a refund of $3,000, for example, instead of $300—interest will not start to accrue on the overpayment until the IRS officially notifies you that you owe them the $2,700.

Another recent change in the law may work in your favor. The law no longer forbids the IRS from forgiving interest on underpayments of tax attributable to its own administrative efforts or delays.

In an audit, for instance, you might concede that a deduction was a bit aggressive and agree to pay the additional tax. But it takes the IRS a year to get around to mailing you the bill. The agency now may abate the interest attributable to the one-year delay that was its fault.

Tip: These interest abatement rules apply retroactively to 1979, so if you've paid interest to Uncle Sam any time since then, you may be due a refund. Check it out.

Q: My return was late. But I had a good excuse. I was in the hospital in a coma when April 15 rolled around. do I still have to pay a penalty?

The IRS does accept some excuses. And yours probably qualifies. If you can show that your return was late not out of willful neglect but due to reasonable cause, you may escape the penalty.

Being too busy isn't considered reasonable cause. If, however, you're seriously ill or if your tax records are destroyed by fire, you may qualify as having a reasonable cause. But it's up to you to convince the IRS that what is reasonable to you should also be reasonable to them.

Q: I received a notice from the IRS that I failed to report $100 in interest income. I failed to report that amount because I never received a 1099 from my bank. I don't think I should have to pay a penalty to the IRS. Do I have any recourse?

You certainly do. You can ask the IRS to waive the penalty. In 1987 the IRS assessed some $14.2 billion in penalties—but forgave $3.9 billion.

Explain your situation to the IRS in a letter. Include a copy of the notice that the agency sent you, plus a check for any taxes and interest you owe. Don't pay the penalty until you hear from the Uncle Sam. You'll hear from the IRS one way or the other.

CHAPTER 29

What to Do When the IRS Says Prove It

You filed your tax forms, mailed them off with your payment, and the cancelled check has come back from the bank. Now you can breathe easy. Right?

Wrong. The fact that the IRS cashes your check, or sends you the refund you claim as your due, means that the post office didn't lose the correspondence, the IRS computers aren't on the fritz, and you didn't make any obvious math errors on the return.

But it doesn't mean that the IRS is necessarily happy with your return or that it won't be asking questions. It doesn't mean, in other words, that you've escaped an audit.

If your pulse doesn't race at the very thought of an audit, you're an unusual soul. The unhappy fact is that the IRS may audit your return at any time.

You do get one break, though—a statute of limitations. Uncle Sam is prevented by law from assessing any additional tax after three years have passed from April 15 or the date you filed your return, whichever is later.

But there are exceptions to this rule: You're subject to audit after three years if you didn't pay all the tax you owed, you failed to report all your income on your return, or you filed a fraudulent return.

And, in any case, the IRS may disallow any deductions or credits that you carried forward to a future return. The result: You'd have to pay more tax later.

Never been audited before? You're lucky. The odds are that most taxpayers will face the IRS across a desk at some time. So, given that eventuality, we're going to suggest ways that will help you get through this unpleasantness when your turn comes.

Provided you haven't deliberately tried to shortchange Uncle Sam, an audit needn't be any worse than unpleasant. And look on the bright side. If you did make an honest mistake, it might have been in the IRS' favor. You could get money back as a result of the audit.

But don't count on it. IRS statistics show that only 4.59 percent of tax returns examined in 1987 led to a refund.

THE ODDS OF AN AUDIT   All told, the government audits about 1.1 million of the 102 million tax returns filed every year. That means the odds of being picked for an audit in a given year are only about one percent.

However, you're much more likely to face an audit if you fall into one of the taxpayer categories that the IRS watches closely or if your return upsets IRS computers.

What triggers IRS scrutiny?

When you mail your completed 1040 to one of the agency's regional service centers, a clerk enters the numbers from your return into a computer. The computer compares your numbers— your deductions, for instance—with the average deductions claimed by other taxpayers.

The computer then assigns a score to your return based on how much greater your write-offs are than the average. And the IRS selects returns for audit on the basis of these scores—that is, it selects all returns above a certain score.

At that point, a human takes over again. An IRS employee looks over your return and decides whether an audit might be worth the agency's time and expense.

How far off the averages do your claims have to be before the computer picks out your return for this special attention? Not surprisingly, the IRS won't say.

But our experience tells us that you can gauge the likelihood of an audit from your answers to the following questions.

How much income did you report?

The odds of your being audited go up with your earnings. In 1987, for instance, the IRS examined 0.50 percent of returns with gross income of less than $10,000 but 2.24 percent of returns with gross income of $50,000 or more.

Did you itemize deductions?

People who itemize are almost twice as likely to be audited as individuals who file a short form.

Are you self-employed?

Individuals in business for themselves are audited far more frequently than those collecting a salary from someone else. That's because the IRS frequently finds abusers among this group.

Are your travel and entertainment deductions significant?

The IRS scrutinizes these write-offs because, it has found, taxpayers frequently claim improper travel and entertainment deductions.

Do you pay or receive alimony?

The IRS has found that not all taxpayers report alimony payments as income. As a result, a number of the agency's offices now match deductions for alimony payments by one former spouse with reports of alimony income by the other.

Are you a tax shelter investor?

If so, your chances of being audited increase dramatically. Often the IRS earmarks tax shelter investors for audit after it has examined the return of the tax shelter itself or has found recurring problems with the promoter who sold them the investment.

NONAUDIT INQUIRIES Not every letter from the IRS is cause for panic. The notice of an audit may be, but there's another letter the IRS mails. It simply says the agency thinks that you've made a mistake and asks that you send them more money.

Don't send the money—not right away.

But don't ignore the letter either. Instead, pull your return out of the file and go over it. Or, have your tax preparer go over it for you. Did you make a mistake?

The data-entry clerk at the IRS may have incorrectly keypunched a number. Maybe you just forgot to file an obscure form. In any case, don't assume that the IRS computer that sent you this letter is right. Check it out. If you do owe the money the IRS claims you owe, send it along.

But if, after checking, you find that you don't owe, or that you still don't understand the agency's claim, write the IRS a letter. Explain why you disagree.

To be helpful, you should enclose a copy of the correspondence the agency sent you. That way the IRS employee who gets your letter doesn't have to search through the agency files, and he or she has a better chance of matching your response with your IRS file.

PREPARING FOR THE AUDIT The IRS doesn't actually use the word "audit" when it writes to tell you you're going to be audited. It's much more polite. The letter just says that the agency wants to verify the accuracy of your return, and it asks for a meeting.

Do not ignore this letter.

The two most common types of audits—other than audits conducted exclusively through the mail—are office audits and field audits. If you must be audited, you would prefer the office audit. It is often less detailed.

For an office audit, the IRS asks you to meet with its auditor at a specific time and place. The letter you get will specify the areas of your return that the IRS is questioning. And it will ask you to bring records to back up deductions or credits you've claimed, income you've reported, or any other item that has a bearing on the tax you've computed.

The letter also asks you to bring along a copy of your tax return for the year in question, plus a copy of your prior year's return.

For the more formidable field audit, however the agency will announce that it's sending its representative to you. That's probably because the auditor will want to see more records than you can conveniently bring to him or to her. The field audit isn't a minor affair.

If the date and time the IRS sets for either a field or an office audit is inconvenient, immediately call the agency's office and ask for a change. Chances are the agent will accommodate you.

Now, start getting ready. Preparation and organization are the keys to getting through the audit as painlessly as possible.

You should have the answers—and the backup—to all questions about which the IRS has indicated an interest. But let yourself be guided by this general rule: Provide only what's requested and answer only what's asked—nothing more. Otherwise, the audit may extend into areas of your return that you're not prepared to discuss.

WHO GOES TO THE AUDIT? The issue of who actually goes to the audit is left, by and large, up to you. If your return is a joint one, you or your spouse or both of you may go. But neither of you has to. You may send your accountant to represent you.

In fact, almost anyone who has your authorization (IRS Form 2848D) or your power of attorney (IRS Form 2848) may represent you at an audit.

Theoretically, you can go to the audit with your accountant, your attorney, and an army of advisers in tow. But it's not a good idea.

Too many troops gives the impression that you're worried and have a great deal to hide. And all those reinforcements are charging you for their time. Also, most audits are routine, so you don't need to roll out your heavy artillery.

If the matter seems simple, with the right preparation and backup documents you may be able to handle it yourself. If it's complicated, ask your adviser to be there with you. In any case, discuss the matter with your tax adviser before you decide you should go.

THE BIG DAY   The day of the audit is at hand. How should you behave? To begin with, be prompt. When the audit begins, pay attention to what's going on.

If the person you meet says anything to indicate that the examination of your return is anything but routine—or if he or she is introduced as a "special" IRS agent—stop the proceedings right there and seek legal help.

Special agents work for the IRS criminal division, and they don't participate in audits unless you're suspected of serious wrongdoing. By law, a special agent is supposed to inform you before the audit begins that this is something more than a routine check.

But listen carefully for the warning. You don't want to miss it. If in doubt, you can always request to see the person's IRS identification card. And you can copy down his or her name and any other information printed on it.

But assuming that your audit is routine, how do you behave? Pleasantly, of course, but don't be lulled into letting your guard down. Speak when you're spoken to. Answer the questions you're asked.

Above all, don't become abusive, railing against the unfairness of the tax system. Keep your politics to yourself. If you know of a neighbor who's getting away with tax murder, this isn't the time to call attention to him or her. It won't distract the auditor's attention away from you.

Listen carefully to the auditor's questions, and consider your answer before making it. IRS employees are skilled. They may probe a bit in hopes of identifying additional problem areas on your return.

In short, stay calm. Don't get flustered. Be patient. It will all be over in time.

AND IF YOU DISAGREE: STAGES OF APPEAL   When it's over, however, you may not agree with the auditor's finding. What can you do about it? There are several stages of appeal, beginning with the IRS itself, and eventually, if it comes to that, the courts.

Step one: Ask for a meeting with your auditor's supervisor. Perhaps you can persuade him or her of the correctness of your position. Or you may receive a more satisfactory explanation for the finding than the auditor gave.

If you're still not happy, though, ask for a meeting with a representative of the Office of the Regional Director of Appeals. Your tax adviser should get involved if you decide to go this route. Filing a protest is a formal procedure that you should not attempt on your own.

IRS statistics show that about 85 percent of cases that go to the Regional Director are settled at that level. Settlement often involves compromise—on both Uncle Sam's part and the taxpayer's. But it will be worth your while to go through this process if you've taken a supportable—though not necessarily 100 percent correct—position on your tax return.

If the appeals process doesn't work, well, there are always the courts. In fact, you can take your appeal to the courts at any time. You don't have to exhaust the IRS internal appeal steps. But here's a word of caution about court appeals.

They're expensive. If the attorney's fees are going to be greater than the IRS claims, you may want to swallow your pride and principles and pay the government what it wants. It could be cheaper in the long run. If you think you want to try an appeal, though, seek qualified counsel.

QUESTIONS AND ANSWERS

QUESTION: Does the IRS ever do random audits?

Most IRS audits aren't entirely random events—but some, in fact, are. Every three years the IRS chooses 50,000 individual returns completely at random for audit in connection with its Taxpayer Compliance Measurement Program (TCMP).

The unfortunate souls who filed these targeted returns must justify every entry, line by line. The government isn't picking on them out of any specific suspicion. It just wants to see, by sampling, what proportion of taxpayers aren't complying with the laws and how they're not complying.

And if, by the way, just knowing that one might have to endure such an audit helps keep the rest of us honest, the IRS considers that a useful secondary effect.

One additional note: The last TCMP audit was done in 1985. That means another TCMP audit is scheduled for 1988.

These random audits are also done on partnership tax returns and on information returns filed by businesses. For example, the IRS may check the accuracy of returns that report the payment of interest income. And these audits may indirectly influence your individual return.

Q: Any advice on how to avoid an audit?

Perhaps the best advice we can give you: Fill out your returns as honestly and completely as you can. That way if an audit does come your way, you know your heart—and your 1040—are pure. And that knowledge will help you more than anything else in breezing through IRS scrutiny.

CHAPTER 30

How to Get Ready for Your Tax Preparer

A tax return is, in many people's eyes, like a postmortem. It's undertaken after the damage is already done. Alas, we have little control over what happens to us when we're gone. But we *are* in the driver's seat when it comes to our taxes.

That's why it's important to begin tax planning before the year ends. That way there's still time to trim your tax liability.

A critical point to keep in mind: Your tax adviser is not just a tax preparer. You should work with him or her throughout the year to ensure optimum tax savings.

But don't forget. Uncle Sam holds you—not your tax preparer—ultimately responsible for the accuracy of your return.

GET ORGANIZED One of the keys to sound tax planning: good organization. And the sooner you tackle your organizing chores, the better.

As we've seen, to reap benefits from year-end tax planning, you have to act before the tax year ends. January 1 of the following tax year is far too late.

The bottom line: It's never too soon for you and your adviser to start developing tax-saving strategies for the current year.

GOOD RECORDS SAVE TIME AND EXPENSE Finally it's time to assemble the correct data for Uncle Sam. Remember, all the careful tax planning you've done will count for naught if you can't produce the records and the facts that you need at tax filing time.

Keep in mind too: A tax advisers's main function is to help you make the most of the tax law, so you can save money. You don't want to waste your adviser's time—and your cash—sorting through slips of paper.

One question we're frequently asked: Is it important to file on time? It's true that Uncle Sam lets you extend your return past April 15. But having your tax preparer file a request for an extension (Form 4868) with the IRS can cost you more in tax preparation fees.

Besides, filing for an extension doesn't really get you off the hook. The rules require you to pay 90 percent of your tax liability by April 15, even if you don't file your tax return until August 15 or later. So it makes sense to gather together all your data as soon as you can. Don't put off the job because you still need information on, say, one trust account.

Here's another incentive to early preparation. Many tax preparers will be able to file your 1988 return electronically. Uncle Sam says that if your preparer does file by computer, you'll receive any refund you have coming to you in as little as 17 days, not the now common four to eight weeks. So if your tax data is ready, you could be that much closer to a refund check.

In the following pages we've compiled a checklist of the records and information that you'll want to pull together before you or your tax preparer begins work on your return. So get started. A tidy sum in tax savings might well be your reward.

Note: Many tax preparers send their clients forms listing income and deductions for the previous year and asking for data for the current year. If your preparer sends such a form, use it in addition to our checklist. It may well jog your memory for deductions you might otherwise forget.

RECORDS DETAILING INCOME   Let's start with the records you need to gather to account for your income—whatever the source. Keep in mind that your employer, bank, broker, or a dividend-paying corporation in which you own stock is required by law to mail W-2's or 1099's by January 31. So if you haven't received the information by February 10 (a date that allows for mail delays), start making inquiries.

Wages
    Bring copies of all W-2 forms.

Dividends
    Bring all copies of your 1099's.

Interest

Again, bring all copies of your 1099's, and if you've made loans to friends or relatives, make sure you have information on those loans too.

Self-Employment Income

Bring along any 1099's you've received from customers or clients, your checkbooks for the year, any other books you've kept, and your bank statements. Also, don't forget to collect all your travel, meal, entertainment, and automobile records, including your charge card slips.

Capital Gains and Losses

Bring the transaction slips for any securities that you may have bought or sold. You can save some steps if you make sure the sell slips agree with the Form 1099-B that you received from your broker. (The 1099-B may also remind you of what you sold during the year.)

Did you sell your personal residence or any other real estate? Bring along your closing statement and receipts for your fixing-up expenses.

Partnerships, Estates, Trusts, S Corporations

Be sure that you have the Form K-1's that you should have received from any of these entities. The form lists your share of income or deductions.

Also, for partnerships and S corporations, know the date you made your investment and be ready to explain to your tax preparer whether your involvement is active or passive.

And if the funds you invested were borrowed, keep in mind that the new tax law has specific rules governing interest deductions.

Real Estate Rental Activities

Gather your receipts and expenses (with cancelled checks or invoices) for the year, and summarize them by category on a piece of paper. If you bought the property this year, bring your closing statement.

You'll also want a list of any improvements made to the property this year. And if you or any family members used the property during the year, be sure that you know how many days of personal and rental use were involved.

Other Income

Bring along all the other slips of paper starting with a W or 1099 that organizations have been sending you, and list them on a sheet of paper. For instance, you may have received:

- State tax refunds
- Fully taxable pensions
- Taxable Social Security benefits
- Unemployment insurance
- Alimony
- Gambling winnings

Supplemental Gains and Losses

If you disposed of or sold equipment that you use in self-employment, or if you sold a car that you've used for work as an employee, bring any information you have relating to those transactions. You'll also need records of when you bought the equipment.

RECORDS DETAILING EXPENSES Up to this point the records you've been collecting will help you account for your income from whatever sources. Now you want to be sure that you also have the records you'll need to justify the deductions that you've got coming to you—deductions that will help you offset some of this income.

IRA's and Keoghs

Under certain conditions your IRA contribution is fully deductible from your gross income. And you may always deduct the money you have socked away in a Keogh. So have on hand your records of these investments.

Alimony

You may deduct above the line—that is, directly from your income—any alimony you pay. And you should have your cancelled checks as proof of your payments.

Interest You Forfeit

You may not know it, but interest you forfeit is also deductible above the line. When might you have forfeited income?

Say you take out a two-year CD at 6 percent. A year later interest rates rise to 8.5 percent. You cash in your CD prematurely and buy a new one with a higher payout.

When you do, your bank imposes a penalty—you lose three months of interest you've already earned. The good news: You may write the amount off.

Keep the bank's statement handy.

Medical Expenses

Do you think your medical expenses will top the new 7½ percent floor? If so, collect all your receipts to doctors, dentists, hospitals, pharmacies, and labs—anything related to your good health and well being.

If you had to modify your house for medical reasons, bring the signed statement from the doctor and the receipt from the improvement.

Don't forget to include information about insurance reimbursements you might have received during the year. You're also entitled to a deduction for medical mileage.

Taxes

Although sales tax is no longer deductible, other taxes such as state and local income taxes, real property taxes on all residences, and personal property taxes are. You should have the cancelled checks or validated tax bills to substantiate your claim.

Gather your payroll withholding statements. Also, bring the cancelled checks for current or previous years' state or local income taxes you paid, including amended state or local return payments. If you paid property taxes on a vacation home, bring the cancelled check or the bill.

Contributions

Bring along cancelled checks or the receipts you received for the current year's charitable contributions. If you gave old clothes or secondhand goods to a church drive, say, or Goodwill, bring the list you made or the receipt you received.

And note: If you donated more than $500 worth of used goods during the year, the IRS wants to know how much these goods originally cost you, when you bought them, and how you determined their value when you gave them away.

If you donated stock to your favorite charity, note the day you made the donation and the price that you originally paid for the securities.

If you donated a highly valued piece of jewelry, you should have an appraisal and an acknowledgment (Form 8283) from the organization to which you made the donation.

Interest

Under the reformed tax laws, interest deductions can be very complicated. In fact, interest deductibility depends on how you use the borrowed money, not on where you borrowed it. In any case, you should be able to relate each loan to its specific use.

To assist yourself or your tax preparer, separate your interest expenses into the following categories:

- Principal residence interest
- Second residence interest
- All other residence interest
- Mortgage points
- Credit card interest
- Investment interest
- Other personal loan interest
- Passive investment activity interest

Investment interest includes interest on money you borrowed to buy, say, stocks or bonds—margin accounts, for example.

Because not all mortgage interest may be deductible, you should be able to answer these questions for your tax preparer: Have you ever refinanced your original mortgage? If so, when did you refinance? What was the amount of your original mortgage? Your refinanced mortgage?

Also, if you've sold your house, have in hand the records you need to substantiate the amount you paid for your home plus the cost of any improvements. (You'll find more information about interest deductions in Chapter 4.)

If so, when, why, and how much?

If you have more than two residences, be sure to talk with your tax preparer about which one you want to consider your second residence to maximize your deduction.

Miscellaneous Deductions

Here's where you should list your out-of-pocket employee expenses and investment advisory expenses. If you used your car as an employee and the actual expenses topped the amount you were reimbursed, bring those records.

If you used your club for business entertainment, have those records handy. You'll also need receipts for your unreimbursed business meals. (See Chapter 8 for a complete list of these miscellaneous deductions.)

SUMMARY: WHY IT'S BETTER TO BE PREPARED   Why is it so important to gather together all this information? The answer is simple: The more organized your data, the easier it is for your tax adviser to save you tax dollars.

And keep in mind that the earlier you start your planning, the better the tax-saving opportunities. In fact, the best plan is to keep your records organized on an ongoing basis.

And stay in touch with your adviser as your financial circumstances change—you get married, say, you sell your home, or you make a killing in the stock market. Remember, you must invest your time today if you are to save tax dollars tomorrow.

APPENDIX

1. 1988 TAX RATE SCHEDULES

Single Individuals		Married Filing Jointly and Surviving Spouse	
Taxable Income	Rate	Taxable Income	Rate
$ 0 to $17,850	15%	$ 0 to $29,750	15%
17,851 to 43,150	28%	29,751 to 71,900	28%
43,151 to 89,560	33%	71,901 to 149,250	33%
89,561* and above	28%	149,251* and above	28%

Heads of Household		Married Filing Separately	
Taxable Income	Rate	Taxable Income	Rate
$ 0 to $23,900	15%	$ 0 to $14,875	15%
23,901 to 61,650	28%	14,876 to 35,950	28%
61,651 to 123,790	33%	35,951 to 113,300	33%
123,791* and above	28%	113,301* and above	28%

*The benefit of the personal exemptions, as discussed in Chapter 2, also phases out beginning at the indicated income level for each filing status. This phase-out should be taken into account when calculating your tax.

2. BUSINESS MILEAGE LOG

MONTH OF: _____

DATE	DESTINATION & PURPOSE	BUSINESS MILES	PERSONAL MILES	COMMUTE MILES	BUSINESS TOLLS/PARKING
TOTAL					

ODOMETER READING - BEGINNING OF MONTH _____

ODOMETER READING - END OF MONTH _____

TOTAL MONTHLY MILES _____

3. ANNUAL LEASE VALUE TABLE*

Fair Market Value	Annual Lease Value
$ 0 to 999	$ 600
1,000 to 1,999	850
2,000 to 2,999	1,100
3,000 to 3,999	1,350
4,000 to 4,999	1,600
5,000 to 5,999	1,850
6,000 to 6,999	2,100
7,000 to 7,999	2,350
8,000 to 8,999	2,600
9,000 to 9,999	2,850
10,000 to 10,999	3,100
11,000 to 11,999	3,350
12,000 to 12,999	3,600
13,000 to 13,999	3,850
14,000 to 14,999	4,100
15,000 to 15,999	4,350
16,000 to 16,999	4,600
17,000 to 17,999	4,850
18,000 to 18,999	5,100
19,000 to 19,999	5,350
20,000 to 20,999	5,600
21,000 to 21,999	5,850
22,000 to 22,999	6,100
23,000 to 23,999	6,350
24,000 to 24,999	6,600
25,000 to 25,999	6,850
26,000 to 27,999	7,250
28,000 to 29,999	7,750
30,000 to 31,999	8,250
32,000 to 33,999	8,750
34,000 to 35,999	9,250
36,000 to 37,999	9,750
38,000 to 39,999	10,250
40,000 to 41,999	10,750
42,000 to 43,999	11,250
44,000 to 45,999	11,850
46,000 to 47,999	12,250
48,000 to 49,999	12,750
50,000 to 51,999	13,250

Fair Market Value	Annual Lease Value
52,000 to 53,999	13,750
54,000 to 55,999	14,250
56,000 to 57,999	14,750
58,000 to 59,999	15,250

For vehicles having a fair market value in excess of $59,999, the Annual Lease Value is equal to: (.25 × the fair market value of the automobile) + 500.

*IRS table used to determine the amount of annual compensation to include as income, based upon the original fair market value of the automobile provided.

4. INDIVIDUAL AMT SYSTEM AT A GLANCE

Regular Taxable Income
+/– Post-1986 depreciation
+/– Sale of depreciable assets
+   Passive losses allowed by phase-in
+   Research and development expenses
+   Itemized deductions denied

> State & local income taxes
> Real estate taxes
> Medical expenses in excess of 10% of AGI
> Miscellaneous deductions
> Personal interest expense
> Excess home mortgage interest expense
> Excess investment interest expense
>
> or
>
> Standard deduction

+ Preferences

> Percentage depletion
> Intangible drilling costs
> Incentive stock options
> Net ''private activity'' bond interest
> Appreciated property contributions
> Pre-1987 depreciation on real property

–   AMT net operating loss deduction

Alternative Minimum Taxable Income (AMTI)
+   Personal exemption deduction
–   AMT exemption deduction

AMTI Subject to AMT
×   21 percent

Tentative Minimum Tax Before Credits
–   Foreign tax credit

Tentative Minimum Tax (TMT)
–   Regular tax after foreign tax credit

Alternative Minimum Tax (AMT)

5. IRA DEDUCTION WORK SHEET*

Upper phase-out limit:
Married filing jointly	$50,000	
Married filing separately	10,000	\} _____
Other returns	35,000	

Less: Adjusted gross income
before IRA deduction   (_____)

Equals: Amount under the
upper phase-out limit (if
zero or less, stop: no
amount is deductible)   _____

Divide by $10,000

Equals: Percentage of the maximum contribution that can
be deducted (not more than 100%)   _____%

Times $2,000 ($2,250 spousal)

Equals: Deductible limit before
rounding and minimum limit   _____

(If the deductible limit is not an
even multiple of $10, round up
to the next $10)   _____

(If the deductible limit is less than
$200, increase the amount to the
minimum limit of $200)   _____

*The formula is used to determine deductible IRA contributions
when a taxpayer (or spouse) is an active participant in a qualified
retirement plan.

INDEX